THE
DOG LOVER'S
LITERARY
COMPANION

THE
DOG LOVER'S
LITERARY
COMPANION

JOHN RICHARD STEPHENS

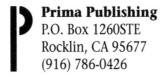

Prima Publishing
P.O. Box 1260STE
Rocklin, CA 95677
(916) 786-0426

The author wishes to express special appreciation to Martha and Jim Goodwin, Mollie Seibert, Bill and Norene Hilden, Frank and Marybeth DiVito, Doug and Shirley Strong, and Marty Goeller.

Typography by Janet Hansen, Alphatype
Copyediting by Elizabeth Judd
Production by Janelle Rohr, Bookman Productions
Interior design by Judith Levinson, Hal Lockwood,
    and Michael Yazzolino
Cover design by The Dunlavey Studio

Cover illustration ANNE VALLAYER-COSTER, *Les Petits Favoris, (The Little Favorites)* ca. 1775–1780. Oil on canvas, 16 $^{11}/_{16}$" by 20 $^9/_{16}$" (45 by 52 cm). Shown are two King Charles Spaniel puppies and a whippet.

Frontispiece BRITON RIVIÈRE, *Sympathy*, 1877. British painter. (Royal Holloway College, London)

Library of Congress Cataloging-in-Publication Data

The Dog lover's literary companion / [edited by] John Richard Stephens.
    p.   cm.
    Includes index.
    ISBN 1-55958-218-9 : $14.95
    1. Dogs—Literary collections.   I. Stephens, John Richard.
PN6071.D6D638   1992
808.8'036—do20   92-24278
                           CIP

92   93   94   95   RRD   10   9   8   7   6   5   4   3   2   1

Printed in the United States of America

Acknowledgments in the credits on pages 391–393 constitute an extension of the copyright page.

This book is dedicated to
Scott Douglas Stephens
and all his dogs.

How to Order:

Quantity discounts are available from the publisher, Prima Publishing, P.O.Box 1260STE, Rocklin, CA 95677; telephone (916) 786-0449. On your letterhead, include information concerning the intended use of the books and the number of books you wish to purchase.

CONTENTS

DOG ENCOUNTERS

There is no man so poor but what he can afford to keep one dog. And I have seen them so poor that they could afford to keep three.

Josh Billings (H. W. Shaw), *On Poverty,* 1865.

When an animal has feelings that are delicate and refined, and when they can be further perfected by education, then it becomes worthy of joining human society. To the highest degree the dog has all these inner qualities that merit human attention.

Count of Buffon, *Histoire Naturelle,* 1749–1804.

D ogs have been living with people for a long time, possibly for as many as 25,000 years. No one knows when the first dog came into existence, but many stories speculate on this.

While the Bible claims God created dogs before people, the creation myth of the Kato Indians of California says the dog existed even earlier, since the creator already had his dog before he began creating the world. Xolotl, a god of the Aztecs and the twin of Quetzalcoatl, was represented as a dog or a dog-headed man. He created the present human cycle of life when he recovered the bones of people who lived and died in previous cycles from the underworld. He was pursued by the furious god of death and accidentally dropped the bones, shattering them. The pieces were scattered and each became a different tribe. Another myth—from the Pit River Indians—says the world was actually created by relatives of the dog: a fox and a coyote.

Other myths say the dog played a direct role in the creation of the first humans. The Jicarilla Apache Indians say people were created because the dog asked for a companion. The Chinese, Southeast Asians, Native Americans, and Eskimos all tell stories of how dogs are actually the ancestors of humans; others say dogs are really people and that they will be restored to human form in the afterlife. And the ancient Mbayá Indians of the Gran Chaco in South America maintain that people originally lived underground until a dog smelled them and dug them up.

The dog appears in myths all over the world as a helper and teacher. Dogs are said to have given people their first food, their first bow and arrows, caused them to speak, introduced them to fire, and showed them how to cultivate crops. The Chinese relate how humankind was starving from a famine caused by a flood until someone noticed some seeds in a dog's tail. The person planted them, and they turned out to be rice. Many Chinese families still express their gratitude by giving the family dog some rice at the beginning of every meal.

The Nandi people of Uganda recount how death resulted from mistreatment of a dog. The dog was sent to tell people of their immortality, but they tried to play tricks on him and insulted him. The dog responded, "All men will die like the moon, but you will not be reborn like the moon unless you give me food and drink." The people just laughed. Since they did not give the dog the respect a divine messenger deserved, the dog left, saying, "All men shall die—only the moon shall be reborn."

The Shawnee Indians, who lived in the Eastern forests of North America, describe how a dog postpones the end of the world. When the Creatress has woven a basket in which to gather up all the spirits of the good, the world will be destroyed. Every day she works at her weaving, but every night her constant companion—a dog—unravels all her work. In this way, a dog is the world's savior.

Ever since dogs and people first crossed paths, dogs have influenced people's lives. Their importance is reflected in these myths. On a more personal level, people's introduction to their first dog often results in memories that stay with them for the rest of their lives. And once they become a part of people's world, dogs' impact can be profound.

My Dog

JOHN KENDRICK BANGS, from *Foothills of Parnassus,* 1914. American
humorist and author of over 30 books.

I have no dog, but it must be
Somewhere there's one belongs to me—
A little chap with wagging tail,
And dark brown eyes that never quail,
But look you through, and through, and through,
With love unspeakable and true.

Somewhere it must be, I opine,
There is a little dog of mine
With cold black nose that sniffs around
In search of what things may be found
In pocket or some nook hard by
Where I have hid them from his eye.

Somewhere my doggie pulls and tugs
The fringes of rebellious rugs,
Or with the mischief of the pup
Chews all my shoes and slippers up,
And when he's done it to the core,
With eyes all eager, pleads for more.

Somewhere upon his hinder legs
My little doggie sits and begs,
And in a wistful minor tone
Pleads for the pleasures of the bone—
I pray it be his owner's whim
To yield, and grant the same to him.

THOMAS GAINSBOR-
OUGH, *A Cottage Girl
with Dog and Pitcher,*
1785. English portrait
and landscape painter.

Somewhere a little dog doth wait;
It may be by some garden gate.
With eyes alert and tail attent—
You know the kind of tail that's meant—
With stores of yelps of glad delight
To bid me welcome home at night.

Somewhere a little dog is seen,
His nose two shaggy paws between,
Flat on his stomach, one eye shut
Held fast in dreamy slumber, but
The other open, ready for
His master coming through the door.

Why Mr. Dog Is Tame (excerpt)

JOEL CHANDLER HARRIS, from *Told by Uncle Remus,* 1905. American author famous for his Uncle Remus stories.

"Well, ol' Brer Dog wuz e'en about like he is deze days, scratchin' fer fleas, an' growlin' over his vittles stidder sayin' grace, an' berryin' de bones when he had one too many. He wuz des like he is now, 'ceppin' dat he wuz wil'. He galloped wid Brer Fox, an' loped wid Brer Wolf, an' cantered wid Brer Coon. He went all de gaits, an' he had des ez good a time ez any un um, an' des ez bad a time.

"Now, one day, somers 'twix' Monday mornin' an' Saddy night, he wuz settin' in de shade scratchin' hisse'f, an' he wuz tooken wid a spell er thinkin'. He'd des come thoo a mighty hard winter wid de yuther creeturs, an' he up an' say ter hisse'f dat ef he had ter do like dat one mo' season, it'd be de een' er him an' his fambly. You could count his ribs, an' his hip-bones stuck out like de horns on a hat-rack.

"Whiles he wuz settin' dar, scratchin' an' studyin', an' studyin' an' scratchin', who should come meanderin' down de big road but ol' Brer Wolf; an' it 'uz 'Hello, Brer Dog! you look like you ain't seed de inside uv a smokehouse fer quite a whet. I ain't sayin' dat I got much fer ter brag on, kaze I ain't in no better fix dan what you is. De colder it gits, de skacer de vittles grows.' An' den he ax Brer Dog whar he gwine an' how soon he gwine ter git dar. Brer Dog make answer dat it don't make no diffunce whar he go ef he don't fin' dinner ready.

"Brer Wolf 'low dat de way ter git dinner is ter make a fier, kaze 'tain't no use fer ter try ter eat ef dey don't do dat. Ef dey don't git nothin' fer ter cook, dey'll have a place whar dey kin keep warm. Brer Dog say he see whar Brer Wolf is dead right, but whar dey gwine git a fier? Brer Wolf say de quickest way is ter borry a chunk fum Mr. Man er his ol' 'oman. But when it come ter sayin' who gwine atter it, dey bofe kinder hung back, kaze dey know'd dat Mr. Man had a walkin'-cane what he kin p'int at anybody an' snap a cap on it an' blow de light right out.

"But bimeby, Brer Dog say'll go atter de chunk er fier, an' he ain't no mo' dan say dat, 'fo' off he put, an' he travel so peart, dat 'twa'n't long 'fo' he come ter Mr. Man's house. When he got ter de gate he sot down an' done some mo' studyin', an' ef de gate had a been shot, he'd a turned right roun' an' went back like he come; but some er de chillun had been playin' out in de yard, an' dey lef' de gate open, an so dar 'twuz. Study ez he mought, he can't fin' no skuse fer gwine back widout de chunk er fier. An' in he went.

"Well, talk 'bout folks bein' 'umble; you ain't seed no 'umble-come-tumble twel you see Brer Dog when he went in dat gate. He ain't take time fer ter look 'roun', he so skeer'd. He hear hogs a-gruntin' an' pigs a-squealin', he hear hens a-cacklin' an' roosters crowin', but he ain't turn his head. He had sense nuff not ter go in de house by de front way. He went 'roun' de back way whar de kitchen wuz, an' when he got dar he 'fraid ter go any furder. He went ter de do', he did, an' he 'fraid ter knock. He hear chillun laughin' an' playin' in dar, an' fer de fust time in all his born days, he 'gun ter feel lonesome.

"Bimeby, some un open de do' an' den shot it right quick. But Brer Dog ain't see nobody; he 'uz too 'umble-come-tumble fer dat. He wuz lookin' at de groun', an' wonderin' what 'uz gwine ter happen nex'. It must a been one er de chillun what open de do', kaze 'twa'n't long 'fo' here come Mr. Man wid de walkin'-cane what had fier in it. He come ter de do', he did, an' he say, 'What you want here?' Brer Dog wuz too skeer'd fer ter talk; all he kin do is ter des

PIERRE BONNARD, *The Red-Checkered Table-cloth*, 1910. French Postimpressionist painter, lithographer, and illustrator.

wag his tail. Mr. Man, he 'low, 'You in de wrong house, an' you better go on whar you got some business.'

"Brer Dog, he crouch down close ter de groun', an' wag his tail. Mr. Man, he look at 'im, an' he ain't know whedder fer ter turn loose his gun er not, but his ol' 'oman, she hear him talkin', an' she come ter de do', an' see Brer Dog crouchin' dar, 'umbler dan de 'umblest, an' she say, 'Po' feller! you ain't gwine ter hurt nobody, is you?' an' Brer Dog 'low, 'No, ma'am, I ain't; I des come fer ter borry a chunk er fier.' An' she say, 'What in de name er goodness does you want wid fier? Is you gwine ter burn us out'n house an' home?' Brer Dog 'low, 'No, ma'am! dat I ain't; I des wanter git warm.' Den de 'oman say, 'I clean fergot 'bout de col' wedder—come in de kitchen here an' warm yo'se'f much ez you wanter.'

"Dat wuz mighty good news fer Brer Dog, an' in he went. Dey wuz a nice big fier on de h'a'th, an' de chillun wuz settin' all roun' eatin' der dinner. Dey make room fer Brer Dog, an' down he sot in a warm cornder, an' 'twa'n't long 'fo' he wuz feelin' right splimmy-splammy. But he wuz mighty hongry. He sot dar, he did, an' watch de chillun' eatin' der ashcake an' buttermilk, an' his eye-balls 'ud foller eve'y mou'ful dey e't. De 'oman, she notice dis, an' she went ter de cubberd an' got a piece er warm ashcake, an' put it down on de h'a'th.

"Brer Dog ain't need no secon' invite—he des gobble up de ashcake 'fo' you kin say Jack Robberson wid yo' mouf shot. He ain't had nigh nuff, but he know'd better dan ter show what his appetites wuz. He 'gun ter feel good, an' den he got down on his hunkers, an' lay his head down on his fo'paws, an' make like he gwine ter sleep. Atter 'while, he smell Brer Wolf, an' he raise his head an' look todes de do'. Mr. Man he tuck notice, an' he say he b'lieve dey's some un sneakin' 'roun'. Brer Dog raise his head, an' snuff todes de do', an' growl ter hisse'f. So Mr. Man tuck down his gun fum over de fierplace, an' went out. De fust thing he see when he git out in de yard wuz Brer Wolf runnin' out de gate, an' he up wid his gun—bang!—an' he hear Brer Wolf holler. All he got wuz a han'ful er ha'r, but he come mighty nigh gittin' de whole hide.

"Well, atter dat, Mr. Man fin' out dat Brer Dog could do 'im a heap er good, fus' one way an' den an'er. He could head de cows off when dey make a break thoo de woods, he could take keer er de sheep, an' he could warn Mr. Man when some er de yuther creeturs wuz prowlin' 'roun'. An' den he wuz some comp'ny when Mr. Man went huntin'. He could trail de game, an' he could fin' his way home fum anywheres; an' he could play wid de chillun des like he wuz one un um.

" 'Twa'n't long 'fo' he got fat, an' one day when he wuz amblin' in de woods, he meet up wid Brer Wolf. He howdied at 'im, he did, but Brer Wolf won't skacely look at 'im. Atter while he say, 'Brer Dog, why'n't you come back dat day when you went atter fier?' Brer Dog p'int ter de collar on his neck. He 'low, 'You see dis? Well, it'll tell you lots better dan what I kin.' Brer Wolf say, 'You mighty fat. Why can't I come dar an' do like you does?' Brer Dog 'low, 'Dey ain't nothin' fer ter hinder you.'

"So de next mornin', bright an' early, Brer Wolf knock at Mr. Man's do'. Mr. Man peep out an' see who 'tis, an' tuck down his gun an' went out. Brer Wolf try ter be perlite, an' he smile. But when he smile he show'd all his tushes, an' dis kinder skeer Mr. Man. He say, 'What you doin' sneakin' 'roun' here?' Brer Wolf try ter be mo' perliter dan ever, an' he grin fum year ter year. Dis show all his tushes, an' Mr. Man lammed aloose at 'im. An' dat 'uz de las' time dat Brer Wolf ever try ter live wid Mr. Man, an fum dat time on down ter dis day, it 'uz war 'twix' Brer Wolf an' Brer Dog."

THOMAS GAINSBOR-
OUGH, *Study of a
Spaniel,* mid-1760s.
English portrait and
landscape painter.

John Muir's Dog

JOHN MUIR, from *Stickeen,* 1909. American naturalist and conserva-
tionist. Muir Woods National Monument in California and Muir Glacier in Alaska are named after him. This was originally published in a
slightly different form as "An Adventure with a Dog and a Glacier" in
the *Century Magazine,* 1897.

In the summer of 1880 I set out from Fort Wrangel in a canoe to continue the exploration of the icy region of southeastern Alaska, begun in the fall of 1879. After the
necessary provisions, blankets, etc., had been collected and
stowed away, and my Indian crew were in their places
ready to start, while a crowd of their relatives and friends
on the wharf were bidding them good-by and good-luck,
my companion, the Rev. S. H. Young, for whom we were
waiting, at last came aboard, followed by a little black dog,
that immediately made himself at home by curling up in
a hollow among the baggage. I like dogs, but this one
seemed so small and worthless that I objected to his going, and asked the missionary why he was taking him.

"Such a little helpless creature will only be in the way,"
I said; "you had better pass him up to the Indian boys on
the wharf, to be taken home to play with the children. This

11

FREDERIC REMINGTON, *Evening on a Canadian Lake,* 1905. American sculptor, painter, illustrator, and writer. He completed more than 2700 paintings and drawings and was a war correspondent for the Hearst newspapers during the Spanish-American War. (Private collection)

trip is not likely to be good for toy-dogs. The poor silly thing will be in rain and snow for weeks or months, and will require care like a baby."

But his master assured me that he would be no trouble at all; that he was a perfect wonder of a dog, could endure cold and hunger like a bear, swim like a seal, and was wondrous wise and cunning, etc., making out a list of virtues to show he might be the most interesting member of the party.

Nobody could hope to unravel the lines of his ancestry. In all the wonderfully mixed and varied dog-tribe I never saw any creature very much like him, though in some of his sly, soft, gliding motions and gestures he brought the fox to mind. He was short-legged and bunchy-bodied, and his hair, though smooth, was long and silky and slightly waved, so that when the wind was at his back it ruffled, making him look shaggy. At first sight his only noticeable feature was his fine tail, which was about as airy and shady as a squirrel's, and was carried curling forward almost to his nose. On closer inspection you might notice his thin sensitive ears, and sharp eyes with cunning tan-spots above them. Mr. Young told me that when the little fellow was a pup about the size of a woodrat he was pre-sented to his wife by an Irish prospector at Sitka, and that on his arrival at Fort Wrangel he was adopted with enthu-siasm by the Stickeen Indians as a sort of new good-luck totem, was named "Stickeen" for the tribe, and became a universal favorite; petted, protected, and admired wherever he went, and regarded as a mysterious fountain of wisdom.

On our trip he soon proved himself a queer charac-ter—odd, concealed, independent, keeping invincibly quiet, and doing many little puzzling things that piqued my curiosity. As we sailed week after week through the long intricate channels and inlets among the innumerable islands and mountains of the coast, he spent most of the dull days in sluggish ease, motionless, and apparently as unobserving as if in deep sleep. But I discovered that some-how he always knew what was going on. When the Indians were about to shoot at ducks or seals, or when anything along the shore was exciting our attention, he would rest his chin on the edge of the canoe and calmly look out like a dreamy-eyed tourist. And when he heard us talking about making a landing, he immediately roused himself to see what sort of a place we were coming to, and made ready to jump overboard and swim ashore as soon as the canoe neared the beach. Then, with a vigorous shake to get rid of the brine in his hair, he ran into the woods to hunt small game. But though always the first out of the canoe, he was always the last to get into it. When we were ready to start he could never be found, and refused to come to our

GUSTAVE COURBET, *The Greyhound of the Comte de Choiseul (Count of Choiseul)*, 1866. French painter. Courbet received a lot of official criticism, which reached its height when he rejected the cross of the Legion of Honor offered to him by Napoleon III. (St. Louis Art Museum, St. Louis)

call. We soon found out, however, that though we could not see him at such times, he saw us, and from the cover of the briers and huckleberry bushes in the fringe of the woods was watching the canoe with wary eye. For as soon as we were fairly off he came trotting down the beach, plunged into the surf, and swam after us, knowing well that we would cease rowing and take him in. When the contrary little vagabond came alongside, he was lifted by the neck, held at arm's length a moment to drip, and dropped aboard. We tried to cure him of this trick by compelling him to swim a long way, as if we had a mind to abandon him; but this did no good: the longer the swim the better he seemed to like it.

The Sounds of Hounds Barking

WILLIAM SHAKESPEARE, from *A Midsummer Night's Dream,* ca.
1593–1594. English poet and dramatist.

THESEUS:

Go, one of you, find out the forester;
For now our observation is perform'd;
And since we have the vaward of the day,
My love shall hear the music of my hounds.
Uncouple in the western valley; let them go:
Dispatch, I say, and find the forester.
We will, fair queen, up to the mountain's top,
And mark the musical confusion
Of hounds and echo in conjunction.

HIPPOLYTA:

I was with Hercules and Cadmus once,
When in a wood of Crete they bay'd the bear
With hounds of Sparta: never did I hear
Such gallant chiding; for, besides the groves,
The skies, the fountains, every region near
Seem'd all one mutual cry: I never heard
So musical a discord, such sweet thunder.

THESEUS:

My hounds are bred out of the Spartan kind,
So flew'd, so sanded; and their heads are hung
With ears that sweep away the morning dew;
Crook-knee'd, and dew-lapp'd like Thessalian bulls;
Slow in pursuit, but match'd in mouth like bells,
Each under each. A cry more tuneable
Was never holla'd to, nor cheer'd with horn,
In Crete, in Sparta, nor in Thessaly:
Judge when you hear.

ARTHUR RACKHAM, from an edition of Shakespeare's *A Midsummer Night's Dream,* 1908. English illustrator.

LOUIS ICART, *Fanny and Chou-Chou,* 1943. French Art Deco artist. Fanny was his wife.

Fashions in Dogs

E. B. WHITE, from *The Fox of Peapack and Other Stories,* 1932. American writer. Author of *Charlotte's Web.*

An Airedale, erect beside the chauffeur of a Rolls-
    Royce,
Often gives you the impression he's there from
    choice.

In town, the Great Dane
Is kept by the insane.

Today the boxer
Is fashionable and snappy;
But I never saw a boxer
Who looked thoroughly happy.

The Scotty's a stoic,
He's gay and he's mad;
His pace is a snail trot,
His harness is plaid.
I once had a bitch,
Semi-invalid, crazy:
There ne'er was a Scotch girl
Quite like Daisy.

Pekes
Are biological freaks.
They have no snout
And their eyes come out.
Ladies choose'm
To clutch to their bosom.
A Pekinese would gladly fight a wolf or a cougar
But is usually owned by a Mrs. Applegate Krueger.

Cockers are perfect for Elizabeth Barrett Browning,
Or to carry home a package from the A. & P. with-
        out clowning.

The wire-haired fox
Is hard on socks
With or without clocks.

The smooth-haired variety
Has practically vanished from nice society,
And it certainly does irk us
That you never see one except when you go to the
        circus.

GEORGE STUBBS, *A Brown and White Norfolk or Water Spaniel*, 1778. English animal painter. This is probably a Norfolk spaniel. (Private collection)

The dachshund's affectionate,
He wants to wed with you:
Lie down to sleep,
And he's in bed with you.
Sit in a chair,
He's there.
Depart,
You break his heart.

My Christmas will be a whole lot wetter and
    merrier
If somebody sends me a six-weeks-old Boston
    terrier.

JEAN-JACQUES BACHELIER, *Dog of the Havannah Breed,* 1768. French painter. (Bowes Museum, Durham, England)

Sealyhams have square sterns and cute faces
Like toy dogs you see at Macy's.
But the Sealyham, while droll in appearance,
Has no clearance.

Chows come in black, and chows come in red;
They could come in bright green, I wouldn't turn
    my head.
The roof of their mouth is supposed to be blue,
Which is one of those things that might easily be
    true.

To us it has never seemed exactly pleasant
To see a beautiful setter on East Fifty-seventh
    Street looking for a woodcock or a pheasant.

German shepherds are useful for leading the blind,
And for biting burglars and Consolidated Edison
    men in the behind.

Lots of people have a rug.
Very few have a pug.

Adaptability of the Dog

MAURICE MAETERLINCK, from *Our Friend, the Dog,* 1904. Belgian poet. Maeterlinck received the Nobel Prize for Literature in 1911.

This animal, our good familiar dog, simple and unsurprising as may to-day appear to us what he has done, in thus perceptibly drawing nearer to a world in which he was not born and for which he was not destined, has nevertheless performed one of the most unusual and improbable acts that we can find in the general history of life. When was this recognition of man by beast, this extraordinary passage from darkness to light, effected? Did we seek out the poodle, the collie, or the mastiff from among the wolves and the jackals, or did he come spontaneously to us? We cannot tell. So far as our human annals stretch, he is at our side, as at present; but what are human annals in comparison with the times of which we have no witness? The fact remains that he is there in our houses, as ancient, as rightly placed, as perfectly adapted to our habits as though he had appeared on this earth, such as he now is, at the same time as ourselves. . . .

But he loves us not only in his consciousness and his intelligence: the very instinct of his race, the entire unconsciousness of his specie, it appears, think only of us, dream only of being useful to us. To serve us better, to adapt himself better to our different needs, he has adopted every shape and been able infinitely to vary the faculties, the aptitudes which he places at our disposal. Is he to aid us in the pursuit of game in the plains? His legs lengthen inordinately, his muzzle tapers, his lungs widen, he becomes swifter than the deer. Does our prey hide under wood? The docile genius of the species, forestalling our desires, presents us with the basset, a sort of almost footless serpent, which steals into the closest thickets. Do we ask

21

that he should drive our flocks? The same compliant genius grants him the requisite size, intelligence, energy and vigilance. Do we intend him to watch and defend our house? His head becomes round and monstrous, in order that his jaws may be more powerful, more formidable and more tenacious. Are we taking him to the south? His hair grows shorter and lighter, so that he may faithfully accompany us under the rays of a hotter sun. Are we going up to the north? His feet grow larger, the better to tread the snow; his fur thickens, in order that the cold may not compel him to abandon us. Is he intended only for us to play with, to amuse the leisure of our eyes, to adorn or enliven the home? He clothes himself in a sovereign grace and elegance, he makes himself smaller than a doll to sleep on our knees by the fireside, or even consents, should our fancy demand it, to appear a little ridiculous to please us.

You shall not find, in nature's immense crucible, a single living being that has shown a like suppleness, a similar abundance of forms, the same prodigious faculty of accommodation to our wishes. This is because, in the world which we know, among the different and primitive geniuses that preside over the evolution of the several species, there exists not one, excepting that of the dog, that ever gave a thought to the presence of man.

SIR EDWIN LANDSEER, *Dignity and Impudence*, 1839. Landseer was the most popular of the English animal painters and one of the most prolific dog artists. (Tate Gallery, London)

PUPPIES

Puppies are nature's remedy for feeling un-
loved . . . plus numerous other ailments of life.

Richard Allan Palm, "Martha, Princess of
Diamonds", 1963.

A remarkable discovery comes from Siberia, where biologists bred wild silver foxes for their docility. It took them only 20 generations—about two decades—to breed tame, domesticated foxes. The surprising thing is that these tame foxes are very doglike; they seek human company instead of fleeing from it, they wag their tails, they lick people's faces, their ears have become floppy, their coats are multicolored, the females come into heat twice a year (like domestic dogs) instead of once a year (like wild canids), and they even sound like dogs.

Somehow they have spontaneously developed the characteristics of dogs without being crossbred with them (dogs and foxes have a different number of chromosomes, so it's physically impossible for them to interbreed). For some unknown reason, all these doglike characteristics are linked to tameness. It's likely the domestication process triggered the same characteristics in wolves, with dogs being the result. This would mean that whenever you breed wolves for tameness many of the characteristics we associate with dogs will automatically appear, and the same would be true for some of the other wild canids.

All domestic dogs, from the Great Dane to the Pekinese, are descended from the wolf. Although there are not many variations among wolves, dogs come in a great variety of shapes, sizes, and colors. Full grown, they can range in weight from as little as 1½ pounds to over 250 pounds. Some experts estimate that there are currently over 800 different dog breeds—mainly the result of selective breeding by people—and many more will probably emerge in the future.

Most dogs were bred for specific duties such as hunting, tending sheep, or protecting property. Usually this meant emphasizing the development of a single sense or characteristic, which resulted in very specialized dogs that were useful for specific purposes. For example, the sporting breeds were bred for hunting game birds. The pointing breeds (pointers and setters) wander around out in front of the hunter until they smell a bird, then they stop and wait for the hunter with their noses pointed in the direction of the smell. When the hunter arrives, the flushing breeds (spaniels) rush in through underbrush and reeds to drive the birds into the air. After the bird is shot, the retrieving breeds (retrievers and some spaniels) bring the prey to the hunter.

Scent hounds, on the other hand, were bred to hunt by following trails of scent. Their ability to smell has developed to an amazing degree. One bloodhound successfully trailed a scent that was over 13 days old, even though it had rained in the meantime.

All dogs are much better than we are at sensing odors. For some substances the dog's sense of smell is about the same as ours, but for others it is over a million times better. Tests have found that explosive-detecting dogs can sense concentrations as small as one part per billion, and in some tests the dogs detected concentrations smaller than the sensing equipment was able to measure.

Hearing is another sense that is highly developed in dogs. While we can only hear a ticking watch up to about 4 feet away, the average dog can hear it from 40 feet. They are also able to hear sounds of a much higher pitch than we can. This is why dogs can hear a dog whistle and we cannot.

Although some dogs were bred to hunt by sight, their eyesight is generally poorer than ours. Dogs cannot see colors—only shades of gray—and even though they can visually recognize their owner at about 150 yards, they can only see the silhouette and movement. But, they are able to detect movements at a greater distance than we can.

Taste is another sense that is probably poor in dogs. Since dogs swallow their food whole with very little chewing, how their food smells is much more important than how it tastes. This sense is not an attribute that would have been emphasized by dog breeders through the years.

Dogs have been bred to pull carts or sleds (huskies and malamutes), to race (greyhounds), to chase prey down holes (terriers), to protect or guard (mastiffs), to fight (pitbulls), and for their ability to herd (collies and sheepdogs). Herding is a natural instinct in dogs and can be seen in wolves when they hunt caribou. Breeding has been used to improve and refine this instinct. Dogs are also valued solely as companions, which has resulted in the wide variety of small, friendly breeds. The cocker spaniel, for example, was bred to have a fondness for children.

In some dogs, many traits are combined; an example is the German shepherd, which is obedient, intelligent, protective, agile, brave, and very strong. The bite of one of these dogs averages from 400 to 700 pounds per square inch. German shepherds can kill an armed attacker, yet they are gentle with children. They can herd sheep and cattle and are excellent guard dogs. All of these characteristics were developed or enhanced through years of breeding.

In many ways, dogs are now very different from wolves, but in other respects, they are still very similar. Biologist Raymond Coppinger and linguist Mark Feinstein suggest that when dogs were bred to be tame—a juvenile characteristic—they also retained other characteristics of juveniles. Therefore, dogs actually remain immature for their entire lives without ever developing their ancestors' adult characteristics. As a result, they are more playful, form social bonds (among themselves and with other species) more easily, seek contact and someone to care for them, and are noisier. So, even though dogs lose much of the puppy in them, these canine Peter Pans never truly grow up.

JEAN-BAPTISTE OUDRY, *Chienne allaitant ses petits (Bitch Hound Nursing Her Puppies)*, 1752. French animal painter and court painter to Louis XV. (Musée de la Chasse et de la Nature, France)

The New Puppy

D. H. LAWRENCE, from "Rex", *Dial* magazine, 1921. English author. Lawrence wrote *The Rainbow, Sons and Lovers,* and *Lady Chatterley's Lover.*

It was winter-time, and I wore a big-flapped black overcoat, half cloak. Under the cloak-sleeves I hid the puppy, who trembled. It was Saturday, and the train was crowded, and he whimpered under my coat. I sat in mortal fear of being hauled out for traveling without a dog-ticket. However, we arrived, and my torments were for nothing.

The others were wildly excited over the puppy. He was small and fat and white, with a brown-and-black head: a fox terrier. My father said he had a lemon head—some such mysterious technical phraseology. It wasn't lemon at all, but colored like a field bee. And he had a black spot at the root of his spine.

It was Saturday night—bath-night. He crawled on the hearth-rug like a fat white tea-cup, and licked the bare toes that had just been bathed.

"He ought to be called Spot," said one. But that was too ordinary. It was a great question, what to call him.

"Call him Rex—the King," said my mother, looking down on the fat, animated little tea-cup, who was chewing my sister's little toe and making her squeal with joy and tickles. We took the name in all seriousness.

"Rex—the King!" We thought it was just right. Not for years did I realize that it was a sarcasm on my mother's part. She must have wasted some twenty years or more of irony, on our incurable naïveté.

It wasn't a successful name, really. Because my father, and all the people in the street, failed completely to pronounce the monosyllable Rex. They all said Rax. And it always distressed me. It always suggested to me seaweed, and rack-and-ruin. Poor Rex!

We loved him dearly.

PAUL GAUGUIN, *Still Life with Three Puppies,* 1888. French Post-impressionist painter. Originally Gauguin was a banker, but he gave this up at age 35 and devoted himself to art. Although he was not appreciated during his lifetime, he is now considered one of the greatest of the modern masters. (Museum of Modern Art, New York)

Puppies Adopted by Cats

SARAH J. EDDY, *Alexander and Some Other Cats,* 1929.

Beside a mother cat and her four kittens they had placed a mother dog with her four young puppies in the headquarters of the Society for the Prevention of Cruelty to Animals. One by one the mother cat saw the dog and three of her puppies taken away to be destroyed. Then the mother instinct became too strong to be resisted. The mother cat jumped from her box, tenderly caught the remaining puppy by the back of the neck and carried it back to her own litter of kittens.

Now the four kittens and the puppy rest side by side, while the proud mother cat looks on. I found a home for the whole little family.

The following instance was reported in the Boston Herald. The mother of three puppies died when they were three days old, and they were adopted by "Kitty," a Provincetown cat. She found the care of three too much for her, and she took two across the street to "Frisky" a ten year old cat stronger than Kitty. The two cats nursed the motherless puppies.

LOUIS ICART, *Chien et Chat (Dear Friends),* 1929. French Art Deco artist. His wife, Fanny, and two of their pets.

A Dog Imitates Cats

CHARLES DARWIN, from *The Descent of Man and Selection in Relation to Sex*, 1871. English naturalist and originator of the theory of evolution.

Dureau de la Malle gives an account of a dog reared by a cat, who learnt to imitate the well-known action of a cat licking her paws, and thus washing her ears and face; this was also witnessed by the celebrated naturalist Audouin. I have received several confirmatory accounts; in one of these, a dog had not been suckled by a cat, but had been brought up with one, together with kittens, and had thus acquired the above habit, which he ever afterwards practised during his life of thirteen years. Dureau de la Malle's dog likewise learnt from the kittens to play with a ball by rolling it about with his fore paws, and springing on it.

CLAUDE MONET, *Camille au petit chien (Camille with Her Puppy)*, 1866. French Impressionist landscape painter. Shortly after painting this picture, Monet married his model, Camille. (Private collection)

ROBERT ALEXANDER,
The Happy Mother,
1887. Scottish artist.
(National Gallery of
Scotland, Edinburgh)

Wonder

BERNARD RAYMOND.

Collie puppies in a dooryard,
Wheeling along lopsided,
So hard to manage those hind legs,
Standing, blue eyes on nothing,
Noses twitching,
Stubby tails in the air,
Trying to remember what they are thinking about:
Fat puppies that forget everything,
Even the terrible
White teeth their mother yops at them
When she eats her supper:

Fat puppies full of wonder
At round holes where spiders live,
At the wide wings of a yellow butterfly,
And lifting shrill voices of wonder
At the stranger who leans over their gate
Making uncouth noises.

A Puppy in Wonderland

LEWIS CARROLL (CHARLES DODGSON), from *Alice's Adventures in Wonderland,* 1865. English writer and mathematician.

"The first thing I've got to do," said Alice to herself, as she wandered about in the wood, "is to grow to my right size again; and the second thing is to find my way into that lovely garden. I think that will be the best plan."

It sounded an excellent plan, no doubt, and very neatly and simply arranged: the only difficulty was, that she had not the smallest idea how to set about it; and, while she was peering about anxiously among the trees, a little sharp bark just over her head made her look up in a great hurry.

An enormous puppy was looking down at her with large round eyes, and feebly stretching out one paw, trying to touch her. "Poor little thing!" said Alice, in a coaxing tone, and she tried hard to whistle to it; but she was terribly frightened all the time at the thought that it might be hungry, in which case it would be very likely to eat her up in spite of all her coaxing.

Hardly knowing what she did, she picked up a little bit of stick, and held it out to the puppy: whereupon the puppy jumped into the air off all its feet at once, with a yelp of delight, and rushed at the stick, and made believe to worry it: then Alice dodged behind a great thistle, to keep herself from being run over; and, the moment she appeared on the other side, the puppy made another rush at the stick, and tumbled head over heels in its hurry to get hold of it: then Alice, thinking it was very like having a game of play with a cart-horse, and expecting every moment to be trampled under its feet, ran around the thistle again: then the puppy began a series of short charges at the stick, running a very little way forwards each time and a long way back, and barking hoarsely all the while, till at last it sat down a good way off, panting, with its tongue hanging out of its mouth, and its great eyes half shut.

This seemed to Alice a good opportunity for making her escape: so she set off at once, and ran till she was quite tired and out of breath, and till the puppy's bark sounded quite faint in the distance.

"And yet what a dear little puppy it was!" said Alice, as she leaned against a buttercup to rest herself, and fanned herself with one of the leaves. "I should have liked teaching it tricks very much, if—if I'd only been the right size to do it!"

SIR JOHN TENNIEL, from *Alice's Adventures in Wonderland,* 1865. English caricaturist and illustrator.

Remarks from the Pup

BURGES JOHNSON, from *Sonnets from the Pekinese*, 1935.

PIET MONDRIAN, *Puppy*, 1891. Dutch painter who became a leading abstract artist and influenced the Bauhaus movement. (Private collection)

She's taught me that I mustn't bark
    At little noises after dark,
But just refrain from any fuss
    Until I'm sure they're dangerous.
This would be easier, I've felt,
    If noises could be seen or smelt.

She's very wise, I have no doubt,
    And plans ahead what she's about;
Yet after eating, every day,
    She throws her nicest bones away.
If she were really less obtuse
    She'd bury them for future use.

But that which makes me doubt the most
    Those higher powers that humans boast
Is not so much a fault like that,
    Nor yet her fondness for the cat,
But on our pleasant country strolls
    Her dull indifference to holes!

Ah me! what treasures might be found
    In holes that lead to underground!
However vague or small one is,
    It sends me into ecstasies;
While she, alas! stands by to scoff,
    Or meanly comes to call me off.

THOMAS GAINSBOROUGH, *Pomeranian Bitch and Puppy,* ca. 1777.
English portrait and landscape painter. (Tate Gallery, London)

Oh, if I once had time to spend
    To reach a hole's extremest end,
I'd grab it fast, without a doubt,
    And promptly pull it inside out;
Then drag it home with all my power
    To chew on in a leisure hour.

Of all the mistresses there are,
    Mine is the loveliest by far!
For would I wag myself apart
    If I could thus reveal my heart.
But on some things, I must conclude
    Mine is the saner attitude.

A Wolf Pup

JACK LONDON, from *White Fang,* 1905. American writer who was also a seaman, an oyster pirate, a prospector in the Alaska gold rush, and a war correspondent during the Russo-Japanese War and the Mexican Revolution. Depression, alcoholism, and financial problems resulted in his suicide in 1916. *White Fang,* about a wolf whose mother was half dog, is one of the best stories about dogs or wolves ever written. The pups are the center of the wolves' universe and are fed, reared, and defended by the entire pack.

He was different from his brothers and sisters. Their hair already betrayed the reddish hue inherited from their mother, the she-wolf; while he alone, in this particular, took after his father. He was the one little gray cub of the litter. He had bred true to the straight wolf-stock—in fact, he had bred true, physically, to old One Eye himself, with but a single exception, and that was that he had two eyes to his father's one.

The gray cub's eyes had not been open long, yet already he could see with steady clearness. And while his eyes were still closed, he had felt, tasted, and smelled. He knew his two brothers and his two sisters very well. He had begun to romp with them in a feeble, awkward way, and even to squabble, his little throat vibrating with a queer rasping noise, (the forerunner of the growl), as he worked himself into a passion. And long before his eyes had opened, he had learned by touch, taste, and smell to know his mother—a fount of warmth and liquid food and tenderness. She possessed a gentle, caressing tongue that soothed him when it passed over his soft little body, and that impelled him to snuggle close against her and to doze off to sleep.

Most of the first month of his life had been passed thus in sleeping; but now he could see quite well, and he stayed awake for longer periods of time, and he was coming to

HOKUSAI (1760–1849), *Puppies in the Snow.* Japanese painter, draftsman, and wood engraver. Hokusai was the leading figure of the Ukiyo-e (popular school). Even after he became famous, he continued to live in poverty his entire life. This is one of 12 panels in two screens depicting the months of the year. (Smithsonian Institution, Washington, D.C.)

learn his world quite well. His world was gloomy; but he did not know that, for he knew no other world. It was dim-lighted; but his eyes had never had to adjust themselves to any other light. His world was very small. Its limits were the walls of the lair; but as he had no knowledge of the wide world outside, he was never oppressed by the narrow confines of his existence.

But he had early discovered that one wall of his world was different from the rest. This was the mouth of the cave and the source of light. He had discovered that it was different from the other walls long before he had any thoughts of his own, any conscious volitions. It had been an irresistible attraction before ever his eyes opened and looked upon it. The light from it had beat upon his sealed lids, and the eyes and the optic nerves had pulsated to little, sparklike flashes, warm-colored and strangely pleasing. The life of his body, and of every fibre of his body, the life that was the very substance of his body and that was apart from his own personal life, had yearned toward this light and urged his body toward it in the same way that the cunning chemistry of a plant urges it toward the sun.

Always, in the beginning, before his conscious life dawned, he had crawled toward the mouth of the cave. And in this his brothers and sisters were one with him. Never, in that period, did any of them crawl toward the dark corners of the back-wall. The light drew them as if they were plants; the chemistry of the life that composed them demanded the light as a necessity of being; and their little puppet-bodies crawled blindly and chemically, like the tendrils of a vine. Later on, when each developed individuality and became personally conscious of impulsions and desires, the attraction of the light increased. They were always crawling and sprawling toward it, and being driven back from it by their mother.

It was in this way that the gray cub learned other attributes of his mother than the soft, soothing tongue. In his insistent crawling toward the light, he discovered in her a nose that with a sharp nudge administered rebuke, and later, a paw, that crushed him down or rolled him over and over with swift, calculating stroke. Thus he learned hurt; and on top of it he learned to avoid hurt, first, by not incurring the risk of it; and second, when he had incurred the risk, by dodging and by retreating. These were conscious actions, and were the results of his first generalizations upon the world. Before that he had recoiled automatically from hurt, as he had crawled automatically toward the light. After that he recoiled from hurt because he *knew* that it was hurt. . . .

The fascination of the light for the gray cub increased from day to day. He was perpetually departing on yard-long adventures toward the cave's entrance, and as perpetually being driven back. Only he did not know it for an entrance. He did not know anything about entrances—passages whereby one goes from one place to another place. He did not know any other place, much less of a way to get there. So to him the entrance of the cave was a wall—a wall of light. As the sun was to the outside dweller, this wall was to him the sun of his world. It attracted him as a candle attracts a moth. He was always striving to attain it. The life that was so swiftly expanding within him, urged him continually toward the wall of light. The life that was within him knew that it was the one way out, the way he was predestined to tread. But he himself did not know anything about it. He did not know there was any outside at all.

There was one strange thing about this wall of light. His father (he had already come to recognize his father as the one other dweller in the world, a creature like his mother, who slept near the light and was a bringer of meat)—his father had a way of walking right into the white far wall and disappearing. The gray cub could not understand this. Though never permitted by his mother to approach that wall, he had approached the other walls, and encountered hard obstruction on the end of his tender nose. This hurt. And after several such adventures, he left the walls alone. Without thinking about it, he accepted this disappearing into the wall as a peculiarity of his father, as milk and half-digested meat were peculiarities of his mother.

In fact, the gray cub was not given to thinking—at least, to the kind of thinking customary of men. His brain
40

YI OM, *Puppy Playing with a Pheasant Feather,* 16th century. Korean painter.

worked in dim ways. Yet his conclusions were as sharp and distinct as those achieved by men. He had a method of accepting things, without questioning the why and wherefore. In reality, this was the act of classification. He was never disturbed over *why* a thing happened. *How* it happened was sufficient for him. Thus, when he had bumped his nose on the back-wall a few times, he accepted that he would not disappear into walls. In the same way he accepted that his father could disappear into walls. But he was not in the least disturbed by desire to find out the reason for the difference between his father and himself. Logic and physics were no part of his mental make-up. . . .

By the time his mother began leaving the cave on hunting expeditions, the cub had learned well the law that forbade his approaching the entrance. Not only had this law been forcibly and many times impressed on him by his mother's nose and paw, but in him the instinct of fear was developing. Never, in his brief cave-life, had he encountered anything of which to be afraid. Yet fear was in him. It had come down to him from a remote ancestry through a thousand thousand lives. It was a heritage he had received directly from One Eye and the she-wolf; but to them, in turn, it had been passed down through all the generations of wolves that had gone before. Fear!—that legacy of the Wild which no animal may escape nor exchange for pottage.

So the gray cub knew fear, though he knew not the stuff of which fear was made. Possibly he accepted it as one of the restrictions of life. For he had already learned that there were such restrictions. Hunger he had known; and when he could not appease his hunger he had felt restriction. The hard obstruction of the cave-wall, the sharp nudge of his mother's nose, the smashing stroke of her paw, the hunger unappeased of several famines, had borne in upon him that all was not freedom in the world, that to life there were limitations and restraints. These limitations and restraints were laws. To be obedient to them was to escape hurt and make for happiness.

He did not reason the question out in this man-fashion. He merely classified the things that hurt and the things that did not hurt. And after such classification he avoided the things that hurt, the restrictions and restraints, in order to enjoy the satisfactions and the remunerations of life.

Thus it was that in obedience to the law laid down by his mother, and in obedience to the law of that unknown and nameless thing, fear, he kept away from the mouth of the cave. It remained to him a white wall of light. When his mother was absent, he slept most of the time, while during the intervals that he was awake he kept very quiet, suppressing the whimpering cries that tickled in his throat and strove for noise. . . .

But there were other forces at work in the cub, the greatest of which was growth. Instinct and law demanded of him obedience. But growth demanded disobedience. His mother and fear impelled him to keep away from the white wall. Growth is life, and life is forever destined to make for light. So there was no damming up the tide of life that was rising within him—rising with every mouthful of meat he swallowed, with every breath he drew. In the end, one day, fear and obedience were swept away by the rush of life, and the cub straddled and sprawled toward the entrance.

Unlike any other wall with which he had had experience, this wall seemed to recede from him as he approached. No hard surface collided with the tender little nose he thrust out tentatively before him. The substance of the wall seemed as permeable and yielding as light. And as condition, in his eyes, had the seeming of form, so he entered into what had been wall to him and bathed in the substance that composed it.

It was bewildering. He was sprawling through solidity. And ever the light grew brighter. Fear urged him to go back, but growth drove him on. Suddenly he found himself at the mouth of the cave. The wall, inside which he had thought himself, as suddenly leaped back before him to an immeasurable distance. The light had become painfully bright. He was dazzled by it. Likewise he was made dizzy by this abrupt and tremendous extension of space. Automatically, his eyes were adjusting themselves to the brightness, focussing themselves to meet the increased distance of objects. At first, the wall had leaped beyond his vision. He now saw it again; but it had taken upon itself a remarkable remoteness. Also, its appearance had

SIR EDWIN LANDSEER, *Dog with Litter of Puppies*, 1861. English animal painter. (Private collection)

changed. It was now a variegated wall, composed of the trees that fringed the stream, the opposing mountain that towered above the trees, and the sky that out-towered the mountain.

A great fear came upon him. This was more of the terrible unknown. He crouched down on the lip of the cave and gazed out on the world. He was very much afraid. Because it was unknown, it was hostile to him. Therefore the hair stood up on end along his back and his lips wrinkled weakly in an attempt at a ferocious and intimidating snarl. Out of his puniness and fright he challenged and menaced the whole wide world.

Nothing happened. He continued to gaze, and in his interest he forgot to snarl. Also, he forgot to be afraid. For the time, fear had been routed by growth, while growth had assumed the guise of curiosity. He began to notice near objects—an open portion of the stream that flashed in the sun, the blasted pine tree that stood at the base of the slope, and the slope itself, that ran right up to him and ceased two feet beneath the lip of the cave on which he crouched.

Now the gray cub had lived all his days on a level floor. He had never experienced the hurt of a fall. He did not know what a fall was. So he stepped boldly out upon the air. His hind-legs still rested on the cave-lip, so he fell forward head downward. The earth struck him a harsh blow on the nose that made him yelp. Then he began rolling down the slope, over and over. He was in a panic of terror. The unknown had caught him at last. It had gripped savagely hold of him and was about to wreak upon him some terrific hurt. Growth was now routed by fear, and he ki-yi'd like any frightened puppy.

C H A P T E R 3

FRIENDSHIP

'Tis sweet to hear the watch dogs' honest bark
Bay deep-mouthed welcome as we draw near
     home;
'Tis sweet to know there is an eye will mark
Our coming and look brighter when we come.

Lord Byron, *Don Juan*, 1819.

D ogs are generally considered the first animals to have been domesticated (though some believe sheep may have been domesticated earlier).

The association between humans and dogs goes back thousands of years. One skeleton of a Cro-Magnon girl was found surrounded by four dog heads pointing in each direction, as if they were guarding her. This seems to indicate that the association began 20,000 to 25,000 years ago. Remains of domesticated dogs that date from 14,000 years ago have been found in a cave in Iraq, while in Britain and Denmark, 9000-year-old dog skeletons have been found. Similar remains in an Idaho cave are 10,500 years old. In fact, until the 18th century, when Europeans introduced horses to the Americas, dogs were the only domesticated animals of many Native American peoples.

Initially dogs had a primarily utilitarian role, but today they tend to be looked on as companions and friends. Of course, there are still many people who believe that their sole purpose, like that of other animals, is to be used or abused. This self-centered point of view is finally beginning to lose ground, although there is still lots of evidence that it is alive and well, as we will see later in this book. Fortunately for dogs, being viewed as companions has helped save them from some disasters— such as being eaten as food—and sometimes it has even helped them receive special treatment.

Throughout history, many dogs belonging to aristocrats, particularly the miniature or toy breeds, have lived like royalty. Grooming them, perfuming them, feeding them fancy foods, dressing them with jewels, and carrying pampered dogs around on cushions goes back at least as far as the Romans. At one point, Julius Caesar asked if Roman women had begun giving birth to lapdogs instead of children. In China, before the communists took over, the emperor's dogs were tended by eunuchs, and anyone who dared to strike one of these dogs was tortured to death. The babies of some women slaves were killed at birth so the women could nurse the puppies.

It is said that two dogs actually became kings—one became king of Ethiopia in the first century A.D. and the other of Norway in the 11th century. There may have been a third dog king, in Hungary. More recently, a town in California elected a Labrador retriever as its mayor—an office he filled for quite a few years.

Some nonaristocratic dogs also receive special treatment. The hunting dogs of the Nyanga people of Africa have rights equal with those of the hunters and above those of the women and children. In fact, a hunter will do everything he can to protect his dog from even minor injuries or discomforts, often at the expense of his own welfare. So, in some ways, he is even treated better than the hunter himself.

Much of this special treatment came about because of the valuable, unconditional friendship dogs offer. Will Rogers once wrote, "That's one thing the poor country fellow will always have, his pack of dogs, and no man can be condemned for owning a dog. In fact you admire him, 'cause as long as he's got a dog he's got a friend, and the poorer he gets the better friend he has."

In 1603, Rudolf II, emperor of the Holy Roman Empire, was given a dozen dogs by Maximilian, the duke of Bavaria, because the Duke's daughter refused to marry him. He wrote back, "These great animals are my joy and comfort. My admiration for them is greater than my understanding of marriage."

After the Battle of Germantown during the Revolutionary War, General Howe's hungry dog wandered across the lines and into George Washington's tent as he was eating his dinner. General Washington ordered his men to feed the dog and then had him returned under a flag of truce. It seems that there are some who can put aside their differences when the companionship of a dog is involved.

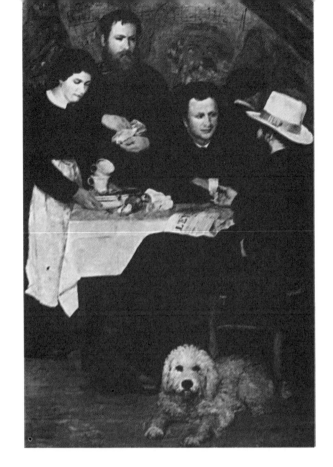

PIERRE-AUGUSTE RENOIR, *At Mother Anthony's,* 1866. French Impressionist painter who is considered one of the great masters. (National Museum, Stockholm)

Hemingway's Dog

ERNEST HEMINGWAY, from "The Christmas Gift", *Look* magazine, 1954. American novelist. Considered one of the great authors of the 20th century, Hemingway is the author of many classics, including *For Whom the Bell Tolls* and *A Farewell to Arms*. He was awarded the Pulitzer Prize for Fiction in 1953 and the Nobel Prize for Literature in 1954. Poor health and depression led to his suicide in 1961.

Thinking about these times and about how fine the night could be when you were allowed to roam freely, I skipped further dreams and decided to think about the past.

This past was never my past life which truly bores me to think about and is often very distasteful due to the mistakes that I have made and the casualties to various human beings involved in that sad affair. I tried to think instead of other people, of the fine deeds of people and animals I have known, and I thought a long time about my dog Black Dog and what the two winters must have been when he had no master in Ketchum, Idaho, having been lost or abandoned by some summer motorist. Any small hardships we had encountered seemed to me to be dwarfed by Blackie's odyssey.

We encountered Blackie when we were living in a log cabin in Ketchum and had two deer, killed, respectively, by Mary and Patrick, hung up in the open door of the barn. There was also a string of mallard ducks hung out of the reach of cats and there were also hung up Hungarian partridges, different varieties of quail and other fine eating birds. It seeming that we were people of such evident solidarity, Blackie abandoned promiscuous begging and attached himself to us as our permanent dog. His devotion was exemplary and his appetite enormous. He slept by the fireplace and he had perfect manners.

When it came time to leave Ketchum and return to Cuba, I was faced with a grave moral problem as I did not know whether a dog bearing such a heavy coat as he had grown living in the snow could be brought to Cuba without making him suffer. But Blackie solved this problem when he saw us start packing by getting into the car and refusing to leave it unless he was lifted out. Lifted out, he would immediately leap back into the car and look at you with those eyes which are possessed only by springer spaniels and certain women.

"Black Dog," I asked him, "can you use a can opener?"

Black Dog appeared to give a negative answer, and I decided against leaving him with several cases of tinned dog food. There was also the first licensing project for dogs on in Ketchum. This was a town where a man was once not regarded as respectable unless he was accompanied by his dog. But a reform movement had set in, led by several local religionists, and gambling had been abolished and there was even a movement on foot to forbid a dog entering a public eating place with his master. Blackie had always tugged me by the trouser leg as we passed a combination gambling and eating place called the Alpine where they served the finest sizzling steak in the West. Blackie wanted me to order the giant sizzling steak and it was difficult to pass the Alpine and go to a place called the Tram where the steak while good was much smaller. We decided to make a command decision and take Blackie to Cuba.

To Flush, My Dog

ELIZABETH BARRETT BROWNING, from the *Athenaeum*, 1843. English poet. Browning is considered one of the greatest women poets. She was an invalid, and Flush—a cocker spaniel—was her constant companion for almost 14 years.

I

Loving friend, the gift of one
Who her own true faith has run
   Through thy lower nature,
Be my benediction said
With my hand upon thy head,
   Gentle fellow-creature!

II

Like a lady's ringlets brown,
Flow thy silken ears adown
   Either side demurely
Of thy silver-suited breast
Shining out from all the rest
   Of thy body purely.

III

Darkly brown thy body is,
Till the sunshine striking this
   Alchemize its dulness,
When the sleek curls manifold
Flash all over into gold
   With a burnished fulness.

IV

Underneath my stroking hand,
Startled eyes of hazel bland
   Kindling, growing larger,
Up thou leapest with a spring,
Full of prank and curveting,
   Leaping like a charger.

V

Leap! thy broad tail waves a light,
Leap! thy slender feet are bright,
   Canopied in fringes;
Leap! those tasselled ears of thine
Flicker strangely, fair and fine
   Down their golden inches.

JEAN-BAPTISTE GREUZE (1725–1805), *Madame de Porcin*. French genre and portrait painter. Greuze was very popular and even did a portrait for Napoleon, but he lost his fortune and popularity in the French Revolution and died in poverty.

VI

Yet, my pretty, sportive friend,
Little is 't to such an end
   That I praise thy rareness;
Other dogs may be thy peers
Haply in these drooping ears
   And this glossy fairness.

VII

But of *thee* it shall be said,
This dog watched beside a bed
   Day and night unweary,
Watched within a curtained room
Where no sunbeam brake the gloom
   Round the sick and dreary.

VIII

Roses, gathered for a vase,
In that chamber died apace,
   Beam and breeze resigning;
This dog only, waited on,
Knowing that when light is gone
   Love remains for shining.

IX

Other dogs in thymy dew
Tracked the hares and followed through
   Sunny moor or meadow;
This dog only, crept and crept
Next a languid cheek that slept,
   Sharing in the shadow.

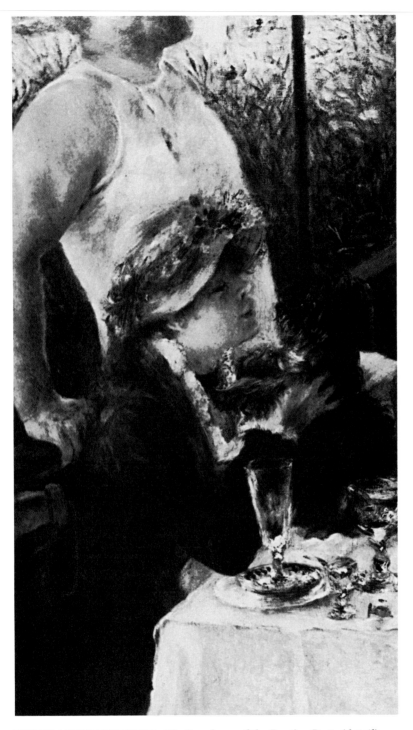

PIERRE-AUGUSTE RENOIR, *The Luncheon of the Boating Party* (detail), 1881. French Impressionist painter. This picture is one of Renoir's most famous works. (Phillips Collection, Washington, D.C.)

X

Other dogs of loyal cheer
Bounded at the whistle clear,
    Up the woodside hieing;
This dog only, watched in reach
Of a faintly uttered speech
    Or a louder sighing.

XI

And if one or two quick tears
Dropped upon his glossy ears
    Or a sigh came double,
Up he sprang in eager haste,
Fawning, fondling, breathing fast,
    In a tender trouble.

XII

And this dog was satisfied
If a pale thin hand would glide
    Down his dewlaps sloping,—
Which he pushed his nose within,
After,—platforming his chin
    On the palm left open.

XIII

This dog, if a friendly voice
Call him now to blither choice
    Than such chamber-keeping,
'Come out!' praying from the door,—
Presseth backward as before,
    Up against me leaping.

XIV

Therefore to this dog will I,
Tenderly not scornfully,
    Render praise and favor:
With my hand upon his head,
Is my benediction said
    Therefore and for ever.

XV

And because he loves me so,
Better than his kind will do
    Often man or woman,
Give I back more love again
Than dogs often take of men,
    Leaning from my Human.

XVI

Blessings on thee, dog of mine,
Pretty collars make thee fine,
    Sugared milk make fat thee!
Pleasures wag on in thy tail,
Hands of gentle motion fail
    Nevermore, to pat thee!

XVII

Downy pillow take thy head,
Silken coverlid bestead,
    Sunshine help thy sleeping!
No fly's buzzing wake thee up,
No man break thy purple cup
    Set for drinking deep in.

SIR EDWIN LANDSEER, *Macaw, Love Birds, Terrier, and Spaniel Puppies, Belonging to Her Majesty* (also called *Islay and Tilco with a Red Macaw and Two Love Birds*), 1819. English animal painter. Shown are some of Queen Victoria's pets. (Her Majesty the Queen)

XVIII

Whiskered cats arointed flee,
Sturdy stoppers keep from thee
   Cologne distillations;
Nuts lie in thy path for stones,
And thy feast-day macaroons
   Turn to daily rations!

XIX

Mock I thee, in wishing weal?—
Tears are in my eyes to feel
   Thou art made so straitly,
Blessing needs must straiten too,—
Little canst thou joy or do,
   Thou who lovest *greatly*.

XX

Yet be blessèd to the height
Of all good and all delight
   Pervious to thy nature;
Only *loved* beyond that line,
With a love that answers thine,
   Loving fellow-creature!

On a Little Dog

MARTIAL (MARCUS VALERIUS MARTIALIS), from *Epigrammata (Epigrams),* A.D. 86–102. Roman epigrammatist who was made an honorary military tribune by Emperor Titus. *Epigrammata* is a 12-volume work containing 1172 epigrammatic poems. This poem was written about a Maltese named Issa who belonged to Publius, the Roman governor of Malta.

TITIAN (TIZIANO VE-CELLIO), *The Venus of Urbino,* 1538. Venetian painter. This is a portrait of Eleanora Gonzaga, the Duchess of Urbino, with her papillon. (Uffizi Gallery, Florence)

Cattullus of a sparrow sung:
    But Issa's neater.
A kiss is sweet from ringdove's tongue:
    But Issa's sweeter.
She's nicer than the nicest girl,
    She's dearer than the dearest pearl,
      No pet can beat her.

Whene'er she whines, you'd think that she
    Was talking sadly.
Sometimes she cries, sometimes in glee
    She barks out gladly.
And when she needs herself to ease,
    She lifts her paw, and says—"Sir, please,
      I want to badly."

If she is sleeping on your bed
    You do not hear her;
Nor will she soil the blanket spread,
    You need not fear her.
So modest is she, we can't find
  A suitor of the canine kind
    To let come near her.

Lest death should take her from our eyes,
    A picture giving
Her very self in shape and size
    Portrays her striving
Put dog and picture both together
  You'll wonder which is paint, or whether
    They both are living.

LOUIS ICART, *Les Yeux
(Two Beauties),* 1931.
French Art Deco artist.
His wife, Fanny, and
their dog, Dollar.

A Dog and a Cat

SARAH EDDY, from *Alexander and Some Other Cats,* 1929.

A woman in a city in Ohio tells a very interesting story of how she learned from her dog a humane lesson which she says will stay by her during her entire life.

The dog for some time was the only pet in the family, but owing to the infringement of rats and mice upon the place, they decided to add a cat to the household. Like many other people who have not learned to consider the value of a cat from many standpoints, as soon as her work was done the woman decided she was of no further use, and was somewhat of a nuisance. She therefore insisted that her husband should carry the cat away to a remote section of the city and drop it, leaving it to find a home for itself, and trusting that some heart would be kinder than hers.

Her insistence brought about the desired result. The dog, who at first had not been in sympathy with the addition of a cat to the family circle, had later become much attached to her and seemed to miss her. Later in the year when winter had set in, the woman was one day sitting at her window, sewing. It had been snowing hard throughout the day, and she looked out upon a world of trackless white. In the distance she saw the dog floundering through the snow with something in his mouth. When he reached the gate she discovered that it was a cat, and at the threshold that it was the puss which she had abandoned. The dog had brought the cat safely home, carrying it well up out of the snow, without injury. Whether he found it on its way home, or whether he had searched until he found it at the place where it had been dropped, is not known. He could not tell, but the wagging of his tail was expressive of his satisfaction in having found his old friend.

PABLO PICASSO, Left: *Fillette au chien (étude pour Les Bateleurs) [Little Girl with a Dog (Study for The Saltimbanques)]*, 1905, Right: *L'Enfant au chien (Boy with a Dog)*, 1905. Spanish painter. Picasso was one of the inventors of the Cubist style. (Left: Private collection, Right: Hermitage Museum, St. Petersburg)

A Dog and a Raven

REV. JOHN WESLEY, from *The Journal of Rev. John Wesley*, 1790. English evangelical preacher and founder of the Methodist Church writing about a visit to some friends in Chester, England.

Here I met with one of the most extraordinary phenomena that I ever saw or heard of. Mr. Sellers has in his yard a large Newfoundland dog, and an old raven. These have fallen deeply in love with each other, and never desire to be apart. The bird has learnt the bark of the dog, so that few can distinguish them. She is inconsolable when he goes out; and if he stays out a day or two, she will get up all the bones and scraps she can, and hoard them up for him, till he comes back.

Walking with a Dog

THOMAS MANN, from *Herr und Hund (A Man and His Dog)*, 1918. German novelist and essayist who moved to the United States after the Nazis came to power. He was awarded the Nobel Prize for Literature in 1929 and is considered one of the greatest German writers of the 20th century.

When spring, the fairest season of the year, does honour to its name, and when the trilling of the birds rouses me early because I have ended the day before at a seemly hour, I love to rise betimes and go for a half-hour's walk before breakfast. Strolling hatless in the broad avenue in front of my house, or through the parks beyond, I like to enjoy a few draughts of the young morning air and taste its blithe purity before I am claimed by the labours of the day. Standing on the front steps of my house, I give a whistle in two notes, tonic and lower fourth, like the beginning of the second phrase of Schubert's Unfinished Symphony; it might be considered the musical setting of a two-syllabled name. Next moment, and while I walk towards the garden gate, the faintest tinkle sounds from afar, at first scarcely audible, but growing rapidly louder and more distinct; such a sound as might be made by a metal licence-tag clicking against the trimmings of a leather collar. I face about, to see Bashan rounding the corner of the house at top speed and charging towards me as though he meant to knock me down. In the effort he is making he has dropped his lower lip, baring two white teeth that glitter in the morning sun.

He comes straight from his kennel, which stands at the back of the house, between the props of the veranda floor. Probably, until my two-toned call set him in this violent motion, he had been lying there snatching a nap after the adventures of the night. The kennel has curtains of sacking and is lined with straw; indeed, a straw or so may be

CLAUDE MONET (1840–1926), *Man with a Parasol*. French Impression-ist landscape painter. (Kunsthaus, Zurich)

clinging to Bashan's sleep-rumpled coat or even sticking between his toes—a comic sight, which reminds me of a painstakingly imagined production of Schiller's *Die Räuber* that I once saw, in which old Count Moor came out of the Hunger Tower tricot-clad, with a straw sticking pathetically between his toes. Involuntarily I assume a defensive posi-tion to meet the charge, receiving it on my flank, for Bashan shows every sign of meaning to run between my legs and trip me up. However at the last minute, when a collision is imminent, he always puts on the brakes, exe-cuting a half-wheel which speaks for both his mental and his physical self-control. And then, without a sound—for he makes sparing use of his sonorous and expressive voice—he dances wildly round me by way of greeting, with immoderate plungings and waggings which are not confined to the appendage provided by nature for the purpose but bring his whole hind quarters as far as his ribs into play. He contracts his whole body into a curve, he hurtles into the air in a flying leap, he turns round and round on his own axis—and curiously enough, whichever way I turn, he always contrives to execute these manoeuvres behind my back. But the moment I stoop down and put out my hand he jumps to my side and stands like a statue, with his shoulder against my shin, in a slantwise posture, his strong paws braced against the ground, his face turned upwards so that he looks at me upside-down. And his utter immobility, as I pat his shoulder and murmur encouragement, is as concentrated and fiercely passionate as the frenzy before it had been.

●   ●   ●

Here for a while I stroll along the paths, and Bashan revels in the freedom of unlimited level space, galloping across and across the lawns like mad with his body inclined in a centrifugal plane; sometimes, barking with mingled pleasure and exasperation, he pursues a bird which flutters as though spellbound, but perhaps on purpose to tease him, along the ground just in front of his nose. But if I sit down on a bench he is at my side at once and takes up a position on one of my feet. For it is a law of his being that he only runs about when I am in motion too; that when I settle down he follows suit. There seems no obvious reason for this practice; but Bashan never fails to conform to it.

I get an odd, intimate, and amusing sensation from having him sit on my foot and warm it with the blood-heat of his body. A pervasive feeling of sympathy and good cheer fills me, as almost invariably when in his company and looking at things from his angle. He has a rather rustic slouch when he sits down; his shoulder-blades stick out and his paws turn negligently in. He looks smaller and squatter than he really is, and the little white boss on his chest is advanced with comic effect. But all these faults are atoned for by the lofty and dignified carriage of the head, so full of concentration. All is quiet, and we two sit there absolutely still in our turn. The rushing of the water comes to us faint and subdued. And the senses become alert for all the tiny, mysterious little sounds that nature makes: the lizard's quick dart, the note of the bird, the burrowing of a mole in the earth. Bashan pricks up his ears—in so far as the muscles of naturally drooping ears will allow them to be pricked. He cocks his head to hear the better; and the nostrils of his moist black nose keep twitching sensitively as he sniffs.

Then he lies down, but always in contact with my foot. I see him in profile, in that age-old, conventionalized pose of the beast-god, the sphinx: head and chest held high, forelegs close to the body, paws extended in parallel lines.

HOKUSAI, *Japanese Spaniel* (a fan print), 1833. Japanese painter, draftsman, and wood engraver.

The Dog and the Water-Lily

WILLIAM COWPER, from the *Gentleman's Magazine,* 1791. English poet.

NO FABLE

The noon was shady, and soft airs
   Swept Ouse's silent tide,
When, 'scap'd from literary cares,
   I wander'd on his side.

My spaniel, prettiest of his race,
   And high in pedigree,
(Two nymphs, adorn'd with ev'ry grace
   That spaniel found for me)

Now wanton'd lost in flags and reeds,
   Now starting into sight
Pursued the swallow o'er the meads
   With scarce a slower flight.

It was the time when Ouse display'd
   His lilies newly blown;
Their beauties I intent survey'd;
   And one I wish'd my own.

With cane extended far I sought
   To steer it close to land;
But still the prize, though nearly caught,
   Escap'd my eager hand.

Beau marked my unsuccessful pains
   With fixt consid'rate face,
And puzzling set his puppy brains
   To comprehend the case.

GIUSEPPE CASTIGLIONE (1688–1766), *Dog under Flowering Branches.* Italian court painter. Castiglione became a Jesuit missionary to China, where he adopted the Chinese style.

But with a chirrup clear and strong,
   Dispersing all his dream,
I thence withdrew, and follow'd long
   The windings of the stream.

My ramble finish'd, I return'd.
   Beau trotting far before
The floating wreath again discern'd,
   And plunging left the shore.

I saw him with that lily cropp'd
   Impatient swim to meet
My quick approach, and soon he dropp'd
   The treasure at my feet.

Charm'd with the sight, the world, I cried,
   Shall hear of this thy deed,
My dog shall mortify the pride
   Of man's superior breed;

But, chief, myself I will enjoin,
   Awake at duty's call,
To show a love as prompt as thine
   To Him who gives me all.

Bum

W. DAYTON WEDGEFARTH.

He's a little dog, with a stubby tail, and a moth-eaten coat
   of tan,
   And his legs are short, of the wabbly sort;
I doubt if they ever ran;
And he howls at night, while in broad daylight he sleeps
   like a bloomin' log,
And he likes the food of the gutter breed; he's a most
   irregular dog.

I call him Bum, and in total sum he's all that his name
   implies,
For he's just a tramp with a highway stamp that culture
   cannot disguise;
And his friends, I've found, in the streets abound, be they
   urchins or dogs or men;
   Yet he sticks to me with a fiendish glee. It is truly
   beyond my ken.

I talk to him when I'm lonesome-like, and I'm sure that
   he understands
When he looks at me so attentively and gently licks my
   hands;
Then he rubs his nose on my tailored clothes, but I never
   say nought thereat,
For the good Lord knows I can buy more clothes, but
   never a friend like that!

Mexican Indian vessel,
A.D. 300–1000.

Owd Roä[1] (excerpt)

LORD TENNYSON (ALFRED TENNYSON), from *Demeter and Persephone*, 1889. English poet laureate who wrote "The Charge of the Light Brigade" and *Idylls of the King*. This excerpt from "Owd Roä" represents the opening lines of a lengthy poem where a man explains to his son how their house, Howlaby Daale, burned down on Christmas 10 years earlier and how Old Rover was severely injured saving the son's life.

Naäy, noä mander[2] o' use to be callin' 'im
    Roä, Roä, Roä,
Fur the dog's stoän-deäf, an' 'e 's blind, 'e
    can naither stan' nor goä.

But I meäns fur to maäke 'is owd aäge as
    'appy as iver I can,
Fur I owäs owd Roäver moor nor I iver
    owäd mottal man.

Thou 's rode of 'is back when a babby,
    afoor thou was gotten too owd,
Fur 'e 'd fetch an' carry like owt, 'e was
    allus as good as gowd.

Eh, but 'e 'd fight wi' a will *when* 'e fowt;
    'e could howd[3] 'is oän,
An' Roä was the dog as knaw'd when an'
    wheere to bury his boäne.

An' 'e kep his heäd hoop like a king, an'
    'e 'd niver not down wi' 'is taäil,
Fur 'e 'd niver done nowt to be shaämed
    on, when we was i' Howlaby Daäle.

---

[1]Old Rover.

[2]Manner.

[3]Hold.

The Harper

THOMAS CAMPBELL, from *The Pleasures of Hope,* 1799. Scottish poet.
Campbell became famous in Britain with his first book, *The Pleasures of
Hope,* at the age of 21.

On the banks of Shannon when Sheelah was nigh,
No blithe Irish lad was so happy as I;
No harp like my own could so cheerily play
And wherever I went was my poor dog Tray.

When at last I was forced from my Sheelah to part,
She said, (while the sorrow was big at the heart,)
"Oh! remember your Sheelah when far, far away;
And be kind, my dear Pat, to our poor dog Tray."

GEORGE STUBBS, *An Old Pony and a Hound,* ca. 1777. English painter. Stubbs is especially famous for his horse paintings. (Private collection)

"Oh! Poor dog! he was faithful and kind to be sure,
And he constantly loved me although I was poor;
When the sour-looking folk sent me heartless away,
I had always a friend in my poor dog Tray.

When the road was so dark, and the night was so cold,
And Pat and his dog were grown weary and old,
How snugly we slept in my old coat of gray,
And he licked me for kindness—my old dog Tray.

Though my wallet was scant I remembered his case,
Nor refused my last crust to his pitiful face;
But he died at my feet on a cold winter day,
And I play'd a sad lament for my poor dog Tray.

Where now shall I go, poor, forsaken, and blind?
Can I find one to guide me, so faithful and kind?
To my sweet native village, so far, far away,
I can never more return with my poor dog Tray.

The Power of the Dog

RUDYARD KIPLING, from *Actions and Reactions*, 1909. English poet, novelist, and short story writer who wrote about India. He was the author of *The Jungle Book, Kim, Captains Courageous, Just So Stories,* the poem "Gunga Din", and the short story "The Man Who Would Be King". He was awarded the Nobel Prize for Literature in 1907.

There is sorrow enough in the natural way
From men and women to fill our day;
And when we are certain of sorrow in store,
Why do we always arrange for more?
Brothers and Sisters, I bid you beware
Of giving your heart to a dog to tear.

Buy a pup and your money will buy
Love unflinching that cannot lie—
Perfect passion and worship fed
By a kick in the ribs or a pat on the head.
Nevertheless it is hardly fair
To risk your heart for a dog to tear.

When the fourteen years which Nature permits
Are closing in asthma, or tumor, or fits,
And the vet's unspoken prescription runs
To lethal chambers or loaded guns,
Then you will find—it's your own affair—
But . . . you've given your heart to a dog to tear.

When the body that lived at your single will,
With its whimper of welcome, is stilled (how still!).
When the spirit that answered your every mood
Is gone—wherever it goes—for good,
You will discover how much you care,
And will give your heart to a dog to tear.

We've sorrow enough in the natural way,
When it comes to burying Christian clay.
Our loves are not given, but only lent,
At compound interest of cent per cent.
Though it is not always the case, I believe,
That the longer we've kept 'em, the more do we grieve:
For, when debts are payable, right or wrong,
A short-time loan is as bad as a long—
So why in—Heaven (before we are there)
Should we give our hearts to a dog to tear?

ÉDOUARD MANET, *The Spaniel*, 1866. French Impressionist painter.
Manet's work was attacked by critics his entire life. He is now considered one of the masters. (Private collection)

Waking from a Nightmare

EDGAR ALLAN POE, from "The Narrative of A. Gordon Pym of Nantucket", *Harper's* magazine, 1838. American author, editor, and critic. Author of the short stories "The Tell-Tale Heart", "The Murders in the Rue Morgue", and "The Pit and the Pendulum" and the poem "The Raven". Alcoholism led to his death at the age of 40. Unappreciated in his time, Poe is now considered "one of America's greatest literary geniuses."

Stifling in a paroxysm of terror, I at last found myself partially awake. My dream, then, was not all a dream. Now, at least, I was in possession of my senses. The paws of some huge and real monster were pressing heavily upon my bosom—his hot breath was in my ear—and his white and ghastly fangs were gleaming upon me through the gloom.

Had a thousand lives hung upon the movement of a limb or the utterance of a syllable, I could have neither stirred nor spoken. The beast, whatever it was, retained his position without attempting any immediate violence, while I lay in an utterly helpless, and, I fancied, a dying condition beneath him. I felt that my powers of body and mind were fast leaving me—in a word, that I was perishing, and perishing of sheer fright. My brain swam—I grew deadly sick—my vision failed—even the glaring eyeballs above me grew dim. Making a last strong effort, I at length breathed a faint ejaculation to God, and resigned myself to die. The sound of my voice seemed to arouse all the latent fury of the animal. He precipitated himself at full length upon my body; but what was my astonishment, when, with a long and low whine, he commenced licking my face and hands with the greatest eagerness, and with the most extravagant demonstration of affection and joy! I was bewildered, utterly lost in amazement—but I could not forget the peculiar whine of my Newfoundland dog Tiger, and the odd manner of his caresses I well knew. It

SIR EDWIN LANDSEER, *Portrait of Neptune, the Property of William Ellis Gosling, Esq.,* 1824. English animal painter. Landseer's paintings of Newfoundlands were so popular that the black and white versions are now called Landseers, and some people even consider them to be a separate breed. It is said that Napoleon—who could not swim—fell into the sea when he left exile for his return to power and that his life was saved by a Newfoundland. (Philadelphia Museum of Art, Philadelphia)

was he. I experienced a sudden rush of blood to my temples—a giddy and overpowering sense of deliverance and reanimation. I rose hurriedly from the mattress upon which I had been lying, and, throwing myself upon the neck of my faithful follower and friend, relieved the long oppression of my bosom in a flood of the most passionate tears. . . . Most people love their dogs, but for Tiger I had an affection far more ardent than common; and never, certainly, did any creature more truly deserve it. For seven years he had been my inseparable companion, and in a multitude of instances had given evidence of all the noble qualities for which we value the animal. I had rescued him, when a puppy, from the clutches of a malignant little villain in Nantucket, who was leading him, with a rope around his neck, to the water; and the grown dog repaid the obligation, about three years afterward, by saving me from the bludgeon of a street robber.

A Case Against a Dog Killer

SENATOR GEORGE GRAHAM VEST, address before a jury, 1870. A farmer had his nephew kill his neighbor's foxhound, Old Drum, for coming onto his land. Old Drum's owner sued. After three trials, Vest (not yet a senator) was hired by Old Drum's owner, while the farmer hired Francis Cockrell (who would also become a senator) and Thomas Crittenden (who became the governor credited with breaking up the Jesse James gang). Vest showed no interest in the testimony and took no notes. The trial looked as if it could go either way. Then he made his closing arguments.

"Gentlemen of the Jury:

"The best friend a man has in the world may turn against him, and become his enemy. His son or daughter that he has reared with loving care may prove ungrateful. Those who are nearest and dearest to us, those whom we trust with our happiness and our good name, may become traitors to their faith. The money that a man has, he may lose. It flies away from him, perhaps when he needs it most. A man's reputation may be sacrificed in a moment of ill-considered action. The people who are prone to fall on their knees to do us honor when success is with us may be the first to throw the stone of malice when failure settles its cloud upon our heads.

"The one absolutely unselfish friend that man can have in this selfish world, the one that never deserts him, the one that never proves ungrateful or treacherous, is his dog. A man's dog stands by him in prosperity and in poverty, in health and in sickness. He will sleep on the cold ground, where the wintry winds blow and the snow drives fiercely, if only he may be near his master's side. He will kiss the hand that has no food to offer; he will lick the wounds and sores that come in encounter with the roughness of the world. He guards the sleep of his pauper master as if he were a prince. When all other friends desert,

SIR EDWIN LANDSEER, *The Poor Dog* (also called *The Shepherd's Grave*), 1829. English animal painter. (Private collection)

he remains. When riches take wings, and reputation falls to pieces, he is as constant in his love as the sun in its journey through the heavens.

"If fortune drives the master forth an outcast in the world, friendless and homeless, the faithful dog asks no higher privilege than that of accompanying him, to guard him against danger, to fight against his enemies. And when the last scene of all comes, and death takes his master in its embrace and his body is laid away in the cold ground, no matter if all other friends pursue their way, there by the grave-side will the noble dog be found, his head between his paws, his eyes sad, but open in alert watchfulness, faithful and true even in death."

After hearing this argument, the jury deliberated for only two minutes before deciding in favor of Old Drum's owner, telling the judge they wanted to send the dog killer to prison. Unfortunately the law would not allow it. Monuments to Old Drum, with Vest's argument inscribed on them, were erected outside the courthouse in Warrensburg, Missouri, and at the site where his body was found.

JOHN SINGER SARGENT, *Beatrice Townsend,* ca. 1882. American painter. Though Sargent was an American citizen, he spent almost his entire life in Britain and Europe. (Private collection)

LOYALTY

*If you pick up a starving dog and make him pros-
perous, he will not bite you. This is the principal
difference between a dog and man.*

Mark Twain, *Pudd'nhead Wilson*, 1894.

*Histories are more full of examples of fidelity of
dogs than of friends.*

Alexander Pope in a letter to H. Cromwell,
1709.

One of the best-known characteristics of dogs is their unflinching loyalty. Even today, it is not unusual to find that the rich and famous—who are often surrounded by people with ulterior motives—are very devoted to their dogs. In earlier periods, the need to depend on dogs was sometimes even greater.

Some political and military leaders have been forced to rely heavily on dogs for their protection. The Byzantine emperor Andronicus I (ca. 1110–1185) scandalized Constantinople with his romances, murders, and treason. His acts of treachery and betrayal, which brought him to power and kept him there, provoked so much enmity that he could not even trust his bodyguards when he slept at night. He had to rely on a large Albanian hound for his protection. This hound turned out to be very effective at keeping everyone away from his sleeping master.

King Henry III of France (1551–1589) had three dogs who guarded him at night in shifts. When a shift ended, the dog on duty would go and wake up his replacement. One night a monk came to see the king and was attacked by the dog on duty. After the king locked the dog in another room, the monk stabbed him. The dogs raised the alarm, and the king was able to explain what happened before he died. Earlier, Alexander the Great (356–323 B.C.) had also kept his dog, Perites, near him while he slept. When Perites died, Alexander honored this dog by naming a city after him.

Dogs were very popular among the Egyptian pharaohs. One pharaoh had over 600 dogs. Cheops, the Egyptian king who ruled from 2590 to 2568 B.C. and built the Great Pyramid at Giza, had a dog named Abakaru as his companion and protector. And there are other

Egyptian dogs who lie among the royal tombs at Giza. One was mummified and given a full ceremonial burial, complete with his own coffin and incense, in about 3000 B.C. His stone slab bears this inscription: "The dog who was the guard of the king. Abuwtiyuw was his name. . . ." Many pharaohs were buried with effigies of their dogs. Ramses II was buried with the names and statues of four of his dogs, and Tutankhamen was buried with images of two of his dogs.

The Egyptians were not the only ones to inter dogs with their royalty. The Hittites, who lived in what is now Turkey, buried dogs in tombs along with their kings and queens. The Chinese emperors of the Shang dynasty (ca. 1523–1028 B.C.) may also have been interred with their watchdogs, though effigies—such as straw dogs— appear to have been substituted after this period.

Some ancient Egyptian cities, such as those named Cynopolis, had special cemeteries for dogs and jackals. (Cynopolis is their Hellenistic name and means "Dogtown". One Cynopolis had the Egyptian name Pi-anup, or "City of Anubis", and is now the modern city Asyut. There appear to be two others that were also dedicated to Anubis; one is now called Samallut and the other was located in the Nile delta. A fourth Egyptian city had the Hellenistic name Lycopolis, or "Wolf City".) People would sometimes bring their dogs long distances to have them mummified and interred in these cities with the proper ceremonies. Some dog mummies have been found wearing masks and collars made of flowers. Modern Americans also have special cemeteries where people can bury their dogs with ceremonies and elaborate monuments.

Actually, it is not surprising to find dogs receiving such honors. They are among the few creatures who will unquestioningly put the well-being of a member of another species above their own safety and comfort.

In 1979, Ray Thomas was spending the afternoon in a forest near Cleveland, Ohio, with his fiancée and her dog, which was part collie and part German shepherd. As he was trying to take a photograph, he slipped and fell off an 80-foot cliff. He landed at the edge of the river below, breaking his back. The dog immediately went after him, leaping off the cliff into thin air. The fall broke both her hips, and so she had to slowly drag herself over to where Thomas was lying unconscious, face down in the water. She pulled his head from the water, saving him from drowning, and then watched over him until help arrived.

Heroism in dogs is not a recent phenomenon. Excavators digging through the volcanic ash that buried the ruins of Pompeii in A.D. 79 discovered a dog lying across a child. The dog, whose name was Delta, wore a collar that told how he had saved the life of his owner, Severinus, three times. Once Delta had pulled Severinus from the sea, preventing him from drowning. On another occasion, the dog had fought off four men attempting to rob his master. Finally, Delta had saved Severinus when he was attacked by a wolf in the sacred grove of Diana, near Herculaneum. As Vesuvius erupted, the dog was apparently trying to protect the child underneath him from the hot ash when they were both overcome by the volcano's poisonous gases. Nearly 2000 years later, Delta's unselfish deeds still stand as an excellent example of a dog's loyalty.

Faithful and Trusty Companion

PLINY THE ELDER (GAIUS PLINIUS SECUNDUS, A.D. 23–79). Roman naturalist. Pliny died from volcanic gases while investigating the eruption of Mt. Vesuvius that buried Pompeii and Herculaneum in A.D. 79. This selection is from *Natural History,* which consists of 37 books dealing with geography, anthropology, biology, and other fields.

Among those domesticated creatures that converse with us, there be many things worth the knowledge: and namely, as touching dogs (the most faithful and trusty companions of all others to a man) and also horses. And in very truth, I have heard it credibly reported, of a dog, that in defence of his master, fought hard against thieves robbing by the highwayside: and albeit he were sore wounded even to death, yet would he not abandon the dead body of his master, but drave away both wild foule and savage beast, from seizing of his carcass. Also of another in Epirus, who in a great assembly of people knowing the man that had murdered his master flew upon him with open mouth, barking and snapping at him so furiously, that he was ready to take him by the throat, until he at length confessed the fact that should cause the dog thus to rage and foam against him. . . .

But this passeth all, which happened in our time, and standeth upon record in the public registers, namely, in the year that Appius Julius and P. Silius were Consuls, at what time as T. Sabinus and his servants were executed for an outrage committed upon the person of Nero,[1] son of Germanicus: one of them that died had a dog which could not be kept from the prison door, and when his master was thrown down the stairs (called Scalae Gemoniae) would not depart the dead corpse, but kept a most piteous howling lamentation about it, in the sight of a great multitude of Romans that stood round about to see the execution and the manner of it: and when one of the company threw the dog a piece of meat, he straight ways carried it to the mouth of his master lying dead. Moreover, when the carcass was thrown into the river Tiberis, the same dog swam after, and made all the means he could to bear it up afloat that it should not sink: and to the sight of this spectacle and fidelity of the poor dog to his master, a number of people ran forth by heaps out of the city to the waterside.

---

[1]Nero was Roman emperor from A.D. 54 to 68.

SIR EDWIN LANDSEER, *Attachment*, 1829. English animal painter. This painting was based on the same story that inspired the accompanying poems by Wordsworth and Scott. (Private collection)

Fidelity

WILLIAM WORDSWORTH, from *Poems in Two Volumes*, 1807. English poet laureate.

"The young man whose death gave occasion to this poem was named Charles Gough, and had come early in the spring to Patterdale for the sake of angling. While attempting to cross over Helvellyn to Grasmere he slipped from a steep part of the rock where the ice was not thawed, and perished. His body was discovered as is told in this poem. Walter Scott heard of the accident, and both he and I, without either of us knowing that the other had taken up the subject, each wrote a poem in admiration of the dog's fidelity. His contains a most beautiful stanza:—

How long didst thou think that his silence was slumber?
When the wind waved his garment, how oft didst thou
　　　start?

I will add that the sentiment in the last four lines of the last stanza in my verses was uttered by a shepherd with such exactness, that a traveller, who afterwards reported his account in print, was induced to question the man whether he had read them, which he had not."

A barking sound the Shepherd hears,
A cry as of a dog or fox;
He halts—and searches with his eyes
Among the scattered rocks:
And now at distance can discern
A stirring in a brake of fern;
And instantly a dog is seen,
Glancing through that covert green.

The Dog is not of mountain breed;
Its motions, too, are wild and shy;
With something, as the Shepherd thinks,
Unusual in its cry:
Nor is there any one in sight
All round, in hollow or on height;
Nor shout, nor whistle strikes his ear;
What is the creature doing here?

It was a cove, a huge recess,
That keeps, till June, December's snow;
A lofty precipice in front,
A silent tarn below!
Far in the bosom of Helvellyn,
Remote from public road or dwelling,
Pathway, or cultivated land;
From trace of human foot or hand.

There sometimes doth a leaping fish
Send through the tarn a lonely cheer;
The crags repeat the raven's croak,
In symphony austere;
Thither the rainbow comes—the cloud—
And mists that spread the flying shroud;
And sunbeams; and the sounding blast,
That, if it could, would hurry past;
But that enormous barrier holds it fast.

Not free from boding thoughts, a while
The Shepherd stood; then makes his way
O'er rocks and stones, following the Dog
As quickly as he may;
Nor far had gone before he found
A human skeleton on the ground;
The appalled Discoverer with a sigh
Looks round, to learn the history.

From those abrupt and perilous rocks
The Man had fallen, that place of fear!
At length upon the Shepherd's mind
It breaks, and all is clear:
He instantly recalled the name,
And who he was, and whence he came;
Remembered, too, the very day
On which the Traveller passed this way.

But hear a wonder, for whose sake
This lamentable tale I tell!
A lasting monument of words
This wonder merits well.
The Dog which still was hovering nigh,
Repeating the same timid cry,
This Dog had been through three months' space
A dweller in that savage place.

Yes, proof was plain that, since the day
When this ill-fated Traveller died,
The Dog had watched about the spot,
Or by his master's side:
How nourished here through such long time
He knows, who gave that love sublime;
And gave that strength of feeling, great
Above all human estimate!

SIR EDWIN LANDSEER, *The Ptarmigan Hill,* by 1869. English animal painter. Showing two Gordon setters. (Private collection)

Hellvellyn

SIR WALTER SCOTT, 1805. Scottish novelist and poet.

I climb'd the dark brow of the mighty
    Hellvellyn,
  Lakes and mountains beneath me
    gleam'd misty and wide;
All was still, save by fits, when the
    eagle was yelling,
  And starting around me the echoes
    replied.
On the right, Striden-edge round the
    Red-tarn was bending,
And Catchedicam its left verge was
    defending,
One huge nameless rock in the front
    was ascending,
  When I mark'd the sad spot where
    the wanderer had died.

Dark green was that spot 'mid the
brown mountain-heather,
Where the Pilgrim of Nature lay
stretch'd in decay,
Like the corpse of an outcast abandon'd
to weather,
Till the mountain winds wasted
the tenantless clay.
Nor yet quite deserted, though lonely
extended,
For, faithful in death, his mute
favourite attended,
The much-loved remains of her master
defended,
And chased the hill-fox and the
raven away.

How long didst thou think that his
silence was slumber?
When the wind waved his garment,
how oft didst thou start?
How many long days and long weeks
didst thou number,
Ere he faded before thee, the friend
of thy heart?
And, oh, was it meet, that—no re-
quiem read o'er him—
No mother to weep, and no friend
to deplore him,
And thou, little guardian, alone
stretch'd before him—
Unhonour'd the Pilgrim from life
should depart?

A Dog on Duty

DR. JOHN CAIUS, from *De Canibus Britannicus* (also known as *Of Englishe Dogges*), 1570. Doctor of Physic at Cambridge University and court physician to King Edward VI.

And when fires happen in the evening or at night, dogs a year old will bark even though prohibited until the servants wake and perceive the fire; and then stop of their own accord. This has been proved in England. And that dog was not less faithful who would not leave his master, who while hunting fell into a deep well, until by his own sagacity he had been drawn up by a rope on to which, when he was close to the top, the dog leapt to take him into his arms as it were, impatient of more delay. There are some who will not allow a fire to go out, but move coal on to it with their paws, having previously watched and wondered how it is done. If the coal is too hot, they cover it with ash and then shove it into the place with the nose.[2]

---

[2]Perhaps this is why andirons are also called *firedogs*.

ALBRECHT DÜRER, *Big Dog in Repose,* 1520. German painter, draftsman, and engraver. He is considered one of the greatest engravers. (British Museum, London)

Dogs Save the King

A 12TH-CENTURY LATIN BESTIARY compiled from a variety of earlier sources.

So much do dogs adore their owners, that one can read how, when the king of Garamantes[3] was captured by his enemies and sold into slavery, two hundred of his hounds, having made up a party, rescued him from exile out of the middle of the whole battle-line of his foes, and fought those who resisted.

---

[3]Garamantes is now Libya.

HENRY DANCKERTS (1630–1678), *Pineapple Picture*. Charles II, king of England, Scotland, and Ireland, is shown here being presented with the first pineapple grown in England. With him are two of his spaniels. Some of his contemporaries felt he spent too much time with his dogs, at the expense of his royal duties. This breed, made popular by the king, became known as King Charles spaniels (in America they are called English toy spaniels). In the 1920s it was noted that the modern breed—being more snub nosed and round headed—no longer resembled its ancestors depicted in paintings, and so they were rebred to resemble the original. These are called Cavalier King Charles spaniels. (Private collection)

Saved by a Spaniel

JOHN LOTHROP MOTLEY, from *The Rise of the Dutch Republic,* 1856. American historian. Motley relates an incident that occurred when William the Silent, Prince of Orange, was leading the Dutch rebels who were rising up against Spanish rule. In 1572 the Duke of Alva, a Spanish general, sent assassins to kill the prince. Prince William was a founder of Dutch independence.

A chosen band of six hundred harquebusiers, attired, as was customary in these nocturnal expeditions, with their shirts outside their armor, that they might recognize each other in the darkness, were led by Julien Romero within the lines of the enemy. The sentinels were cut down, the whole army surprised and for a moment powerless, while, for two hours long, from one o'clock in the morning until

SIR EDWIN LANDSEER, *Dash,* 1836. English animal painter. This was Landseer's first royal commission. Dash was Princess Victoria's King Charles spaniel. (Her Majesty the Queen)

SIR EDWIN LANDSEER, *King Charles Spaniels* (also called *The Cavalier's Pets*), 1845. English animal painter. It is said that this picture was completed in one or two days. (Tate Gallery, London)

three, the Spaniards butchered their foes, hardly aroused from their sleep, ignorant by how small a force they had been thus suddenly surprised, and unable in the confusion to distinguish between friend and foe. The boldest, led by Julien in person, made at once for the prince's tent. His guards and himself were in profound sleep, but a small spaniel, who always passed the night upon his bed, was a more faithful sentinel. The creature sprang forward, barking furiously at the sound of hostile footsteps, and scratching his master's face with his paws. There was but just time for the prince to mount a horse which was ready saddled, and to effect his escape through the darkness, before his enemies sprang into the tent. His servants were cut down, his master of the horse and two of his secretaries, who gained their saddles a moment later, all lost their lives, and but for the little dog's watchfulness, William of Orange, upon whose shoulders the whole weight of his country's fortunes depended, would have been led within a week to an ignominious death. To his dying day, the prince ever afterward kept a spaniel of the same race in his bedchamber.

Napoleon and a Dog

NAPOLEON BONAPARTE as reported by Count of Las Cases (Emmanuel), *Mémorial de Sainte-Hélène,* 1815. French emperor and one of the greatest conquerors in history. The Comte de Las Cases was the French historian to whom Napoleon dictated his memoirs. The night after the Battle of Bassano in 1796, during his Italian campaign, Napoleon took a stroll through the corpse-laden battlefield.

We were alone, in the profound solitude of a beautiful moonlit night. Suddenly a dog leaped out from under the cloak of a corpse, came running toward us, and almost immediately afterward ran back to its shelter, howling piteously. He licked his master's face, ran back to us, and repeated this several times: he was seeking help and revenge at the same time. I don't know whether it was the mood of the moment, or the place, or the time, or the action in itself, or what—at any rate, it's a fact that nothing I saw on any other battlefield ever produced a like impression on me. I stopped involuntarily to contemplate this spectacle. This man, I said to myself, has friends, perhaps. He may have some at the camp, in his company—and here he lies, abandoned by all except his dog. What a lesson nature was teaching us through an animal!

What a strange thing is man! How mysterious are the workings of his sensibility! I had commanded in battles that were to decide the fate of a whole army, and I had felt no emotion. I had watched the execution of maneuvers that were bound to cost the lives of many among us, and my eyes had remained dry. And suddenly I was shaken, turned inside out, by a dog howling in pain!

The Legend of Gelert

FROM THE STONE MARKING GELERT'S GRAVE. This legend was created by an innkeeper of the village of Beddgelert in 1793–94, when he combined a 2000-year-old tale from India with that of Gelert. The resulting tale was popularized in the ballad by William Spencer. This legend is sometimes presented as being factual.

GELERT'S GRAVE

IN THE 13TH CENTURY, LLEWELYN, PRINCE OF NORTH WALES, HAD A PALACE AT BEDDGELERT. ONE DAY HE WENT HUNTING WITHOUT GELERT "THE FAITHFULL HOUND" WHO WAS UNACCOUNTABLY ABSENT. ON LLEWELYN'S RETURN, THE TRUANT STAINED AND SMEARED WITH BLOOD, JOYFULLY SPRANG TO MEET HIS MASTER. THE PRINCE ALARMED HASTENED TO FIND HIS SON, AND SAW THE INFANT'S COT EMPTY, THE BEDCLOTHES AND FLOOR COVERED WITH BLOOD. THE FRANTIC FATHER PLUNGED HIS SWORD INTO THE HOUND'S SIDE THINKING IT HAD KILLED HIS HEIR. THE DOG'S DYING YELL WAS ANSWERED BY A CHILD'S CRY. LLEWELYN SEARCHED AND DISCOVERED HIS BOY UNHARMED. BUT NEAR BY LAY THE BODY OF A MIGHTY WOLF WHICH GELERT HAD SLAIN, THE PRINCE FILLED WITH REMORSE IS SAID NEVER TO HAVE SMILED AGAIN HE BURIED GELERT HERE THE SPOT IS CALLED

BEDDGELERT

Beth-Gêlert

WILLIAM ROBERT SPENCER, 1800. Beth-Gêlert (or Gelert) was a grey-hound given to Llewellyn the Great (a Welsh prince) in 1205 by his father-in-law, King John (of England). It is said that Beth-Gêlert means "brightest of the smartest" in Old Saxon.

The spearmen heard the bugle sound,
   And cheerily smiled the morn;
And many a brach, and many a hound
   Obeyed Llewellyn's horn.

And still he blew a louder blast,
   And gave a lustier cheer,
"Come, Gêlert, come, wert never last
   Llewellyn's horn to hear.

"O where does faithful Gêlert roam
   The flower of all his race;
So true, so brave—a lamb at home,
   A lion in the chase?"

In sooth, he was a peerless hound,
   The gift of royal John;
But now no Gêlert could be found,
   And all the chase rode on.

That day Llewellyn little loved
   The chase of hart and hare;
And scant and small the booty proved,
   For Gêlert was not there.

Unpleased, Llewellyn homeward hied,
   When, near the portal seat,
His truant Gêlert he espied
   Bounding his lord to greet.

REMBRANDT VAN RIJN, *Self-Portrait in an Oriental Costume with a Dog,* 1631. Dutch painter and etcher. Rembrandt's popularity declined after his wife's death in 1642, and he eventually went bankrupt. He spent the last years of his life in poverty. He is now considered one of the masters and the world's greatest etcher. (Petit Palais, Paris)

But when he gained the castle-door,
  Aghast the chieftain stood;
The hound all o'er was smeared with gore;
  His lips, his fangs, ran blood.

Llewellyn gazed with fierce surprise;
  Unused such looks to meet,
His favorite checked his joyful guise,
  And crouched, and licked his feet.

Onward, in haste, Llewellyn passed,
  And on went Gêlert too;
And still, where'er his eyes he cast,
  Fresh blood-gouts shocked his view.

O'erturned his infant's bed he found,
    With blood-stained covert rent;
And all around the walls and ground
    With recent blood besprent.

He called his child—no voice replied—
    He searched with terror wild;
Blood, blood he found on every side,
    But nowhere found his child.

"Hell-hound! my child's by thee devoured,"
    The frantic father cried;
And to the hilt his vengeful sword
    He plunged in Gêlert's side.

Aroused by Gêlert's dying yell,
    Some slumberer wakened nigh;
What words the parent's joy could tell
    To hear his infant's cry!

Concealed beneath a tumbled heap
    His hurried search had missed,
All glowing from his rosy sleep
    The cherub boy he kissed.

Nor scathe had he, nor harm, nor dread,
    But, the same couch beneath,
Lay a gaunt wolf, all torn and dead,
    Tremendous still in death.

Ah, what was then Llewellyn's pain!
    For now the truth was clear;
His gallant hound the wolf had slain
    To save Llewellyn's heir.

BRITON RIVIÈRE, *Fidelity* (also known as *Prisoners*), ca. 1869. Rivière had two of his paintings exhibited in the British Institution before he was 12 years old. (Lady Lever Art Gallery, Port Sunlight)

The Outlaw

ROBERT SERVICE, from *Ballads of a Bohemian,* 1921. Canadian poet and novelist.

"After old men and children I am greatly interested in dogs. I will go out of my way to caress one who shows any desire to be friendly. There is a very filthy fellow who collects cigarette stubs on Boul' Mich', and who is always followed by a starved yellow cur. The other day I came across them in a little side street. The man was stretched on the pavement brutishly drunk and dead to the world. The dog, lying by his side, seemed to look at me with sad, imploring eyes. Though all the world despised that man, I thought, this poor brute loves him and will be faithful unto death.

"From this incident I wrote the verse that follows:"

A wild and woeful race he ran
Of lust and sin by land and sea;
Until, abhorred of God and man,
They swung him from the gallows-tree.
And then he climbed the Starry Stair,
And dumb and naked and alone,
With head unbowed and brazen glare,
He stood before the Judgment Throne.

The Keeper of the records spoke:
"This man, O Lord, has mocked Thy Name.
The weak have wept beneath his yoke,
The strong have fled before his flame.
The blood of babes is on his sword;
His life is evil to the brim:
Look down, decree his doom, O Lord!
Lo: there is none will speak for him."

The golden trumpets blew a blast
That echoed in the crypts of Hell,
For there was Judgment to be passed,
And lips were hushed and silence fell.
The man was mute; he made no stir,
Erect before the Judgment Seat . . .
When all at once a mongrel cur
Crept out and cowered and licked his feet.

It licked his feet with whining cry.
Come Heav'n, come Hell, what did it care?
It leapt, it tried to catch his eye;
Its master, yea, its God was there.
Then, as a thrill of wonder sped
Through throngs of shining seraphim,
The Judge of All looked down and said:
"Lo! here is ONE who pleads for him.

"And who shall love of these the least,
And who by word or look or deed
Shall pity show to bird or beast,
By Me shall have a friend in need.
Aye, though his sin be black as night,
And though he stand 'mid men alone,
He shall be softened by My sight,
And find a pleader by My Throne."

"So let this man to glory win;
From life to life salvation glean;
By pain and sacrifice and sin,
Until he stand before Me—*clean*.
For he who lovest the least of these
(And here I say and here repeat)
Shall win himself an angel's pleas
For Mercy at My Judgment Seat."

LUDWIG KNAUS, *Behind the Curtain*, 1880. German genre painter. (Staatliche Kunstsammlungen Dresden, Gemäldegalerie Neue Meister)

Lost Dog

FRANCES RODMAN, 1932.

He lifts his hopeful eyes at each new tread,
Dark wells of brown with half his heart in each;
He will not bark, because he is well-bred,
Only one voice can heal the sorry breach.
He scans the faces that he does not know,
One paw uplifted, ear cocked for a sound
Outside his sight. Only he must not go
Away from here; by honor he is bound.
Now he has heard a whistle down the street;
He trembles in a sort of ecstasy,
Dances upon his eager, padding feet,
Straining himself to hear, to feel, to see,
And rushes at a call to meet the one
Who of his tiny universe is sun.

SIR EDWIN LANDSEER, *There's No Place Like Home,* 1842. English animal painter. (Victoria and Albert Museum, London)

A Canine View of People

JACK LONDON, from *White Fang,* 1905. American writer.

Twilight drew down and night came on, and White Fang lay by his mother's side. His nose and tongue still hurt, but he was perplexed by a greater trouble. He was homesick. He felt a vacancy in him, a need for the hush and quietude of the stream and the cave in the cliff. Life had become too populous. There were so many of the man-animals, men, women, and children, all making noises and irritations. And there were the dogs, ever squabbling and bickering, bursting into uproars and creating confusions. The restful loneliness of the only life he had known was gone. Here the very air was palpitant with life. It hummed and buzzed unceasingly. Continually changing its intensity and abruptly variant in pitch, it impinged on his nerves and senses, made him nervous and restless and worried him with a perpetual imminence of happening.

He watched the man-animals coming and going and moving about the camp. In fashion distantly resembling the way men look upon the gods they create, so looked White Fang upon the man-animals before him. They were superior creatures, of a verity, gods. To his dim comprehension they were as much wonder-workers as gods are to men. They were creatures of mastery, possessing all manner of unknown and impossible potencies, overlords of the alive and the not alive—making obey that which moved, imparting movement to that which did not move, and making life, sun-colored and biting life, to grow out of dead moss and wood. They were fire-makers! They were gods!

The days were thronged with experience for White Fang. During the time that Kiche was tied by the stick, he ran about over all the camp, inquiring, investigating, learning. He quickly came to know much of the ways of the man-animals, but familiarity did not breed contempt. The more he came to know them, the more they vindicated their superiority, the more they displayed their mysterious powers, the greater loomed their god-likeness.

To man has been given the grief, often, of seeing his gods overthrown and his altars crumbling; but to the wolf and the wild dog that have come in to crouch at man's feet, this grief has never come. Unlike man, whose gods are of the unseen and the overguessed, vapors and mists of fancy eluding the garmenture of reality, wandering wraiths of desired goodness and power, intangible outcroppings of self into the realm of spirit—unlike man, the wolf and the wild dog that have come in to the fire find their gods in the living flesh, solid to the touch, occupying earth-space and requiring time for the accomplishment of their ends and their existence. No effort of faith is necessary to believe in such a god; no effort of will can possibly induce disbelief in such a god. There is no getting away from it. There it stands, on its two hind-legs, club in hand, immensely potential, passionate and wrathful and loving, god and mystery and power all wrapped up and around by flesh that bleeds when it is torn and that is good to eat like any flesh.

And so it was with White Fang. The man-animals were gods unmistakable and unescapable. As his mother, Kiche, had rendered her allegiance to them at the first cry of her name, so he was beginning to render his allegiance. He gave them the trail as a privilege indubitably theirs. When they walked, he got out of their way. When they called, he came. When they threatened, he cowered down. When they commanded him to go, he went away hurriedly. For behind any wish of theirs was power to enforce that wish, power that hurt, power that expressed itself in clouts and clubs, in flying stones and stinging lashes of whips.

PETER PAUL RUBENS,
*Alathea Talbot, Countess
of Shrewsbury,* 1620.

He belonged to them as all dogs belonged to them. His actions were theirs to command. His body was theirs to maul, to stamp upon, to tolerate. Such was the lesson that was quickly borne in upon him. It came hard, going as it did, counter to much that was strong and dominant in his own nature; and, while he disliked it in the learning of it, unknown to himself he was learning to like it. It was a placing of his destiny in another's hands, a shifting of the responsibilities of existence. This in itself was compensation, for it is always easier to lean upon another than to stand alone.

But it did not all happen in a day, this giving over of himself, body and soul, to the man-animals. He could not immediately forego his wild heritage and his memories of the Wild. There were days when he crept to the edge of the forest and stood and listened to something calling him far and away. And always he returned, restless and uncomfortable, to whimper softly and wistfully at Kiche's side and to lick her face with eager, questioning tongue.

DOGS AT WORK

I am secretly afraid of animals—of all animals except dogs, and even some dogs. I think it is because of the us-ness in their eyes, with the underlying not-us-ness which belies it, and is so tragic a reminder of the lost age when we human beings branched off and left them: left them to eternal inarticulateness and slavery. "Why?" their eyes seem to ask us.

Edith Wharton (1862–1937).

Dogs have been serving people in many capacities for over 10,000 years. The Jicarilla Apache Indians say that when the creator was making the dog, he took some white from the morning sky and put it on each paw and took some yellow from the sunset and put a patch of it over each of the dog's eyes. This, the creator said, was a sign that the dog would always protect people, morning and night.

The use of dogs as protectors dates from well before written history, and it is thought that the use of dogs in hunting reaches even further back in time. As their association with humans developed, they began to assist people in a greater variety of ways.

St. Bernard (923–1008) specialized in the use of dogs in rescue operations. In A.D. 962, he founded a hospice in the Alps and organized a rescue/care service for travelers crossing the main pass between Switzerland and Italy. His monks have trained Saint Bernards to use their sense of smell to hunt for people buried in snow ever since. These dogs patrol in packs after a storm and dig victims out of snow. While one dog returns for help, the others lie with the victims to warm them and try to help them regain consciousness by licking them. Contrary to popular belief, they have never carried containers of brandy—this legend was started by a painting by Landseer (see page 115)—but they do sometimes carry first aid kits. These dogs can also sense when an avalanche is about to happen and are able to detect hidden crevasses.

The most famous Saint Bernard was Barry I (1802–1814), who is thought to have rescued 41 people (authors often cite Barry's rescues with numbers ranging anywhere from 15 to 75, but 41 appears to be the most accurate number). Contrary to legends, he was not shot during a rescue but died after two years in retirement. His body was then stuffed and put on display in the Museum of Bern. A later Barry, who fell into a gully in 1910, was also stuffed and put on display at the hospice. Barry I is still considered the greatest of St. Bernard's Saint Bernards.

The incredible sense of smell of dogs led to their use in tracking criminals. The British began training them to detect explosives in the late 1960s for use in Northern Ireland. Dogs are now used around the world to detect both explosives and narcotics. They have become a major tool in stopping terrorists and smugglers.

The military use of dogs dates at least as far back as the ancient Greeks, Romans, and Gauls, all of whom equipped their dogs with armor and a collar of knives or spikes to cut the legs of the enemy's horses. Attila the Hun used dogs to protect his camp. The Spanish conquistadors trained dogs to track and kill Native Americans. Their victims became more afraid of these dogs than they were of the Spaniards or their horses. Juan Ponce de León had one dog who did so much damage to the Native Americans that the dog was given one and a half shares of the booty—50 percent more than a regular soldier. In 1798, Napoleon chained dogs all along the walls of Alexandria, Egypt, knowing they would give his men an early warning of an attack and would help delay the attackers. By World War I, dogs were being used as sentries, scouts, ammunition carriers, sled dogs, messengers, and casualty dogs. These roles expanded even more during the next world war.

It is estimated over 200,000 dogs were used in World War II. As mascots, they flew bombing missions, and they warned ships of approaching aircraft before the introduction of radar. Both the Soviets and the Americans had paratroop dogs, sometimes called *parapups*. Since the dogs refused to jump from the planes, they had to be thrown out.

The Soviets were twice able to stop Nazi spearhead attacks by using suicide squads of antitank dogs. These dogs were starved and then trained to enter tanks and armored cars for food. During actual attacks, electromagnetic mines were strapped to the dogs. This practice was effective but was stopped shortly after the second attack. The Japanese also used kamikaze dogs who pulled carts carrying 50-pound bombs into allied lines.

Although many different breeds served in World War I and World War II, today almost all military dogs are either German shepherds or Belgian Malinois. A few of the sporting breeds are sometimes used in detecting explosives and narcotics. There are currently more than 2000 dogs serving in the U.S. Department of Defense worldwide. It was discovered following World War II that military dogs could not readjust to civilian life, so that now they are put to sleep when they are unable to continue serving in active duty.

Closer to home is the use of dogs in research. The most famous subject was Laika, who was shot into space by the Soviets in 1957 to test the effects of weightlessness. At that time they did not know how to bring her back, and so she was killed by remote control.

In testimony before U.S. Congressional committees, it was revealed that over 3 million dogs are killed in medical research and teaching every year. It is common in American universities for medical students to practice operations on living dogs. Referring to this, one medical doctor said, "Dogs are used in 'teaching labs' out of habit and convenience, and not because it is educationally necessary or even helpful." Another doctor adds, "The only thing I remember learning from this laboratory of butchery was that animals howl when they are tortured."

For centuries dogs have served people faithfully, but unfortunately we do not appreciate this service as we should. It is strange that these practices are allowed to continue in countries where dogs are often considered a member of the family.

Dogs for the Blind

MICHEL DE MONTAIGNE, from *Essais (Essays),* 1580. French essayist.

Everybody, I believe, is glutted with the several sorts of tricks that tumblers teach their dogs; the dances where they do not miss any one cadence of the sound they hear; the many various motions and leaps they make them perform by the command of a word. But I observe with more admiration this effect, which, nevertheless, is very common, in the dogs that lead the blind both in the country and in cities: I have taken notice how they stop at certain doors, where they are wont to receive alms; how they avoid the encounter of coaches and carts, even where they have sufficient room to pass; I have seen them, along the trench of a town, forsake a plain and even path, and take a worse, only to keep their masters further from the ditch. How could a man have made this dog understand that it was his office to look to his master's safety only, and to despise his own convenience to serve him? And how had he the knowledge that a way was large enough for him that was not so for a blind man? Can all this be apprehended without ratiocination?

A blind man and his dog in Times Square, Manhattan.

112

THOMAS GAINSBOR-
OUGH, *Henry, Third
Duke of Buceleuch,* 1770.
English portrait and
landscape painter. (Pri-
vate collection)

Dogs for Protection

DR. JOHN BROWN, from "Rab and His Friends", 1859. Scottish essayist and physician. Here Dr. Brown writes about James, a friend, and his
dog, Rab.

He had left Edinburgh very early [in the morning], and in
coming near Auchindinny, at a lonely part of the road, a
man sprang out on him, and demanded his money. James,
who was a cool hand, said, "Weel a weel, let me get it," and
stepping back, he said to Rab, "Speak till him, my man." In
an instant Rab was standing over him, threatening stran-
gulation if he stirred. James pushed on, leaving Rab in
charge; he looked back, and saw that every attempt to rise
was summarily put down. As he was telling Ailie the story,

113

up came Rab with that great swing of his. It turned out that the robber was a Howgate lad, the worthless son of a neighbor, and Rab knowing him had let him cheaply off; the only thing, which was seen by a man from a field was, that before letting him rise, he quenched (*pro tempore*) the fire of the eyes of the ruffian, by a familiar Gulliverian application of Hydraulics, which I need not further particularize. James, who did not know the way to tell an untruth, or embellish anything, told me this as what he called "a fact *positeevely*."

FRANCISCO JOSÉ DE GOYA Y LUCIENTES, *King Charles III of Spain*, ca. 1780. Goya was a Spanish court painter and etcher. Charles III supported the United States in the Revolutionary War. (Museo del Prado, Madrid)

Saint Bernards

ALBERT HEIM, from a speech delivered in Bern, Switzerland, 1927.
Swiss professor.

Apparently, the first dogs, descendants of the old Roman Molosser, were brought to the Hospice between 1660 and 1670 as watchdogs. The monks took them along on their walks in search for lost travelers and soon discovered their salient qualities of path finding and sense of direction. From then on the dogs were trained for guide and rescue work in which they have assisted the monks for the past 250 years with splendid results.

SIR EDWIN LANDSEER, *Alpine Mastiffs Reanimating a Distressed Traveller,* 1820. English animal painter. This picture started the legend of Saint Bernards carrying casks of brandy. Landseer felt the cask would make the picture more interesting. (Private collection)

The records of the Hospice reveal that the dogs in 1787 protected the Hospice from a gang of burglars. . . . The rescue work of the dogs has repeatedly been described and praised by travelers. The dogs leave the Hospice in groups, they search, find and report in groups, and many of them may have accomplished the same number of rescues (40) as Old Barry did. During the past 250 years a total of 2,000 persons have been rescued with the dogs' assistance.

• • •

The Saint Bernard's qualifications that make him indispensable for the rescue work are the never failing sense of direction and the ability to scent (in clear weather they scent a human more than 800 feet, and against the wind they scent for several miles. They are able to scent people buried 5 to 7 ft. deep in snow). The dogs also feel in advance the approach of a snow storm. About 20 to 40 minutes before the storm they become restless and want to go outside. The dogs further have the amazing ability of sensing the closeness of falling avalanches and have frequently proved this by detouring from the path which only minutes later was covered by an avalanche. Remarkable is the dogs' ability of endurance. They often remain outside for hours in temperatures 10 to 20° below and even violent snow storms do not seem to affect them.

Sledge Dogs

MARCO POLO, from *The Book of Marco Polo*, ca. 1298. Venetian traveler and one of the first Europeans to visit China and Siberia.

You see the ice and mire are so prevalent, that over this tract [Siberia], which lies for those 13 days' journey in a great valley between two mountains, no horses can travel, nor can any wheeled carriage either. Wherefore they [Tartars] make sledges, which are carriages without wheels, and made so that they can run over the ice, and also over mire and mud without sinking too deep in it. Of these sledges indeed there are many in our own country, for 'tis such that are used for carrying hay and straw when there have been heavy rains and the country is deep in mire. On such a sledge then they lay a bear-skin on which the courier sits, and the sledge is drawn by six of those big dogs. The dogs have no driver, but go straight for the next post-house, drawing the sledge famously over ice and mire. The keeper of the post-house, however, also gets on a sledge drawn by dogs, and guides the party by the best and shortest way. And when they arrive at the next station, they find a new relay of dogs and sledges ready to take them on, whilst the old relay turns back; and thus they accomplish the journey across that region, always drawn by dogs.

Illumination from Count Gaston de Foix's *Le Livre de Chasse (The Book of Hunting)*, ca. 1440. (Bibliothèque Nationale, Paris)

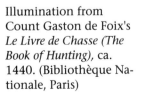

The Bear Hunt

ABRAHAM LINCOLN, ca. 1847. The 16th president of the United
States.

A wild-bear chace, didst never see?
    Then hast thou lived in vain.
Thy richest bump of glorious glee,
    Lies desert in thy brain.

When first my father settled here,
    'Twas then the frontier line:
The panther's scream, filled night with fear
    And bears preyed on the swine.

But wo for Bruin's short lived fun,
    When rose the squealing cry;
Now man and horse, with dog and gun,
    For vengeance, at him fly.

A sound of danger strikes his ear;
    He gives the breeze a snuff:
Away he bounds, with little fear,
    And seeks the tangled *rough*.

On press his foes, and reach the ground,
    Where's left his half munched meal;
The dogs, in circles, scent around,
    And find his fresh made trail.

With instant cry, away they dash,
    And men as fast pursue;
O'er logs they leap, through water splash,
    And shout the brisk halloo.

Now to elude the eager pack,
    Bear shuns the open ground;
Through matted vines, he shapes his track
    And runs it, round and round.

The tall fleet cur, with deep-mouthed voice,
    Now speeds him, as the wind;
While half-grown pup, and short-legged fice,
    Are yelping far behind.

And fresh recruits are dropping in
    To join the merry *corps*;
With yelp and yell,—a mingled din—
    The woods are in a roar.

And round, and round the chace now goes,
    The world's alive with fun;
Nick Carter's horse, his rider throws,
    And more, Hill drops his gun.

Now sorely pressed, bear glances back,
    And lolls his tired tongue;
When as, to force him from his track,
    An ambush on him sprung.

Across the glade he sweeps for flight,
    And fully is in view.
The dogs, new-fired, by the sight,
    Their cry, and speed, renew.

The foremost ones, now reach his rear,
    He turns, they dash away;
And circling now, the wrathful bear,
    They have him full at bay.

At top of speed, the horse-men come,
    All screaming in a row.
"Whoop! Take him Tiger. Seize him Drum."
    Bang,—bang—the rifles go.

And furious now, the dogs he tears,
    And crushes in his ire.
Wheels right and left, and upward rears,
    With eyes of burning fire.

But leaden death is at his heart,
    Vain all the strength he plies.
And, spouting blood from every part,
    He reels, and sinks, and dies.

And now a dinsome clamor rose,
    'Bout who should have his skin;
Who first draws blood, each hunter knows,
    This prize must always win.

But who did this, and how to trace
    What's true from what's a lie,
Like lawyers, in a murder case
    They stoutly *argufy*.

Aforesaid fice, of blustering mood,
    Behind, and quite forgot,
Just now emerging from the wood,
    Arrives upon the spot.

With grinning teeth, and up-turned hair—
    Brim full of spunk and wrath,
He growls, and seizes on dead bear,
    And shakes for life and death.

And swells as if his skin would tear,
  And growls and shakes again;
And swears, as plain as dog can swear,
  That he has won the skin.

Conceited whelp! we laugh at thee—
  Nor mind, that not a few
Of pompous, two-legged dogs there be,
  Conceited quite as you.

HENRY FARNEY, *Indian Hunter,* 1905. American painter. (Midwestern Galleries, Cincinnati)

Sherlock Holmes Tracks a Criminal

SIR ARTHUR CONAN DOYLE, from "The Sign of Four", *Lippencott's Monthly Magazine,* 1890. Scottish author famous for his Sherlock Holmes stories.

"The third house on the right-hand side is a bird-stuffer's; Sherman is the name. You will see a weasel holding a young rabbit in the window. Knock old Sherman up and tell him, with my compliments, that I want Toby at once. You will bring Toby back in the cab with you."

"A dog, I suppose."

"Yes, a queer mongrel with a most amazing power of scent. I would rather have Toby's help than that of the whole detective force of London."

"I shall bring him then," said I. "It is one now. I ought to be back before three if I can get a fresh horse." . . .

Pinchin Lane was a row of shabby, two-storied brick houses in the lower quarter of Lambeth. I had to knock for some time at No. 3 before I could make any impression. At last, however, there was the glint of a candle behind the blind, and a face looked out at the upper window.

"Go on, you drunken vagabone," said the face. "If you kick up any more row, I'll open the kennels and let out forty-three dogs upon you."

"If you'll let one out, it's just what I have come for," said I.

"Go on!" yelled the voice. "So help me gracious, I have a wiper in this bag, and I'll drop it on your 'ead if you don't hook it!"

"But I want a dog," I cried.

"I won't be argued with!" shouted Mr. Sherman. "Now stand clear; for when I say 'three,' down goes the wiper."

"Mr. Sherlock Holmes—" I began; but the words had a most magical effect, for the window instantly slammed down, and within a minute the door was unbarred and open. Mr. Sherman was a lanky, lean old man, with stooping shoulders, a stringy neck, and blue-tinted glasses.

"A friend of Mr. Sherlock is always welcome," said he. "Step in, sir. Keep clear of the badger, for he bites. . . . What was it that Mr. Sherlock Holmes wanted, sir?"

"He wanted a dog of yours."

"Ah! that would be Toby."

"Yes, Toby was the name."

"Toby lives at No. 7 on the left here."

He moved slowly forward with his candle among the queer animal family which he had gathered round him. In the uncertain, shadowy light I could see dimly that there were glancing, glimmering eyes peeping down at us from every cranny and corner. Even the rafters above our heads were lined by solemn fowls, who lazily shifted their weight from one leg to the other as our voices disturbed their slumbers.

Toby proved to be an ugly, long-haired, lop-eared creature, half spaniel and half lurcher, brown and white in colour, with a very clumsy, waddling gait. It accepted, after some hesitation, a lump of sugar which the old naturalist handed to me, and, having thus sealed an alliance, it followed me to the cab and made no difficulties about accompanying me. . . .

Holmes was standing on the doorstep with his hands in his pockets, smoking his pipe.

"Ah, you have him there!" said he. . . .

"Here you are, doggy! Good old Toby! Smell it, Toby, smell it!" He pushed the creosote handkerchief under the dog's nose, while the creature stood with its fluffy legs separated, and with a most comical cock to its head, like a

JOHN CHARLTON, *Earl and Countess Spencer with Hounds in Althorp Park,* 1878. English painter. The Earl and Countess Spencer pictured are the great-grandparents of Princess Diana. Her father was also Earl of Spencer. Althorp (pronounced "Altrup") has been the family's ancestral home since the 16th century. Prince Charles and Princess Diana are both descendants of King James I (1566–1625).

connoisseur sniffing the bouquet of a famous vintage. Holmes then threw the handkerchief to a distance, fastened a stout cord to the mongrel's collar, and led him to the foot of the water-barrel. The creature instantly broke into a succession of high, tremulous yelps and, with his nose on the ground and his tail in the air, pattered off upon the trail at a pace which strained his leash and kept us at the top of our speed.

Pursuit Through the Woods

SIR WALTER SCOTT, an excerpt from *The Lay of the Last Minstrel,* 1805.
Scottish novelist and poet.

For aye the more he sought his way
The farther still he went astray,
Until he heard the mountains round
Ring to the baying of a hound.

And hark! and hark! the deep-mouthed bark
    Comes nigher still and nigher:
Bursts on the path a dark bloodhound,
His tawny muzzle tracked the ground,
    And his red eye shot fire.

Tapestry woven from
the designs of
BERNARD VAN ORLEY,
August (detail), from
the "Maximilian's
Hunts" series, ca. 1530.
Flemish painter who
became a court painter
in Austria and Hun-
gary. (Louvre, Paris)

Hunting Expeditions
of the Kubla Khan

MARCO POLO, from *The Book of Marco Polo,* ca. 1298. Venetian traveler and one of the first Europeans to visit China and Siberia. Kubla Khan was a Mongol emperor of China and the grandson of Genghis Khan. Polo was a member of his court for 17 years.

The Emperor [Kubla Khan] hath two Barons who are his own brothers, one called Baian and the other Mingan; and these two are styled Chinuchi, which is as much as to say "The Keepers of the Mastiff Dogs." Each of these brothers hath 10,000 men under his orders; each body of 10,000 being dressed alike, the one in red and the other in blue, and whenever they accompany the Lord to the chase, they wear this livery, in order to be recognized. Out of each body of 10,000 there are 2,000 men who are in charge of one or more mastiffs, so that the whole number of these

A gold Egyptian fan showing the pharaoh Tutankhamen (King Tut) hunting the ostriches whose feathers were used as the plumes (now gone) on this fan, ca. 1325 B.C. Tutankhamen died before he was 20 years old. This fan was found in his tomb.

is great. And when the Prince goes a-hunting, one of these Barons, with his 10,000 men and something like 5,000 dogs, goes toward the right, whilst the other goes to the left of the party in like manner. They move along all abreast of one another, so that the whole line extends over a full day's journey, and no animal can escape them. Truly it is a glorious sight to see the working of the dogs and the huntsmen on such an occasion. And as the Lord rides a-fowling across the plains, you will see these big hounds come tearing up, one pack after a bear, another pack after a stag, or some other beast, as it may hap, and running the game now on this side and now on that, so it is really a most delightful sport and spectacle.

LEONARDO DA VINCI (1452–1519), *Drawings of Dogs*. Da Vinci is considered one of the great masters. (Left: Windsor Castle, Her Majesty the Queen. Right: British Museum, London)

Dogs of War

PLINY THE ELDER (GAIUS PLINIUS SECUNDUS, A.D. 23–79), from *Natural History*. Roman naturalist. Pliny died of poisonous gases from the eruption of Mt. Vesuvius.

A dog in armor, 16th century. (Museum of Artillery, Madrid)

The Colophonians and Castabulians [the citizens of two towns in Greece], maintained certain squadrons of mastive dogs, for their war service: and those were put in the vaward to make the head and front of the battell, and were never knowne to draw back and refuse fight. These were their trustiest auxiliaries and aid-soldiers, and never so needy as to call for pay.

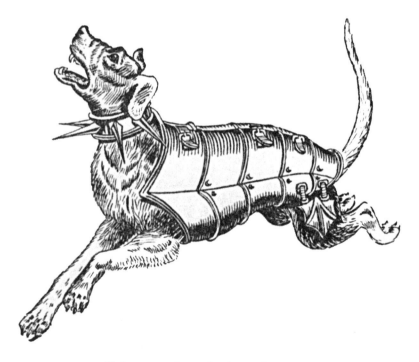

Unknown artist, a dog in ancient armor.

BRITON RIVIÈRE, *Requiescat,* 1889. British painter. (Private collection)

Training Dogs of War

ULISSE ALDROVANDI (ca. 1522–1605). Italian naturalist and professor at the University of Bologna.

Those dogs that defend mankind in the course of private, and also of public conflicts, are called, in Greek, *Symmachi,* or allies, and *Somatophylakes,* or bodyguards. Our authors consider that this kind of dog only differs from the dog which we have just described (the farm-and-sheep-dog) in the matters of training and teaching. The war-dog, according to what is laid down by Blondus, should be a terrifying aspect and look as though he was just going to fight, and be an enemy to everybody except his master; so much so that he will not allow himself to be stroked even by those he knows best, but threatens everybody alike with the fulminations of his teeth, and always looks at everybody as though he was burning with anger, and glares around in every direction with a hostile glance. This dog ought to be trained up to fight from his earliest years. Accordingly some man or other is fitted out with a coat of thick skin, which the dog will not be able to bite through, as a sort of dummy: the dog is then spurred on against this man, upon which the man in the skin runs away and then allows himself to be caught and, falling down on the ground in front of the dog, to be bitten. The day following he ought to be pitted against another man protected in the same manner, and at the finish he can be trained to follow any person upon whose tracks he has been placed. After the fight the dog should be tied up, and fed while tied up, until at the finish he turns out a first-class defender of human beings. Blondus is even of the opinion that from time to time it is a good thing to go for this dog with drawn swords: in this way, he thinks, the dog will develop his spirit and courage to the utmost; and then of course you can lead him against real enemies. And Blondus adds that such dogs are frequently to be met with in Spain of the present day.

Dogs to Fight American Indians

BENJAMIN FRANKLIN, in a letter to Maj. James Read, 1755. American statesman, printer, scientist, and writer. Franklin supported the British during the French and Indian War (1754–1760). Here he was recommending the use of dogs against the Native Americans.

The 50 Arms now sent are all furnish'd with Staples for Sling Straps, that if the Governor should order a Troop or Company of Rangers on Horseback, the Piece may be slung at the Horseman's Back.

If Dogs are carried out with any Party, they should be large, strong and fierce; and every Dog led in a Slip-String, to prevent their tiring themselves by running out and in, and discovering [that is, giving away] the Party by Barking at Squirrels, &c. Only when the Party come near thick Woods and suspicious Places, they should turn out a Dog or two to search them. In Case of meeting a Party of the Enemy, the Dogs are then to be all turn'd loose and set on. They will be fresher and fiercer for having been previously confin'd, and will confound the Enemy a good deal, and be very serviceable. This was the Spanish Method.

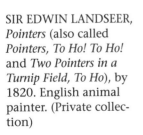

SIR EDWIN LANDSEER, *Pointers* (also called *Pointers, To Ho! To Ho!* and *Two Pointers in a Turnip Field, To Ho*), by 1820. English animal painter. (Private collection)

Dogs to Fight
American Indians

COL. HENRY BOUQUET, in a letter to Pennsylvania lieutenant governor John Penn and the Provincial Commissioners, 1764. Bouquet was getting ready to lead an expedition against the Delaware and Shawnee Indians.

I can not omit to Submit to your Consideration the use that might be made of Dogs against our Savage Enemies; It would be needless to expect that our Foot Soldiers can overtake an Indian in the Woods, and their audacious attempts in attacking our Troops and settlements may, in a great Measure, be ascribed to the certainty of evading our Pursuit by their flight: a few Instances of Indians Seized and worried by Dogs, would, I presume, deter them more effectualy from a War with us, than all the Troops we could raise, and as we have not in this Country the Species of those animals, which would best answer this Purpose, I beg leave to recommend it to you, to have Fifty Couples of proper Hounds imported from Great Britain, with People who understand to train and manage them.

They might be kept on the Frontiers, and a few given to Every Scouting Party, to discover the Ambushes of the Enemy, and direct the Pursuit: This requires that the men intended to follow the Dogs should be well mounted.

Dogs to Fight
American Indians

BENJAMIN FRANKLIN, in a letter to Richard Jackson, 1764. This is apparently in response to Col. Bouquet's request.

I am afraid our Indian War will become perpetual (as they begin to find they can, by Plunder, make a Living of it) without we can effectually Scourge them, and speedily. We have at length concluded to send for 50 Couple of true Bloodhounds to assist in hunting them. If any Gentleman of your Acquaintance has such, I wish you would persuade them to spare 'em to us. Mr. Neate, a Merchant of London, I think, is apply'd to, to collect them. With unchangeable Esteem, I am, Dear Friend, Yours affectionately

B FRANKLIN

Two casualty dogs in the Russo-Japanese War (1904–1905), 1905. Russia and Japan were fighting over Manchuria and North Korea. Russia's defeat was one of the main causes of the Russian Revolution of 1905 (which led to the larger revolution in 1917).

Training dogs to face rifle fire in World War I (1914–1918). About 50,000 dogs were used by the Germans and French in this war. Additional dogs were used by the British, Belgians, and Americans.

A Belgian soldier and his dog wearing gas masks in World War I (1914–1918).

Nazi soldiers and their dogs wearing gas masks during World War II (1939–1945).

U.S. Marines and a scout dog on patrol near Da Nang in the Vietnam War (1964–1975).

Nemo, a U.S. Air Force sentry dog, was shot in the eye during an attack on Tan Son Nhut Air Base in 1966. Twenty-eight Vietcong soldiers, three U.S. airmen, and three dogs were killed in the attack. (U.S. Air Force photograph)

The Turkish Trench Dog

GEOFFREY DEARMER, from *Poems,* 1918. English poet, dramatist, and novelist. Dearmer was a British officer who fought against the Turks in the fierce Gallipoli campaign of 1915.

Night held me as I crawled and scrambled near
The Turkish lines. Above, the mocking stars
Silvered the curving parapet, and clear
Cloud-latticed beams o'erflecked the land with bars;
I, crouching, lay between
Tense-listening armies, peering through the night,
Twin giants bound by tentacles unseen.
Here in dim-shadowed light
I saw him, as a sudden movement turned
His eyes towards me, glowing eyes that burned
A moment ere his snuffling muzzle found
My trail; and then as serpents mesmerize
He chained me with those unrelenting eyes,
That muscle-sliding rhythm, knit and bound
In spare-limbed symmetry, those perfect jaws
And soft-approaching pitter-patter paws.
Nearer and nearer like a wolf he crept—
That moment had my swift revolver leapt—
But terror seized me, terror born of shame,
Brought brooding revelation. For he came
As one who offers comradeship deserved,
An open ally of the human race,
And sniffling at my prostrate form unnerved
He licked my face!

A U.S. airman and his patrol dog in Saudi Arabia during the Gulf War. About 125 dogs served the American military in the Gulf War. (U.S. Air Force photograph, 1990)

Greek ceramic dog's head drinking horn from Falerii, Italy, 500–490 B.C. (Villa Giulia, Rome)

Rags

EDMUND VANCE COOKE.

We called him "Rags." He was just a cur,
    But twice, on the Western Line,
That little old bunch of faithful fur
    Had offered his life for mine.

And all that he got was bones and bread,
    Or the leavings of soldier grub,
But he'd give his heart for a pat on the head,
    Or a friendly tickle and rub.

And Rags got home with the regiment,
    And then, in the breaking away—
Well, whether they stole him, or whether he went,
    I am not prepared to say.

But we mustered out, some to beer and gruel,
    And some to sherry and shad,
And I went back to the Sawbones School,
    Where I still was an undergrad.

One day they took us budding M.D.s
    To one of those institutes
Where they demonstrate every new disease
    By means of bisected brutes.

They had one animal tacked and tied
    And slit like a full-dressed fish,
With his vitals pumping away inside
    As pleasant as one might wish.

I stopped to look like the rest, of course,
    And the beast's eyes leveled mine;
His short tail thumped with a feeble force,
    And he uttered a tender whine.

It was Rags, yes, Rags! who was martyred there,
    Who was quartered and crucified,
And he whined that whine which is doggish prayer
    And he licked my hand—and died.

ARTHUR RACKHAM,
illustration for *Mother Goose Nursery Rhymes,*
1913. English illustra-
tor and water-colorist.

And I was no better in part nor whole
    Than the gang I was found among,
And his innocent blood was on the soul
    Which he blessed with his dying tongue.

Well! I've seen men go to courageous death
    In the air, on sea, on land!
But only a dog would spend his breath
    In a kiss for his murderer's hand.

And if there's no heaven for love like that,
    For such four-legged fealty—well!
If I have any choice, I tell you flat,
    I'll take my chance in hell.

CALL
OF THE WILD

When the long winter nights come on and the wolves follow their meat into the lower valleys, he may be seen running at the head of the pack through the pale moonlight or glimmering bore-alis, leaping gigantic above his fellows, his great throat a-bellow as he sings a song of the younger world, which is the song of the pack.

Jack London, *The Call of the Wild*, 1903.

J ack London wrote two companion novels exploring two major influences on the lives of canines. The first, *The Call of the Wild,* is the story of a dog who is lured into the wilderness, and the second, *White Fang,* describes a wolf who is drawn into human society. In a passage about these two opposing forces, London writes that "there was something calling to him [White Fang] out there in the open. His mother heard it, too. But she heard also that other and louder call, the call of the fire and of man—the call which it has been given alone of all animals to the wolf to answer, to the wolf and the wild-dog, who are brothers."

It was this calling of the wolf to the fire of human beings that resulted in the first dogs, since all dogs, from Saint Bernards to chihuahuas, are basically domesticated wolves. (Some people also believe that there is a little jackal thrown in.) The almost-extinct Indian wolf, gray wolf, and Tibetan wolf are thought to be the direct ancestors of the domestic dog. There are many other relatives to the dog but they are not directly related. They are more like cousins—having descended from a common distant ancestor to the dog and wolf—just as the various monkeys and apes are cousins to people. (Of course, as we look farther back into the past, we will eventually reach a long–extinct animal who is the ancestor of both the primates and the canids. So, in some respect, we are also distant cousins to our dogs.)

Although scientists cannot agree on the exact number, there are at least 39 canid species. All domestic dogs belong to only one of these species—*Canis famillaris.* The family of canids, at the genus level, is broken down into the following groups: wolves and jackals (which includes coyotes and domestic dogs), African wild dogs, red dogs or dholes, raccoon dogs, bush dogs, true foxes, gray foxes, fennec foxes, arctic foxes, and South American foxes. Prairie dogs (also known as *sod poodles*) are not really dogs but members of the squirrel family.

It took many years of selective breeding to produce the more than 400 different breeds of domestic dogs that exist today, but they all came from the wolf. (The current number of breeds is a matter of debate. Some estimates say there are over 800 different breeds.) Dogs and wolves are still close enough relatives that they can mate with each other and produce offspring. In fact, in a German study wolves were actually crossed with poodles, resulting in *puwos*. This crossing of a very independent animal with one that is basically helpless and dependent on humans for its survival had very surprising results. The puwos that looked more poodlelike turned out to act more like wolves, while the wolflike puwos acted more like poodles.

For centuries, people have given wolves a bad name, and they have suffered severely for it. Even though a fear of these animals is common, there has never been a recorded case of healthy wolves attacking people in North America, and it is now thought that the legendary attacks in Europe were actually by rabid wolves and wolf-dog hybrids. The aggressiveness of dogs is not a characteristic inherited from their wolf ancestors; people have bred it into them. Wolves are actually very shy and prefer to retreat from an enemy rather than stand and fight or attack, as dogs have been bred to do. Still, this unfounded fear—coupled with the demand for fur—has contributed to the decimation of the wolf population.

The United States began its predator control program in 1915 with the gray, or timber, wolf as its first target. Because of this program, the wolf was essentially a thing of the past in the West by 1930. The gray wolf, which once roamed over most of the United States, now survives only in Alaska and a portion of Minnesota. In 1974, an attempt was made to reintroduce the gray wolf to northern Michigan, but they were soon killed off. The red wolf once lived throughout the entire southeastern United States but is now extinct in the wild.

Wolves have met a similar fate elsewhere in the world. While they once existed in almost the entire northern hemisphere, they now remain only in the wilderness areas of Canada and Siberia. Several thousand also survive in Eastern Europe and a few in Mexico, South America, Ethiopia, the mountains east of Rome, and Scandinavia.

The Falkland Islands wolf, which was actually more like a fox, had absolutely no fear of people. Charles Darwin wrote that they would often wander into their tents at night and try to pull the stored food from underneath the sleeping men's heads. These friendly wolves never realized they were dealing with the most dangerous creature on earth. People exterminated the species by 1876.

The most heavily hunted canid is the coyote. Often over 250,000 coyotes are killed in the United States in a single year. This is mainly at the behest of sheep ranchers, who feel coyotes cut into their profits. Recent studies indicate that this is an incorrect assumption. Coyotes live mainly on rabbits, rodents, and carrion. They rarely waste energy or risk injury by attacking larger animals. Usually the sheep or calves they do eat have already died from accidents or disease. The removal of coyotes allows populations of rabbits and rodents to soar, and the resulting destruction to crops and grasslands far outweighs any damage the ranchers suffer from the coyotes. Still, millions of tax dollars were spent by the government to kill these animals—far more money than the cost of the damage they are accused of. It is unfortunate for both the taxpayers and the coyotes that they are just as misunderstood as wolves are.

Once a coyote and a raven were actually seen playing together. The delighted coyote was jumping and rolling over the raven. He would then lie on his back as the raven dived at his upraised feet. Perhaps there is something we can learn from these wild relatives of the dog.

Rover

IAN ANDERSON, from *Heavy Horses,* 1978. British musician and leader of the band Jethro Tull.

I chase your every footstep
    and I follow every whim.
When you call the tune I'm ready
    to strike up the battle hymn.
My lady of the meadows
My comber of the beach
You've thrown the stick for your dog's trick
    but it's floating out of reach.
The long road is a rainbow and the pot of gold lies there.
So slip the chain and I'm off again
You'll find me everywhere. I'm a Rover.

As the robin craves the summer
    to hide his smock of red,
I need the pillow of your hair
    in which to hide my head.
I'm simple in my sadness;
    resourceful in remorse.
Then I'm down straining at the lead
    holding on a windward course.

Strip me from the bundle
    of balloons at every fair:
    colourful and carefree
designed to make you stare.
But I'm lost and I'm losing
    the thread that holds me down.
And I'm up hot and rising
    in the lights of every town.

SAMUEL BOUGH (1822–1878), *Young Anglers by a Canal*. English painter.

GEORGE STUBBS, *Hound Coursing a Stag,* ca. 1762–1765. English animal painter. Stubbs was a self-taught artist. (Philadelphia Museum of Art, Philadelphia)

The Forest and the Fire

JACK LONDON, from *The Call of the Wild,* 1903. American author.

He was older than the days he had seen and the breaths he had drawn. He linked the past with the present, and the eternity behind him throbbed through him in a mighty rhythm to which he swayed as the tides and seasons swayed. He sat by John Thornton's fire, a broad-breasted dog, white-fanged and long-furred; but behind him were the shades of all manner of dogs, half-wolves and wild wolves, urgent and prompting, tasting the savor of the meat he ate, thirsting for the water he drank, scenting the wind with him, listening with him and telling him the sounds made by the wild life in the forest, dictating his moods, directing his actions, lying down to sleep with him when he lay down, and dreaming with him and beyond him and becoming themselves the stuff of his dreams.

So peremptorily did these shades beckon him that each day mankind and the claims of mankind slipped farther from him. Deep in the forest a call was sounding, and as often as he heard this call, mysteriously thrilling and luring, he felt compelled to turn his back upon the fire and the beaten earth around it, and to plunge into the forest, and on and on, he knew not where or why; nor did he wonder where or why, the call sounding imperiously, deep in the forest. But as often as he gained the soft unbroken earth and the green shade, the love for John Thornton drew him back to the fire again.

JOSEPH MALLORD WILLIAM TURNER, *Dawn after the Wreck,* ca. 1841. English landscape painter. Turner is considered one of the greatest of the landscape painters. (Courtauld Institute of Art, University of London)

A Rover

JOHN GALSWORTHY, from "Memories", *The Inn of Tranquility*, 1912. English novelist and dramatist. Galsworthy was awarded the Nobel Prize for Literature in 1932. Here he writes about his dog, Chris.

The call of the wild—Spring running—whatever it is—that besets men and dogs, seldom attained full mastery over him [Chris]; but one could often see it struggling against his devotion to the scent of us, and, watching that dumb contest, I have time and again wondered how far this civilisation of ours was justifiably imposed on him; how far the love for us that we had so carefully implanted could ever replace in him the satisfaction of his primitive wild yearnings. He was like a man, naturally polygamous, married to one loved woman.

It was surely not for nothing that Rover is dog's most common name, and would be ours, but for our too tenacious fear of losing something, to admit, even to ourselves, that we are hankering. There was a man who said: Strange that two such queerly opposite qualities as courage and hypocrisy are the leading characteristics of the Anglo-Saxon! But is not hypocrisy just a product of tenacity, which is again the lower part of courage? Is not hypocrisy but an active sense of property in one's good name, the clutching close of respectability at any price, the feeling that one must not part, even at the cost of truth, with what he has sweated so to gain? And so we Anglo-Saxons will not answer to the name of Rover, and treat our dogs so that they, too, hardly know their natures.

The history of his one wandering, for which no respectable reason can be assigned, will never, of course, be known. It was in London, of an October evening, when we were told he had slipped out and was not anywhere.

GEORGE STUBBS, *Fino and Tiny,* 1791. English animal painter. A spaniel and a pomeranian. (Her Majesty the Queen)

Then began those four distressful hours of searching for that black needle in that blacker bundle of hay. Hours of real dismay and suffering—for it is suffering, indeed, to feel a loved thing swallowed up in that hopeless maze of London streets. Stolen or run over? Which was worst? The neighboring police stations visited, the Dog's Home notified, an order for five hundred "Lost Dog" bills placed in the printer's hands, the streets patrolled! And then, in a lull snatched for food, and still endeavoring to preserve some aspect of assurance, we heard the bark which meant: "Here is a door I cannot open!" We hurried forth, and there he was on the top doorstep—busy, unashamed, giving no explanations, asking for his supper; and very shortly after him came his five hundred "Lost Dog" bills. Long I sat looking at him that night after my companion had gone up, thinking of the evening, some years before, when there followed us that shadow of a spaniel who had been lost for eleven days. And my heart turned over within me. But he! He was asleep, for he knew not remorse.

Husky—the Wolf-Dog of the North

JACK LONDON, from *Harper's Weekly,* 1900. American novelist. This is an early essay by London.

Neck, from head to shoulders, a mass of bristling hair; sharp-pointed ears, long-snouted, lips snarling, fangs dripping; yelping rather than barking; wolfish of aspect and not nice to look upon when in anger—this is the husky, or wolf-dog, of the North. Much has been said of the Klondike, but these magnificent brutes, which in the beginning made that frigid El Dorado possible, have received little more than passing comment. Nor has this neglect been due to their being but the humble servants of the master, man. They are far from humble, as their wild ancestry attests. They may be beaten into submission, but that will not prevent them still snarling their hatred. They may be starved into apparent docility, and then die, suddenly, with teeth fast locked in a brother's throat, torn to pieces by their comrades. Rather, has little attention been accorded them because the interest of man has gravitated inexorably toward the natural, mineral, and social features of that far-northerly land.

But the husky is far from uninteresting. As a type of endurance, no better evolved product of natural selection need be sought. If ever a species has been born and bred of hard times, it has. Only the fittest, in a struggle for existence extending through a thousand thousand generations, have survived. And they are well fit. Domesticated by the savage autochthons of that forbidding region, they may not only account their remote ancestors as wild wolves, but often their immediate forebears.

NATHANIEL HONE
(1718–1784), *Miss Julie
Metcalf with Her Dog*.
Irish painter.

It is a North-land aphorism that no man is a fit person to drive a team of huskies who cannot command the intensive adjectives and abjurations of at least two vernaculars, besides the one drunk in with his mother's milk. In fact, a dog-driver is near cousin to the army teamster. A mule is stubborn, and may manifest glimmering adumbrations of cunning; but the husky can be characterized as pertinacious, deceitful, sharp, and above all, well capable of deductive reasoning. He will unerringly connect cause with effect. He is also an actor of no mean ability, concealing the most nefarious designs under the innocent exterior of a new-born lamb. In the old days, before the discovery of the Klondike, the men who freighted grub from Circle City to Birch Creek were wont to charge ten cents per pound more for bacon than for any other merchandise. And even then, so great was the responsibility, they reckoned that they lost on the transaction.

No white man, out of his own brain, ever successfully devised a way of tying up a husky. Rope or thong can resist their sharp teeth, at the best, for a very few minutes. But the Indian, through generations of travail, finally worked out the only method. He ties his dog up with a stick. One end of a pole is fastened so closely to the husky's neck that he cannot get at the thong with his teeth. The other end is made fast by another thong to a stake driven securely into the ground. Unable to free himself from his end, the intervening pole prevents him from getting at the other end. It is a very common sight to see these animals breaking the ice of a water-hole by rearing in the air and coming down upon it with their whole weight on their fore feet. As grub-thieves, they have no equals, and unveracious Klondikers will not stop at telling of the husky which stole a can of condensed milk and traded it off at another camp, where they happened to be short of milk, for a piece of bacon. However, it is a fact that they do open condensed-milk cans and extract the contents.

In the summer-time, when the snow and ice are gone and man travels by canoe and poling-boat, the huskies are thrown upon their own resources. They do not work: wherefore should they be fed? Hence they become splendid scavengers and perform prodigies of benevolence in the matter of sanitation. Nothing escapes them. Not a bone but is cracked for its marrow; not a tin can but shines clean and bright on the inside. They are also excellent fishers, and during the salmon-run no dog goes hungry. This leaving the huskies to shift for themselves, gives rise to peculiar ethics in the North land. A man who steals food from another is shot down without mercy. But it is different in the case of the dogs. Should a man catch one, red-handed, gorging his last piece of bacon, he may not shoot him. If he does, the dog's owner can come down upon him for his value as a draught-animal. A miners' meeting usually settles the amount. Nor is this any insignificant sum, for the prices of sled-dogs range from one to five hundred dollars, and in times of need as high as a thousand.

They are superb travellers. Coming back light, the Circle City freighters thought nothing of making single runs of seventy or eighty miles. Fierce brutes though they be, the closest attachments often spring up between them and their masters, and when a man possesses a good dog or team he is not slow in bragging of it. In the annals of the country may be found the history of one dog-driver who wagered a thousand dollars that his favorite husky could start a thousand pounds on a level trail. Now the steel runners of a stationary sled will quickly freeze to the surface, and by the terms of the bet he was even denied the privilege of breaking the runners loose. But it was stipulated that the dog was to have three trials. The whole camp staked its dust upon one side or the other of the issue, and on the day of trial turned out *en masse*. The dog was hitched to the loaded sled, and everything made ready. "Gee!" the master commanded from a distance. The dog swung obediently to the right, shrewdly throwing his whole weight upon the traces. "Haw!" The manoeuvre was duplicated to the left and the sled broken out. And then, "Mush on!" (the vernacular for "get up!"). The dog whined softly, driving his claws into the frozen trail, calling every muscle into play, digging away like mad. And in answer to this tremendous exertion, the sled slowly got into motion and was dragged several lengths. Let a man try the like and marvel. Of course it was an exceptional dog, but creatures are often measured by their extremes.[1]

It is in fighting that they betray their most wolfish trait. As long as two combatants are on their feet there is

---

[1]London wrote a fictional version of this event in *The Call of the Wild.*

HENRY FARNEY, *After the Evening Meal,* 1902. American painter. (Private collection)

no interference. The onlooking huskies merely crowd interestedly around, ready, however, for the first slip. And the instant one or the other of the dogs goes down, the whole band pitches upon him, and in the snap of a finger he is torn to shreds. The loss of more dogs is due to this than to any or all other causes combined.

A peculiarity they are remarkable for is their howling. It can be likened to nothing on land or sea. When the frost grows bitter and the aurora-borealis trails its cold fires across the heavens, they voice their misery to the night. Heartbreaking, sobbing, it rises like a wail of lost and tortured souls, and when a thousand huskies are in full chorus it is as though the roof had tumbled in and hell stood naked to the stars. No man can hear this for the first time and preserve the equanimity of that portion of his skin which lies contiguous to his spinal column. A certain literary gentleman, whose poems have been praised by Rossetti, by-the-way, but who is here nameless, journeyed into the Klondike during the Fall Rush of 1897. In the boat with him was his partner, also their two wives. All down the Yukon they encountered the most frightful stories of the famine then raging at Dawson. Not only is the Klondiker unveracious, but he is a clever colorist, so these gentlemen believed the lurid tales and were prepared to fight to the last for their grub. Unluckily they approached Dawson during the night. They knew they were very near and were keeping a good lookout. Suddenly, rounding a bend in the Yukon, a faint wail reached them. Straining their ears, it was supplemented by other wails, for all the world like the dying agonies of women and children and grown men. One instant they debated. If this were the famine, as it surely was, they would certainly be torn to pieces in the mad scramble for their grub. They seized their oars in panic and terror and made a wild rush for the bank, landing at Klondike City, and even the few men they there met could not convince them that it was only the nocturnal song of the husky. Nor would the wives permit the journey to continue till the gentleman whose poems had been praised by Rossetti went down on foot and made a personal investigation.

The Coyote

MARK TWAIN (SAMUEL CLEMENS), from *Roughing It*, 1872. American humorist. Twain was the author of *A Connecticut Yankee in King Arthur's Court, The Prince and the Pauper, The Adventures of Tom Sawyer,* and *The Adventures of Huckleberry Finn.*

Another night of alternate tranquillity and turmoil. But morning came, by and by. It was another glad awakening to fresh breezes, vast expanses of level greensward, bright sunlight, an impressive solitude utterly without visible human beings or human habitations, and an atmosphere of such amazing magnifying properties that trees that seemed close at hand were more than three miles away. We resumed undress uniform, climbed a-top of the flying coach, dangled our legs over the side, shouted occasionally at our frantic mules, merely to see them lay their ears back and scamper faster, tied our hats on to keep our hair from blowing away, and leveled an outlook over the world-wide carpet about us for things new and strange to gaze at. Even at this day it thrills me through and through to think of the life, the gladness and the wild sense of freedom that used to make the blood dance in my veins on those fine overland mornings!

Along about an hour after breakfast we saw the first prairie-dog villages, the first antelope, and the first wolf. If I remember rightly, this latter was the regular *cayote* (pronounced ky-*o*-te) of the farther deserts. And if it *was*, he was not a pretty creature or respectable either, for I got well acquainted with his race afterward, and can speak with confidence. The cayote is a long, slim, sick and sorry-looking skeleton, with a gray wolf-skin stretched over it, a tolerably bushy tail that forever sags down with a despairing expression of forsakenness and misery, a furtive and evil eye, and a long, sharp face, with slightly lifted lip and exposed teeth. He has a general slinking expression all over. The cayote is a living, breathing allegory of Want. He is *always* hungry. He is always poor, out of luck and friendless. The meanest creatures despise him, and even the fleas would desert him for a velocipede. He is so spiritless and cowardly that even while his exposed teeth are pretending a threat, the rest of his face is apologizing for it. And he is *so* homely!—so scrawny, and ribby, and coarse-haired, and pitiful. When he sees you he lifts his lip and lets a flash of his teeth out, and then turns a little out of the course he was pursuing, depresses his head a bit, and strikes a long, soft-footed trot through the sagebrush, glancing over his shoulder at you, from time to time, till he is about out of easy pistol range, and then he stops and takes a deliberate survey of you; he will trot fifty yards and stop again—another fifty and stop again; and finally the gray of his gliding body blends with the gray of the sagebrush, and he disappears. All this is when you make no demonstration against him; but if you do, he develops a livelier interest in his journey, and instantly electrifies his heels and puts such a deal of real estate between himself and your weapon, that by the time you have raised the hammer you see that you need a minie rifle, and by the time you have got him in line you need a rifled cannon, and by the time you have "drawn a bead" on him you see well enough that nothing but an unusually long-winded streak of lightning could reach him where he is now. But if you start a swift-footed dog after him, you will enjoy it ever so much—especially if it is a dog that has a good opinion of himself, and has been brought up to think he knows something about speed. The cayote will go swinging gently off on that deceitful trot of his, and every little while he will smile a fraudful smile over his shoulder that will fill that dog entirely full of encouragement and worldly ambition, and make him lay his head still lower to the

JOHN WOODHOUSE
AUDUBON, *Coyote,
Prairie Wolf,* from
*Quadrupeds of North
America,* 1854. J. W.
Audubon was one of
John James Audubon's
sons.

ground, and stretch his neck further to the front, and pant more fiercely, and stick his tail out straighter behind, and move his furious legs with a yet wilder frenzy, and leave a broader and broader, and higher and denser cloud of desert sand smoking behind, and marking his long wake across the level plain! And all this time the dog is only a short twenty feet behind the cayote, and to save the soul of him he cannot understand why it is that he cannot get percep-

159

tibly closer; and he begins to get aggravated, and it makes him madder and madder to see how gently the cayote glides along and never pants or sweats or ceases to smile; and he grows still more and more incensed to see how shamefully he has been taken in by an entire stranger, and what an ignoble swindle that long, calm, soft-footed trot is; and next he notices that he is getting fagged, and that the cayote actually has to slacken speed a little to keep from running away from him—and *then* that town-dog is mad in earnest, and he begins to strain and weep and swear, and paw the sand higher than ever, and reach for the cayote with concentrated and desperate energy. This "spurt" finds him six feet behind the gliding enemy, and two miles from his friends. And then, in the instant that a wild new hope is lighting up his face, the cayote turns and smiles blandly upon him once more, and with a something about it which seems to say: "Well, I shall have to tear myself away from you, bub—business is business and it will not do for me to be fooling along this way all day"—and forthwith there is a rushing sound, and the sudden splitting of a long crack through the atmosphere, and behold that dog is solitary and alone in the midst of a vast solitude!

It makes his head swim. He stops, and looks all around; climbs the nearest sand-mound, and gazes into the distance; shakes his head reflectively, and then, without a word, he turns and jogs along back to his train, and takes up a humble position under the hindmost wagon, and feels unspeakably mean, and looks ashamed, and hangs his tail at half-mast for a week. And for as much as a year after that, whenever there is a great hue and cry after a cayote, that dog will merely glance in that direction without emotion, and apparently observe to himself, "I believe I do not wish any of the pie."

Of Foxes

B. Y. WILLIAMS, from *Far Is the Hill*. American poet.

The gray fox for the mountains—
   The gray fox walks alone
In scorn of any comrade
   Save waterfall and stone.
A sparrow for his dinner,
   A cavern for his bed,
The mist-hung world below him,
   A thin moon overhead;
Long hours for meditation
   On mating time and spring,
On hidden oblique pathways
   Or how the planets swing.
Austerity confirms him
   A proper denizen
     For the fastness of the mountains,
       The solitude of mountains,
         And, keeping to the mountains,
He traffics not with men.

The red fox for the lowlands—
   The red fox has a need
For measuring his cunning,
   For matching speed with speed.
He knows the taste of ducklings
   Made fat by farmers' corn;
He savors the elation
   Of huntsman, hounds and horn.
O splendid hour of testing:
   Outguessing every guess,
Outwitting duller creatures

With delicate finesse!
And when the chase is ended
  He flaunts his brush again,
    A bright torch through the lowlands
      To fire the stolid lowlands,
        A challenge to the lowlands
For the "view halloo" of men.

JOHN JAMES AUDUBON, *Gray Fox,* from *Quadrupeds of North America,*
1854. American ornithologist and animal artist. Audubon is best
known for his bird paintings.

KUNIMASA. Japanese artist. The fox spirits communicate by tipping the table to tap out a code. Table tilting or turning is a Japanese form of divination similar to our ouija boards. (Victoria and Albert Museum, London)

Dogs of the Forest

HENRY DAVID THOREAU, from *Walden,* 1854. American poet, naturalist, and essayist. Thoreau was a Harvard graduate who rejected traditional lifestyles for a more solitary, natural way of living.

Sometimes I heard the foxes as they ranged over the snow crust, in moonlight nights, in search of a partridge or other game, barking raggedly and demoniacally like forest dogs, as if laboring with some anxiety, or seeking expression, struggling for light and to be dogs outright and run freely in the streets; for if we take the ages into our account, may there not be a civilization going on among brutes as well as men? They seemed to me to be rudimental, burrowing men, still standing on their defence, awaiting their transformation. Sometimes one came near to my window, attracted by my light, barked a vulpine curse at me, and then retreated.

WINSLOW HOMER, *The Fox Hunt*, 1893. American landscape, marine, and genre painter. (Pennsylvania Academy of the Fine Arts, Philadelphia)

Four Little Foxes

LEW SERETT, from *Slow Smoke,* 1953. The United States is the world's largest exporter of fur.

Speak gently, Spring, and make no sudden sound;
For, in my windy valley, yesterday I found
New-born foxes squirming on the ground—
                 Speak gently.

Walk softly, March, forbear the bitter blow;
Her feet within a trap, her blood upon the snow,
The four little foxes saw their mother go—
                 Walk softly.

Go lightly, Spring, oh, give them no alarm;
When I covered them with boughs to shelter them from
      harm,
The thin blue foxes suckled at my arm—
                 Go lightly.

Step softly, March, with your rampant hurricane;
Nuzzling one another, and whimpering with pain,
The new little foxes are shivering in the rain—
                 Step softly.

Wolf Chivalry

KONRAD LORENZ, from *Man Meets Dog,* 1955. Austrian behaviorist. Lorenz was awarded the Nobel Prize for Physiology or Medicine in 1973.

There is one particularly endearing canine habit, which has been fixed since early times in the hereditary characters of the central nervous system of the dog. This is the chivalrous treatment of females and puppies. No normal male will bite a female of its species; the bitch is absolutely taboo and can treat a dog as she likes, nipping or even seriously biting him. The dog has at his disposal no means of retaliation other than deferential gestures and the "politeness look," with which he may attempt to divert the attacks of the bitch into play. Masculine dignity forbids the only other outlet—flight—for dogs are always at great pains to "keep face" in front of bitches. In the wolf, as also in all predominantly wolf-blooded Greenland dogs, this chivalrous self-control is extended only to females of his own pack; in all preponderantly jackal dogs, it applies to every bitch, even if she is a complete stranger.

•　•　•

I once saw a good example of this behavior when, together with Stasi, I visited the gray wolf in his cage. . . . After a short while, the wolf invited me to play and I, feeling flattered, accepted. But Stasi felt slighted because I took more notice of the wolf than of her, and she suddenly attacked my partner in the game. Now chow bitches have a particularly nasty, nagging bark and a special way of nipping when they wish to punish a male dog. They do not bite hard and deep, like fighting males; they apparently only seize the skin, but vigorously enough to make the male howl with pain. The wolf, too, howled, attempting at the

RIEN POORTVLIET, *Fox and Hare,* 1978. Dutch painter.

same time to placate Stasi by attitudes of deference and gestures of politeness. Naturally I did not wish to put his chivalry to the test, for fear that I myself should have to suffer the consequences, so I sternly adjured the angry female to silence. And so, paradoxically, I had to rebuke Stasi to prevent her from injuring the good-natured wolf. Only ten minutes earlier, I had set in readiness outside the cage an iron bar and two buckets of water to save my precious Stasi in case the great beast of prey attacked her. *Sic transit gloria—lupi!*

A Wolf Family

FARLEY MOWAT, from *Never Cry Wolf,* 1963. Canadian writer and biologist. This book was made into a movie with the same title.

As I grew more completely attuned to their daily round of family life I found it increasingly difficult to maintain an impersonal attitude toward the wolves. No matter how hard I tried to regard them with scientific objectivity, I could not resist the impact of their individual personalities. Because he reminded me irresistibly of a Royal Gentleman for whom I worked as a simple soldier during the war, I found myself calling the father of the family George, even though in my notebooks, he was austerely identified only as Wolf "A."

George was a massive and eminently regal beast whose coat was silver-white. He was about a third larger than his mate, but he hardly needed this extra bulk to emphasize his air of masterful certainty. George had presence. His dignity was unassailable, yet he was by no means aloof. Conscientious to a fault, thoughtful of others, and affectionate within reasonable bounds, he was the kind of father whose idealized image appears in many wistful books of human family reminiscences, but whose real prototype has seldom paced the earth upon two legs. George was, in brief, the kind of father every son longs to acknowledge as his own.

His wife was equally memorable. A slim, almost pure-white wolf with a thick ruff around her face, and wide-spaced, slightly slanted eyes, she seemed the picture of a minx. Beautiful, ebullient, passionate to a degree, and devilish when the mood was on her, she hardly looked like the epitome of motherhood; yet there could have been no better mother anywhere. I found myself calling her Angeline, although I have never been able to trace the origin of that name in the murky depths of my own subconscious. I respected and liked George very much, but I became deeply fond of Angeline, and still live in hopes that I can somewhere find a human female who embodies all her virtues.

Angeline and George seemed as devoted a mated pair as one could hope to find. As far as I could tell they never quarreled, and the delight with which they greeted each other after even a short absence was obviously unfeigned.

HOWARD PYLE, *A Wolf Had Not Been Seen at Salem for Thirty Years,* from *Harper's Monthly Magazine,* 1909. American illustrator and writer. Pyle also taught at Drexel Institute in Philadelphia where two of his students were Maxfield Parrish and N. C. Wyeth. He is considered the father of modern American illustration.

Wolves Hunting Caribou

FARLEY MOWAT, from *Never Cry Wolf,* 1963. Canadian writer and biologist.

I was in a quandary. My clothes lay by the shore some distance away and I had only my rubber shoes and my binoculars with me on the ridge. If I went back for my clothes, I knew I might lose track of these wolves. But, I thought, who needed clothes on a day like this? The wolves had by now disappeared over the next crest, so I seized my binoculars and hared off in pursuit.

The countryside was a maze of low ridges separated by small valleys which were carpeted with grassy swales where small groups of caribou slowly grazed their way southward. It was an ideal terrain for me, since I was able to keep watch from the crests while the wolves crossed each of these valleys in turn. When they dropped from view beyond a ridge I had only to sprint after them, with no danger of being seen, until I reached another elevated position from which I could watch them traverse the succeeding valley.

Sweating with excitement and exertion I breasted the first ridge to the north, expecting to see some frenzied action as the three wolves came suddenly down upon the unsuspecting caribou below. But I was disconcerted to find myself looking out over a completely peaceful scene. There were about fifty bucks in view, scattered in groups of three to ten animals, and all were busy grazing. The wolves were sauntering across the valley as if they had no more interest in the deer than in the rocks. The caribou, on their part, seemed quite unaware of any threat. Three familiar dogs crossing a farm pasture would have produced as much of a reaction in a herd of domestic cattle as the wolves did among these caribou.

WILLIAM R. LEIGH (1866–1955), *Struggle for Existence.* American painter. (Grand Central Art Galleries)

The scene was all wrong. Here was a band of wolves surrounded by numbers of deer; but although each species was obviously fully aware of the presence of the other, neither seemed perturbed, or even greatly interested.

Incredulously, I watched the three wolves trot by within fifty yards of a pair of young bucks who were lying down chewing their cuds. The bucks turned their heads to watch the wolves go by, but they did not rise to their feet, nor did their jaws stop working. Their disdain for the wolves seemed monumental.

The two wolves passed on between two small herds of grazing deer, ignoring them and being ignored in their turn. My bewilderment increased when, as the wolves swung up a slope and disappeared over the next crest, I jumped up to follow and the two bucks who had been so apathetic in the presence of the wolves leaped to their feet, staring at me in wild-eyed astonishment. As I sprinted past them they thrust their heads forward, snorted unbelievingly, then spun on their heels and went galloping off as if pursued by devils. It seemed completely unjust that they should have been so terrified of *me*, while remaining so blasé about the wolves. However, I solaced myself with the thought that their panic might have resulted from unfamiliarity with the spectacle of a white man, slightly pink, and clad only in boots and binoculars, racing madly across the landscape.

I nearly ran right into the wolves over the next crest. They had assembled in a little group on the forward slope and were having a social interlude, with much nose smelling and tail wagging. I flung myself down behind some rocks and waited. After a few moments the white wolf started off again and the others followed. They were in no hurry, and there was considerable individual meandering as they went down the slopes toward the valley floor where scores of deer were grazing. Several times one or another of the wolves stopped to smell a clump of moss, or detoured to one side to investigate something on his own. When they reached the valley they were strung out in line abreast and about a hundred feet apart, and in this formation they turned and trotted along the valley floor.

Only those deer immediately in front of the wolves showed any particular reaction. When a wolf approached to within fifty or sixty yards, the deer would snort, rise on their hind feet and then spring off to one side of the line of advance. After galloping a few yards some of them swung around again to watch with mild interest as the wolf went past, but most returned to their grazing without giving the wolf another glance.

Within the space of an hour the wolves and I had covered three or four miles and had passed within close range of perhaps four hundred caribou. In every case the reaction of the deer had been of a piece—no interest while the wolves remained at a reasonable distance; casual interest if the wolves came very close; and avoiding-tactics only when a collision seemed imminent. There had been no stampeding and no panic.

Up to this time most of the deer we had encountered had been bucks; but now we began to meet numbers of does and fawns, and the behavior of the wolves underwent a change.

One of them flushed a lone fawn from a hiding place in a willow clump. The fawn leaped into view not twenty feet ahead of the wolf, who paused to watch it for an instant, then raced off in pursuit. My heart began to thud with excitement as I anticipated seeing a kill at last.

It was not to be. The wolf ran hard for fifty yards without gaining perceptibly on the fawn, then suddenly broke off the chase and trotted back to rejoin his fellows.

I could hardly believe my eyes. That fawn should have been doomed, and it certainly would have been if even a tenth of the wolfish reputation was in fact deserved; yet during the next hour at least twelve separate rushes were made by all three wolves against single fawns, a doe with a fawn, or groups of does and fawns, *and in every case the chase was broken off almost before it was well begun.*

I was becoming thoroughly exasperated. I had not run six miles across country and exhausted myself just to watch a pack of wolves playing the fool.

WRIGHT BARKER, *Circe*, 1912. Circe is a goddess and sorceress mentioned in Homer's *Odyssey*. She and her beasts welcomed Odysseus's men to her palace. After giving them drugged wine, she turned them into hogs. (Bradford Art Galleries and Museums)

When the wolves left the next valley and wandered over the far crest, I went charging after them with blood in my eye. I'm not sure what I had in mind—possibly I may have intended to chase down a caribou fawn myself, just to show those incompetent beasts how it was done. In any event I shot over the crest—and straight into the middle of the band.

They had probably halted for a breather, and I burst in among them like a bomb. The group exploded. Wolves went tearing off at top speed in all directions—ears back, tails stretching straight behind them. They ran scared, and as they fled through the dispersed caribou herds the deer finally reacted, and the stampede of frightened animals which I had been expecting to witness all that afternoon became something of a reality. Only, and I realized the fact with bitterness, it was not the wolves who had been responsible—it was I.

The Shepherd Dog and the Wolf

JOHN GAY, from *The Fables: First Series*, 1728. English playwright and poet. Gay is most famous for *The Beggar's Opera*.

A wolf, with hunger fierce and bold,
Ravaged the plains, and thinned the fold:
Deep in the wood secure he lay,
The thefts of night regaled the day.
In vain the shepherd's wakeful care
Had spread the toils, and watched the snare:
In vain the dog pursued his pace,
The fleeter robber mocked the chase.
As Lightfoot ranged the forest round,
By chance his foe's retreat he found.
"Let us awhile the war suspend
And reason as from friend to friend."
"A truce?" replies the wolf. 'Tis done.
The dog the parley thus begun:
"How can that strong intrepid mind
Attack a weak defenceless kind?
Those jaws should prey on nobler food,
And drink the boar's and lion's blood;
Great souls with generous pity melt,
Which coward tyrants never felt.
How harmless is our fleecy care!
Be brave, and let thy mercy spare."
"Friend," says the wolf, "the matter weigh;
Nature designed us beasts of prey;
As such when hunger finds a treat,
'Tis necessary wolves should eat.
If mindful of the bleating weal,
Thy bosom burn with real zeal;

Hence, and thy tyrant lord beseech;
To him repeat the moving speech;
A wolf eats sheep but now and then,
Ten thousands are devoured by men.
An open foe may prove a curse,
But pretended friend is worse."

BEATRIX POTTER, *"Kep" the Sheep Dog,* 1909. English author and illustrator. She is best known for her Peter Rabbit series of children's books.

Antiwolf Sentiments

FARLEY MOWAT, from *Never Cry Wolf*, 1963. Canadian writer and biologist.

Antiwolf feelings at Brochet (the northern Manitoba base for my winter studies) when I arrived there from Wolf House Bay were strong and bitter. As the local game warden aggrievedly described the situation to me: the local people had been able to kill 50,000 caribou each winter as recently as two decades past, whereas now they were lucky if they could kill a couple of thousand. Caribou were becoming scarce to the point of rarity, and wolves were unanimously held to be to blame. My rather meek remonstrance to the effect that wolves had been preying on caribou, without decimating the herds, for some tens of thousands of years before the white men came to Brochet, either fell on deaf ears or roused my listeners to fury at my partisanship.

One day early in the winter a trader burst into my cabin in a state of great excitement.

"Listen," he said challengingly, "you've been screaming for proof wolves butcher the herds. Well, hitch up your team and get out to Fishduck Lake. You'll get your proof! One of my trappers come in an hour ago and he seen fifty deer down on the ice, all of 'em killed by wolves—and hardly a mouthful of the meat been touched!"

Accompanied by a Cree Indian companion I did as I was bid, and late that afternoon we reached Fishduck Lake. We found a sickening scene of slaughter. Scattered on the ice were the carcasses of twenty-three caribou, and there was enough blood about to turn great patches of snow into crimson slush.

FREDERIC REMINGTON, *Wolf in the Moonlight,* ca. 1909. American
sculptor, painter, illustrator, and writer. (Addison Gallery of American
Art, Andover, Massachusetts)

The trapper had been correct in stating that no use had been made of the carcasses. Apart from some minor scavenging by foxes, jays and ravens, all but three of the animals were untouched. Two of those three were bucks—minus their heads; while the third, a young and pregnant doe, was minus both hindquarters.

Unfortunately for the "proof," none of these deer could have been attacked by wolves. There were no wolf tracks anywhere on the lake. But there were other tracks: the unmistakable triple trail left by the skis and tail-skid of a plane which had taxied all over the place, leaving the snow surface scarred with a crisscross mesh of serpentine lines.

These deer had not been pulled down by wolves, they had been shot—some of them several times. One had run a hundred yards with its intestines dragging on the ice as a result of a gut wound. Several of the others had two or more bullet-broken limbs.

The explanation of what had actually happened was not far to seek.

Two years earlier, the tourist bureau of the Provincial Government concerned had decided that Barren Land caribou would make an irresistible bait with which to lure rich trophy hunters up from the United States.[2] Accordingly a scheme was developed for the provision of fully organized "safaris" in which parties of sportsmen would be flown into the subarctic, sometimes in Government-owned planes, and, for a thousand dollars each, would be guaranteed a first-rate set of caribou antlers.

During the winter sojourn of the caribou inside the timberline they feed in the woods at dawn and dusk and spend the daylight hours yarded on the ice of the open

----

[2]In 1963 the Newfoundland Government is using the same gambit.

lakes. The pilot of the safari aircraft, therefore, had only to choose a lake with a large band of caribou on it and, by circling for a while at low altitude, bunch all the deer into one tight and milling mob. Then the aircraft landed; but kept under way, taxiing around and around the panic-stricken herd to prevent it from breaking up. Through open doors and windows of the aircraft the hunters could maintain a steady fire until they had killed enough deer to ensure a number of good trophies from which the finest might be selected. They presumably felt that, since the jaunt was costing a great deal of money, they were entitled to make quite certain of results; and it is to be assumed that the Government officials concerned agreed with them.

When the shooting was over the carcasses were examined and the best available head taken by each hunter, whose permit entitled him to "the possession of" only a single caribou. If the hunters were also fond of venison a few quarters would be cut off and thrown aboard the plane, which would then depart southward. Two days later the sports would be home again, victorious.

The Cree who accompanied me had observed this sequence of events for himself the previous winter while acting as a guide. He did not like it; but he knew enough of the status of the Indian in the white man's world to realize he might just as well keep his indignation to himself.

I was more naïve. The next day I radioed a full report of the incident to the proper authorities. I received no reply—unless the fact that the Provincial Government raised the bounty on wolves to twenty dollars some weeks afterwards could be considered a reply.

YOSHITOSHI, *Musashino no Tsuki (The Moon on Masashi Plain),* from the series *Tsuki no Hyakushi (One Hundred Aspects of the Moon),* 1892. Japanese artist. Yoshitoshi began his apprenticeship at the age of 11 and produced his first print at the age of 14. His early prints were much more complex than the one shown here, which was one of his last.

The Extinction of the Wolf in England

DR. JOHN CAIUS, from *De Canibus Britannicus* (also known as *Of Englishe Dogges*), 1570. Doctor of Physic at Cambridge University and court physician to King Edward VI.

We have no wolves owing to the beneficial policy of Edgar, who imposed an annual tribute of 300 wolves on the Cambri as a tax (they were most frequent amongst them).

Writers say that King Lud of Cambria paid King Edgar an annual tax of 300 wolves (as we have said before), and so in four years all Cambria and all England were rid of them. Edgar reigned A.D. 959 about. Now since that date, we never read that a native wolf was seen in England; but by way of making money we have often seen one brought from abroad, simply to be seen as a rare and unfamiliar animal.

[A few wolves actually remained in the wilder parts of England until the early 1500s. They became extinct in Scotland in about 1740.]

TOYEN, *Au Château Lacoste,* 1946. Czech painter.

DOGS
AND RELIGION

*I would not give much for that man's religion
whose cat and dog are not the better for it.*

Abraham Lincoln (1808–1865).

Beware of dogs.

New Testament, Philippians 3:2, ca. A.D. 60.

When it comes to religion, dogs have had a mixed reception. Though they have often been considered sacred and deserving of special treatment, they have also frequently been regarded as "unclean" or have been sacrificed to please a god. Neither the Old nor the New Testament treats dogs particularly favorably. For the most part they refer to them with derision.

One early Christian legend tells of a woman's only son, who was possessed by the devil. The boy would bite anyone who came near him, and if he could not get ahold of anybody, he would bite himself. His body was covered with terrible wounds. The mother heard that a boy named Jesus could cure those possessed, and so she went to talk to Mary. While they were talking, the possessed boy went over to Jesus and sat down next to him. When Jesus touched him, a mad dog came out of the boy's mouth and fled. This boy was Judas Iscariot. This is an example of how the early Christians associated dogs with Satan, an association that led to the brutal deaths of many dogs down to the 19th century.

Islam has a somewhat similar view of dogs, but unlike many Christians, Muslims at least believe dogs can reach paradise. Muslim legend says Tobias's dog (see page 192) went to paradise along with Al Raqim (also known as Kasmir, Katmir, and so on), who was the dog of the Seven Sleepers (see page 202). Al Raqim's name is used as a kind of talisman, and Muslims write it on their mail to protect it from loss or theft.

Many Catholic saints are associated with dogs, including St. Eustace (2nd century A.D.), St. Vitus (3rd century), St. Anthony (ca. 251–350), St. Hubert (656–727), St. Bernard (923–1008), St. Dominic (ca.

1170–1221), St. Roche (ca. 1298–1327), and, in Brazil, São Lázaro (St. Lazarus, who was resurrected by Christ; the Brazilians confuse St. Lazarus with the Lazarus in Jesus' parable). St. Dominic was the founder of the Dominican order. Because of their involvement in the Inquisition, the Dominicans became known as the "Hounds of the Lord." St. Dominic is occasionally depicted as a dog with flames shooting out of his mouth.

Although many religions have considered dogs sacred, dogs have rarely been worshipped in themselves; instead, gods have manifested themselves through dogs. Dogs have also been sacred because they either represented gods, as in the case of most of the ancient Egyptians, or because they were closely associated with the gods.

Maria Leach's book *God Had a Dog* lists over 75 gods associated with dogs. This does not exhaust the list; there are many others. The Ifugaos of the Philippines had 60 deities associated with dogs, and many African gods have also been linked with these animals.

Several Egyptian gods were represented as dogs or as being dog-headed. Hapi was one of the four sons of Horus and the great god of the Nile. The Egyptians regarded the Nile as the source of life and prosperity from which all gods and all creation sprang. Hapi was associated with all of the other gods, and their attributes were all ascribed to him, including those of the great and unknown God. The second of Horus's four sons was the jackal-headed Tuamautef. The four sons of Horus were originally represented as the four pillars that held up the sky, but they later became associated with the cardinal points, with Hapi as the god of the north and Tuamautef as the god of the east. The four sons also helped guide the deceased in their journey to the afterworld.

Set was pictured as a greyhound with a forked tail as far back as 4240 B.C. and Khentamentiou, who was later identified with Osiris, was also depicted as a dog.

Anubis was the god of the tomb and protector of the deceased; he was depicted as a jackal or as jackal-headed. (During the 19th century, Anubis was thought to be dog-headed and even though today it is generally accepted that he is jackal-headed, some still argue that he looks very similar to the Ibizan hound.) Ap-uat was Anubis in another form, and sometimes they are depicted together as two jackals. In the afterworld, the doorkeeper of the Sixth Mansion, Atek-au-kehaq-kheru, was another god with the head of a jackal, while the mansion's watcher, An-hra, and herald, Ates-hra, were both dog-headed gods.

One religion that gives dogs special treatment, even though it does not consider them sacred, is Zoroastrianism. Zoroastrianism was founded in Persia (now Iran) by Zoroaster (Zarathustra) in about 1500 B.C. (though some authorities feel the date might be as late as 600 B.C.). If the Greeks, who were outnumbered, had not won the Battle of Marathon against the Persians in 490 B.C., it is very likely that Zoroastrianism would be the dominant religion of Europe and the Americas today. The Muslim takeover of Persia in the 7th century A.D. forced many Persians to flee to India, where they became known as Parsis and practiced the Parsi faith. The religion still exists today, mainly in India.

Zoroastrianism recognizes a supreme diety called Ahura Mazda (Wise Lord). Though Zoroastrians do not worship their dogs, they do consider a dog's life to be as valuable as that of a human. The *Zend Avesta*, the Zoroastrian scriptures, says that there are only five sins that result in being cast into outer darkness after death. Two of these involve dogs: giving them food that is too hot to eat and denying them food while humans are eating.

Sacred dogs can be found in many different religions. All of the Egyptian cities named Cynopolis had hordes of sacred municipal dogs. In the 3rd century A.D., Sicily had sacred dogs to protect the temples and serve the gods. Some Native American peoples have considered either dogs or wolves to be their totem animals. And early Chinese writers said that their first temple for dogs was built during the Ch'in dynasty (221–207 B.C.).

Lhasa apsos originally came from Tibet's sacred capital city, Lhasa, where they were once sacred dogs at the huge temple overlooking the city. Lhasa was the home of the Dalai Lama (the Buddhist equivalent of the Pope) until the Chinese invaded in 1950 and destroyed much of Tibet. The Chinese still refuse to give Tibet back its independence, and so Lhasa apsos and the Dalai Lama are forced to live in exile.

The Bible on Dogs

From *The Old Testament* (King James version). These books are considered to be sacred by Judaism, Christianity, and Islam.

Exodus 11:6–7, 1000–500 B.C.
Attributed to Moses (ca. 1200 B.C.), the father of Judaism.

And there shall be a great cry throughout all the land of Egypt, such as there was none like it, nor shall be like it any more. But against any of the children of Israel shall not a dog move his tongue, against man or beast: that ye may know how that the Lord doth put a difference between the Egyptians and Israel.

Exodus 22:31

[The Lord said] And ye shall be holy men unto me: neither shall ye eat any flesh that is torn of beasts in the field; ye shall cast it to the dogs.

Deuteronomy 23:18, 800–700 B.C.
Attributed to Moses.

Thou shall not bring the hire of a whore, or the price of a dog, into the house of the Lord thy God for any vow: for even both these are abomination unto the Lord thy God.

TINTORETTO (JACOPO ROBUSTI, 1518–1594), *Christ Washing the Apostles' Feet*. Venetian painter. Tintoretto is considered one of the greatest and most original of Italy's decorative painters. (Prado, Madrid)

Thus saith the Lord God of Israel. . . . I will bring evil upon the house of Jeroboam, and will cut off from Jeroboam him that pisseth against the wall, and him that is shut up and left in Israel, and will take away the remnant of the house of Jeroboam, as a man taketh away dung, till it be all gone. Him that dieth of Jeroboam in the city shall the dogs eat; and him that dieth in the field shall the fowls of the air eat: for the Lord hath spoken it.[1]

[The Lord said to Elijah] And thou shalt speak unto him [Ahab, the king of Israel], saying, Thus saith the Lord, In the place where dogs licked the blood of Naboth shall dogs lick thy blood, even thine. . . . And of Jezebel also spake the Lord, saying, The dogs shall eat Jezebel by the wall of Jezreel. Him that dieth of Ahab in the city the dogs shall eat.[2]

[Job said] But now they that are younger than I have me in derision, whose father I would have disdained to have set with the dogs of my flock.

Psalms 22:16–21, 700–100 B.C.
Attributed to David, the king of Israel,
who reigned ca. 1000-962 B.C.

For dogs have compassed me: the assembly of the wicked have inclosed me: they pierced my hands and feet. I may tell all my bones: they look and stare upon me. They part my garments among them, and cast lots upon my vesture.

---

[1]A similar curse appears in 1 Kings 16:1–4.

[2]See also 2 Kings 9: 8–10.

But be not thou far from me, O Lord: O my strength, haste thee to help me. Deliver my soul from the sword; my darling from the power of the dog. Save me from the lion's mouth: for thou hast heard me from the horns of the unicorns.

Psalms 68:22–23
Attributed to King David.

The Lord said, I will bring again from Bashan, I will bring my people again from the depths of the sea: That thy foot may be dipped in the blood of thine enemies, and the tongue of thy dogs in the same.

Proverbs 26:10–11, 17, 700–200 B.C.

The great God that formed all things both rewardeth the fool, and rewardeth transgressors. As a dog returneth to his vomit,[3] so a fool returneth to his folly. . . . He that passeth by, and meddleth with strife belonging not to him, is like one that taketh a dog by the ears.

Proverbs 30:29–31

There be three things which go well, yea, four are comely in going: A lion which is strongest among beasts, and turneth not away for any; a greyhound; an he goat also; and a king, against whom there is no rising up.

Ecclesiastes 9:4–5, ca. 150 B.C.

For to him that is joined to all the living there is hope: for a living dog is better than a dead lion. For the living know they shall die: but the dead know not any thing, neither have they any more a reward; for the memory of them is forgotten.

---

[3]Also in 2 Peter 2:22.

Jeremiah 15:1, 3, 605–200 B.C.

Then said the Lord unto me, Though Moses and Samuel stood before me, yet my mind could not be toward this people [Israel]: cast them out of my sight, and let them go forth. . . . And I will appoint over them four kinds, saith the Lord: the sword to slay, and the dogs to tear, and the fowls of the heaven, and the beasts of the earth, to devour and destroy.

From *The Apocrypha* (Douay version). The books of *The Apocrypha* were originally part of the early Christian Bible. They were removed in the 1600s partly because of demands from the Puritans. These books were never part of the Hebrew Bible, but they are still part of the Roman Catholic Bible. In some translations of *Tobias,* the father's name is translated as Tobit and the son's as Tobias; in others, both father and son are called Tobias. The book is sometimes called *The Book of Tobit.* The dog of Tobias the son appears in many works of Christian art.

Tobias 5:22 and 6:1, ca. 250 B.C.

Then all things being ready, that were to be carried in their [Tobias the son and the Archangel Raphael disguised as a man] journey, Tobias bade his father [Tobias the father] and his mother farewell: and they set out both together. . . . And Tobias went forward; and the dog followed him.

Tobias 11:9

[When Tobias returned to his father's house in Nineveh from his long journey] the dog, which had been with them in the way, ran before; and coming as if he had brought the news, shewed his joy by his fawning and wagging his tail.

From *The New Testament* (King James version). These books are considered to be sacred by Christianity and Islam.

Matthew 7:6, A.D. 85

[Jesus said] give not that which is holy unto the dogs, neither cast ye your pearls before swine, lest they trample them under their feet, and turn again and rend you.

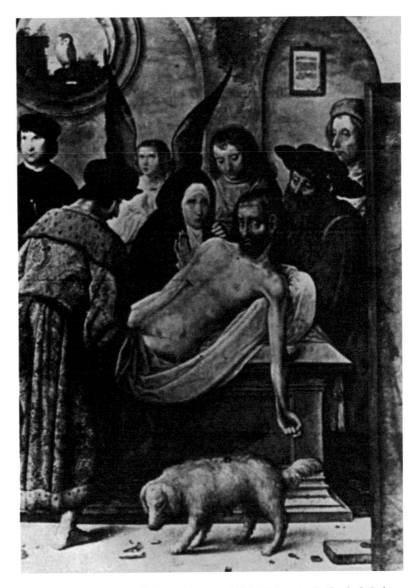

JUAN DE FLANDES, *The Entombment,* 1505. (Palencia Cathedral, Palencia, Spain)

And, behold, a woman of Canaan came out of the same coasts, and cried unto him, saying, Have mercy on me, O Lord, thou Son of David; my daughter is greviously vexed with a devil. But he answered her not a word. And his disciples came and besought him, saying, Send her away; for she crieth after us. But he answered and said, I am not sent but unto the lost sheep of the house of Israel. Then came she and worshipped him, saying, Lord, help me. But he answered and said, It is not meet to take the children's bread, and to cast it to dogs. And she said, Truth, Lord: yet the dogs eat of the crumbs which fall from their masters' table. Then Jesus answered and said unto her, O woman, great is thy faith: be it unto thee even as thou wilt. And her daughter was made whole from that very hour.[4]

Luke 16:20–22, 80–90 A.D.

[Jesus said] And there was a certain beggar named Lazarus, which was laid at his [the rich man's] gate, full of sores, And desiring to be fed with the crumbs which fell from the rich man's table: moreover the dogs came and licked his sores. And it came to pass, that the beggar died, and was carried by the angels into Abraham's bosom.

Revelations 22:13–15, A.D. 95
Attributed to St. John, the apostle.

[Jesus said] I am Alpha and Omega, the beginning and the end, the first and the last. Blessed are they that do his commandments, that they may have right to the tree of life, and may enter in through the gates into the city [the Jerusalem that will descend from heaven]. For without are dogs, and sorcerers, and whoremongers, and murderers, and idolaters, and whosoever loveth and maketh a lie.

---

[4]This story also appears in Mark 7:25–30.

The Legend of St. Christopher

From *Gadla Hawâryât (Contendings of the Apostles),* ca. 1350. This Ethiopian text is based on legends from the 5th century A.D. St. Christopher is referred to as the "dog-headed saint" by the Eastern Orthodox Church, and until recently he was the patron saint of travelers for the Roman Catholic Church.

Then did our Lord Jesus Christ appear unto (Andrew and Bartholomew) and say, ". . . Now depart into the desert, and I will be with you; and be not afraid, for I will send unto you a man whose face is like unto that of a dog, and whose appearance is exceedingly terrible, and ye shall take him with you into the city."

And the Apostles went forth into the desert, being exceedingly sorrowful because the men of the city had not believed; and they had only sat down for a little space to rest themselves when they slumbered and fell asleep, and the Angel of God lifted up the Apostles and brought them unto the City of Cannibals. . . . There came from the City of Cannibals a certain man who was looking for a man to eat. . . . And the Angel of God appeared and said unto him, "O thou whose face is like unto that of a dog, I say unto thee, Behold, thou shalt find two men sitting under a rock, and with them are their disciples; and when thou hast arrived at the place where they are let no evil thing befall them through thee (for they are the servants of God). . . ."

And it came to pass that, when the man whose face was like unto that of a dog heard these things, he trembled exceedingly and he answered and said unto the angel, "Who art Thou? I know neither Thee nor thy God; but tell me who is the God concerning Whom thou speakest unto me?"

195

And the angel answered and said unto him, "He Who hath created the heavens and the earth is God in very truth. . . ."

. . . Then the man with the face like unto that of a dog said unto him, "I wish to see (some sign) so that I may believe in all His miraculous powers. . . ." Then in that same hour fire came down from heaven and surrounded the man whose face was like unto that of a dog, and he was unable to withdraw himself therefrom, for he was standing in the midst of the fire . . . and he cried out with a loud voice saying, "O Thou God, Whom I know not, have compassion upon me, and save me from this tribulation, and I will believe in Thee."

And the angel answered and said unto him, "If God saveth thee from the affliction of this fire, wilt thou follow the Apostles into every place whithersoever they may go, and wilt thou hearken unto everything they shall command thee?"

And the man with a face like unto that of a dog answered and said, "O my Lord, I am not like all the other men, and I have no knowledge of their speech. . . . And if I be hungry, where shall I find men to eat? I should certainly then fall upon them and devour them. . . ."

And the angel said unto him, "God will give unto thee the nature of the children of men, and He will restrain in thee the nature of the beasts," and in that same hour the angel stretched out his hands and brought the man with a face like unto that of a dog from the fire and he made over him the sign of the cross and cried out unto him in the name of the Father, of the Son and of the Holy Ghost. Then straightway did the nature of the beast go forth out of him and he became as gentle as a lamb. . . .

Then the man with a face like unto that of a dog rose up and went unto the place wherein the Apostles were, and

Icon of St. Christopher, A.D. 330–1453. (Byzantine Museum, Athens)

he was rejoicing and was glad because he had learned to know the right faith. Now his appearance was exceedingly terrible. He was four cubits in height and his face was like unto that of a great dog, and his eyes were like unto lamps of fire which burned brightly, and his teeth were like unto the tusks of a wild boar, or the teeth of a lion, and the nails of his hands were like unto curved reaping hooks, and the nails of his toes were like unto the claws of a lion, and the hair had came down over his arms to look like the mane of a lion, and his whole appearance was awful and terrifying. . . .

And it came to pass that when the man with the face like unto that of a dog had come to where they had been, he found there (Andrew's) disciples who had become as it were dead men through fear of him. Then he laid hold upon them with his hands, and said unto them, "Be not afraid, O my spiritual fathers," and thereupon God removed fear from their hearts. . . .

. . . Then (the Apostle) Andrew said unto him "May God bless thee, O my son! . . . But tell me, what is thy name." And the man with a face like unto that of a dog said unto him, "My name is Abominable [Hasum]." And Andrew said unto him, "Rightly thou speakest, for thy name is ever as thyself; but here there is a hidden mystery . . . for from this day onwards shall thy name be 'Christian.' "

And on the third day they arrived at the city of Bartos and they sat down outside the city to rest themselves. Now Satan had gone before them unto the men of the city. . . .

And Andrew rose up and prayed, saying, "Let all the gates of the city be opened quickly." And as Andrew spoke these words the gates of the city fell down, and the Apostles and the man with a face like unto that of a dog entered in. . . .

Then the Governor commanded . . . (the townspeople) to bring hungry and savage beasts to attack them . . . and when he that had a face of a dog saw all that they were doing, he said unto Andrew, "O good servant of God, wilt thou command me to uncover my face (for he had covered it before entering)? And Andrew said unto him, "Whatsoever God commandeth thee, that do." Then he whose face was like unto that of a dog prayed saying, "I beseech thee, O my Lord Jesus Christ, Who didst take from me my vile nature . . . turn me back into my former nature . . . and strengthen Thou me with Thy power, so that they may know there is no other God beside Thee."

And in that same hour his former nature returned unto him, and he became exceedingly wroth, and anger filled his heart, and he uncovered his face and looked at the people with great fury, and he leaped upon all the wild beasts that were among the multitudes of people who were gathered together, and he slew them forthwith, and tore out their bowels and devoured their flesh.

And it came to pass that when the men of the city saw this act they feared exceedingly . . . and seven hundred men and three of the nobles of the city died. . . . And God sent from heaven a great fire which surrounded the city, and not one of its people was able to flee from it. Then the people said, "We believe and we know that there is no other God but your God, our Lord Jesus Christ, above the heavens and above the earth. And we entreat you to have compassion upon us, and to save us from this death and from the double affliction of the fire and of him whose face is like unto that of a dog. . . ." And the Apostles had compassion upon them. . . .

And the Apostles drew nigh unto the man whose face was like unto that of a dog, and they laid their hands upon him, and said unto him, "In the name of our Lord Jesus Christ, let the nature of the wild beast remove itself from thee, and let the nature of the children of men return unto thee; what thou hast done is sufficient for thee, O my son, for behold, thou hast completed the purpose wherefore thou wast sent."

And in the same hour the nature of the children of men returned unto him, and he became as gentle as a lamb. . . . And when the people and the governor saw this wonderful thing, they took olive branches in their hands and bowed before the Apostles, and said unto them, "Have compassion upon us (and bless us) with your blessing and baptize us." And the Apostles said unto them, "Preserve ye your souls in patience; behold, the grace of God hath descended upon you."

The Curate Thinks You Have No Soul

ST. JOHN LUCAS.

The curate thinks you have no soul;
   I know that he has none. But you,
Dear friend, whose solemn self-control,
   In our foursquare familiar pew,
Was pattern to my youth—whose bark
   Called me in summer dawns to rove—
Have you gone down into the dark
   Where none is welcome—none may love?
I will not think those good brown eyes
   Have spent their life of truth so soon;
But in some canine paradise
   Your wraith, I know, rebukes the moon,
And quarters every plain and hill,
   Seeking his master . . . As for me,
This prayer at least the gods fulfill:
   That when I pass the flood and see
Old Charon by the Stygian coast
   Take toll of all the shades who land,
Your little, faithful, barking ghost
   May leap to lick my phantom hand.

JOHN SINGLETON COPLEY, *The Three Daughters of George III,* 1785. American portrait painter. A portrait of Princesses Mary, Sophia, and Amelia. (Windsor Castle, Her Majesty the Queen)

PIERRE BONNARD, *Woman and Dog*, 1922. French Postimpressionist painter, lithographer, and illustrator. (Phillips Collection, Washington, D.C.)

A Malemute Dog

PAT O'COTTER.

You can't tell me God would have Heaven
    So a man couldn't mix with his friends—
That we are doomed to meet disappointment
    When we come to the place the trail ends.

That would be a low-grade sort of Heaven,
    And I'd never regret a damned sin
If I rush up to the gates white and pearly,
    And they don't let my malemute in.

For I know it would never be homelike,
    No matter how golden the strand,
If I lose out that pal-loving feeling
    Of a malemute's nose on my hand.

Islam on Dogs

From *The Koran,* 598–632. This is the primary sacred book of the Muslims.

Dost thou consider that the companions of the cave and al Rakim, were one of our signs, as well as a great miracle? When the young men took refuge in the cave, they said, O Lord, grant us mercy from before thee, and dispose our business for us to a right issue. Wherefore we struck their ears with deafness, so that they slept without disturbance in the cave for a great number of years. . . . And thou wouldest have judged them to have been awake, while they were sleeping; and we caused them to turn themselves to the right hand, and to the left. And their dog stretched forth his forelegs in the mouth of the cave. . . . Some say the sleepers were three; and their dog was the fourth: and others say, They were five: and their dog was the sixth; guessing at a secret matter: and others say, They were seven; and their dog was the eighth. Say, My Lord best knoweth their number: none shall know them, except a few. . . . And they remained in their cave three hundred years, and nine years over.

Islam on Dogs

From *The Sunna* (or *Holy Traditions of Mohammed*), 850–890. The books of the *Sunna* are also considered to be sacred by Muslims. While the Koran is said to be God's revelations to Mohammed, the *Sunna* is about Mohammed himself and is to Muslims what the Gospels are to Christians.

Fear God in respect of animals: ride them when they are fit to be ridden, and get off when they are tired. . . .

Verily there are rewards for our doing good to animals, and giving them water to drink. An adulteress was forgiven who passed by a dog at a well; for the dog was holding out his tongue from thirst, which was near killing him; and the woman took off her boot, and tied it to the end of her garment, and drew water for the dog, and gave him to drink; and she was forgiven because of that act.

JAMES WARD, *Persian Greyhounds,* ca. 1807. The Saluki is one of the oldest dog breeds. It is said King Solomon, Cleopatra, and Mohammad all owned Salukis. (Private collection)

A Sufi Philosopher

SADI, from *Gulistan (Garden of Roses)*, 1258. Persian poet. Sadi is one of the most famous of the Sufi philosophers, who also include Omar Khayyam. Sufism is a mystical movement that uses esthetic practices to experience God. The Whirling Dervishes are part of this semi-monastic order. *Gulistan* is considered Sadi's masterpiece.

In the concurring opinion of the wise, a dog, thankful for his food, is more worthy than a human being who is void of gratitude.—A dog will never forget the crumb thou gavest him, though thou mayst afterward throw a hundred stones at his head; but foster with thy kindness a low man for an age, and on the smallest provocation he will be up against thee in arms.

VITTORE CARPACCIO, *St. Augustine in His Study,* late 15th century. Venetian painter. (Scuola di San Giorgio degli Schiavoni, Venice)

Sacred Dogs of Japan

DR. ENGELBERT KAEMPFER, from *History of Japan,* 1690–1692. Dutch physician.

The temples which we had on our right, as we went up, being built in the ascent of the neighboring green hills, were illuminated with many lamps, and the priests, beating some bells with iron hammers, made such a noise as could be heard at a considerable distance. I took notice of a large white dog, perhaps made of plaster, which stood upon an altar on our left, in a neatly adorned chapel, or small temple, which was consecrated to the Patron of the dogs.

● ● ●

Since the now-reigning Emperor came to the throne there are more dogs bred in Japan than, perhaps in any country whatsoever, and than there were before even in this empire. They have their masters, indeed, but lie about the streets and are very troublesome to passengers and travellers. Every street must, by special command of the Emperor, keep a certain number of these animals and provide them with victuals. There are huts built in every street, where they are taken care of when they fall sick. Those that die must be carried up to the tops of the hills as the usual burying places, and very decently interred. Nobody may, under severe penalties, insult or abuse them, and to kill them is a capital crime, whatever mischief they do. In this case, notice of their misdemeanours must be given to their keepers, who are alone empowered to chastise and to punish them.

● ● ●

[We] went by the place where publick orders and proclamations were put up, not far from the ditch of the castle, where we saw a new proclamation put up lately and twenty shuits of silver nailed to the post to be given as a reward to anybody that would discover the accomplices of a murder lately committed upon a dog.

A Chinese silk picture, 1700s. The Pekinese was considered a sacred dog that only the Chinese emperor could own. Anyone caught trying to steal one of these dogs was sentenced to "death by a thousand cuts". For over 1500 years, this breed remained in the emperor's palaces, except for a pair presented to the Dalai Lama in A.D. 900 and five captured by the British when the Summer Palace in Beijing was taken in 1860. Pekinese were bred to resemble lions and were called the "lions of Buddha". (British Museum)

A statue of Anubis as it was found in 1923, guarding the entrance to the innermost treasury of the tomb of Pharaoh Tutankhamen, ca. 1325 B.C.

Dogs of the Ancient Egyptians

DIODORUS SICULUS, from *On Egypt,* ca. 60 B.C. Sicilian historian.

The dog is useful both for hunting and for guarding; wherefore they depict the god whom they call Anubis with the head of a dog, to show that he was one of the bodyguards of Isis and Osiris. And some say that the dogs which guided Isis in her search for Osiris not only protected her from wild beasts and from the people she encountered, also, being sympathetic to her plight, joined with howling in her search. It is for this reason that dogs lead the solemn procession during the Isis Festival, since those who established the custom thus commemorate the ancient kindness of this animal.

The four sons of Horus. At the left is the jackal-headed Tuamautef and to the right is the dog-headed Hapi. (Mansell Collection)

The Egyptian Book of the Dead

From the *Papyrus of Ani,* ca. 1500 B.C.

"O Rā-Tmu, lord of the Great House, prince, life, strength and health of all the gods, deliver thou [me] from the god whose face is like unto that of a dog, whose brows are as those of a man, and who feedeth upon the dead, who watcheth at the Bight of the Fiery Lake, and who devoureth the bodies of the dead and swalloweth hearts, and who shooteth forth filth, but he himself remaineth unseen."

From the *Nebseni Papyrus,* 1580–1350 B.C.

Anubis, who dwelleth in the region of the embalmed, the chief of the holy house, layeth his hands upon the lord of life (*i.e.,* the mummy), and provideth him with all that belongeth unto him, and saith: "Hail to thee, thou beautiful one, the lord! Thou hast been gazed upon by the Sun's eye, thou hast been bound up by Ptah-Seker, thou hast been made whole by Anubis."

Dogs and Zoroastrianism

From the *Vendidad*, 600–400 B.C. The *Vendidad* is one of the five sacred books that make up the *Zend Avesta*, the Zoroastrian scriptures.

"Whosoever shall smite either a shepherd's dog, or a house-dog, or a *Vohunazga* dog, or a trained dog, his soul when passing to the other world, shall fly howling louder and more sorely grieved than the sheep does in the lofty forest where the wolf ranges.

"No soul will come and meet his departing soul and help it, howling and grieved in the other world; nor will the dogs that keep the Kinvad bridge help his departing soul howling and grieved in the other world."

• • •

"If those two dogs of mine, the shepherd's dog and the house-dog, pass by any of my houses, let them never be kept away from it.

"For no house could subsist on the earth made by Ahura, but for those two dogs of mine, the shepherd's dog and the house-dog."

O Maker of the material world, thou Holy One! When a dog dies, with marrow and seed dried up, whereto does his ghost go?

Ahura Mazda answered: "It passes to the spring of the waters, O Spitama Zarathushtra! and there out of them two water-dogs are formed: out of every thousand dogs and every thousand she-dogs, a couple is formed, a water-dog and a water she-dog.

"He who kills a water-dog brings about a drought that dries up pastures.

"Until then, O Spitama Zarathushtra! sweetness and fatness would flow out from that land and from those fields, with health and healing, with fulness and increase and growth, and a growing of corn and grass."

Hinduism and a Dog

From the *Mahabharata,* ca. 500 B.C. One of the two great Hindu epics, the *Mahabharata* is the story of Vishnu's incarnation as the Krishna (India's most popular god) and of the war between two families. Here King Yudhishthira arrives at the gates of heaven and tries to convince Indra to allow him to bring his dog with him into heaven.

"But the king answered: 'O thou Wisest One,
Who know'st what was, and is, and is to be,
Still one more grace! This hound hath ate with me,
Followed me, loved me: must I leave him now?'

" 'Monarch,' spake Indra, 'thou art now as we—
Deathless, divine; thou art become a god;
Glory and power and gifts celestial,
And all the joys of heaven are thine for aye:
What hath a beast with these? Leave here thy hound.'

"Yet Yudhishthira answered: 'O Most High,
O thousand-eyed and Wisest! can it be
That one exalted should seem pitiless?
Nay, let me lose such glory: for its sake
I would not leave one living thing I loved.'

"Then sternly Indra spake: 'He is unclean,
And into Swarga such shall enter not.
The Krodhavasha's hand destroys the fruits
Of sacrifice, if dogs defile the fire.
Bethink thee, Dharmaraj, quit now this beast!
That which is seemly is not hard of heart.'

"Still he replied: ' 'Tis written that to spurn
A suppliant equals in offense to slay
A twice-born; wherefore, not for Swarga's bliss
Quit I, Mahendra, this poor clinging dog;
So without any hope or friend save me,
So wistful, fawning for my faithfulness,
So agonized to die, unless I help
Who among men was called steadfast and just. . . .'

"Straight as he spake, brightly great Indra smiled;
Vanished the hound; and in its stead stood there
The Lord of Death and Justice, Dharma's self!
Sweet were the words which fell from those dread lips,
Precious the lovely praise: 'O thou true king! . . .
Hear thou my word! Because thou didst not mount
This car divine, lest the poor hound be shent
Who looked to thee, lo! there is none in heaven
Shall sit above thee, king!—Bhârata's son,
Enter thou now to the eternal joys,
Living and in thy form. Justice and Love
Welcome thee, monarch! thou shalt throne with us!' "

Hinduism and a Dog

THE SISTER NIVEDITA (MARGARET NOBLE) and ANANDA K.
COOMARASWAMY, from *Myths and Legends of the Hindus and Bud-
dhists,* ca. 1913. Sister Nivedita was a disciple of Swami Vivekananda
and a follower of Sri Ramakrishna, two of India's most significant religious leaders in the 19th century. The following excerpt is a commen-
tary on the previous passage from the *Mahabharata.*

In the opinion of some amongst the learned we have here
in the Mahābhārata a recapitulation of all the old wonder
world of the early sky-gazer. Gods, heroes, and demi-gods
jostle each other through its pages, and whence they came
and what has been their previous history we have only a
name here or a sidelight there to help us to discover. As in
some marvellous tapestry, they are here gathered together,
in one case for a battle, in another for a life, and out of
the clash of the foemen's steel, out of the loyalty of vassal
and comrade, out of warring loves and conflicting ideals, is
made one of the noblest of the scriptures of the world. Is
it true that, with the exception of what has been added and
remoulded by a supreme poet, fusing into a single molten
mass the images of æons past, most of the characters that
move with such ease across these inspiring pages have
stepped down from the stage of the midnight sky? However this may be, one thing is certain: the very last scene
that ends the long panorama is that of a man climbing a
mountain, followed by a dog, and finally, with his dog,
translated to Heaven in the flesh.

The five royal heroes for whose sake the battle of their
prime was fought and won have held the empire of India
for some thirty-six years, and now, recognizing that the
time for the end has come, they, with Draupadī their
queen, resign their throne to their successors and set forth
on their last solemn journey—the pilgrimage of death—

followed by a dog who will not leave them. First circling their great realm in the last act of kingly worship, they proceed to climb the heights of the Himālayas, evidently by way of ascending to their rightful places amongst the stars. He who has lived in the world without flaw may hope for translation at the last. But, great as is the glory of the Pāndava brothers, only one of them, Yudhishthira, the eldest, is so unstained by life as to merit this, the honour of reaching Heaven in the flesh. One by one the others, Bhīma, Arjuna, and the twins Nakula and Sahādev, together with Draupadī the queen, faint and fall and die. And still without once looking back, without groan or sigh, Yudhishthira and the dog proceed alone.

Suddenly a clap of thunder arrests their steps, and in the midst of a mass of brightness they see the god Indra, King of Heaven, standing in his chariot. He is there to carry Yudhishthira back with him to Heaven, and immediately begs him to enter the chariot.

ALBERTO GIACOMETTI, *A Dog,* 1951. Swiss sculptor. (Museum of Modern Art, New York)

It is here, in the emperor's answer, that we are able to measure how very far the Hindu people have gone since the early worship of purely cosmic deities, in the moralizing and spiritualizing of their deities and demi-gods. Yudhishthira refuses to enter the chariot unless his dead brothers are all first recalled to enter it with him, and adds, on their behalf, that they will none of them accept the invitation even then unless with them be their queen, Draupadī, who was the first to fall. Only when he is assured by Indra that his brothers and wife have preceded him and will meet him again on his arrival in the state of eternal felicity does he consent to enter the divine chariot, and stand aside to let the dog go first.

But here Indra objected. To the Hindu the dog is unholy. It was impossible to contemplate the idea of a dog in Heaven! Yudhishthira is begged, therefore, to send away the dog. Strange to say, he refuses. To him the dog appears as one who has been devoted, loyal in time of loss and disaster, loving and faithful in the hour of entire solitude. He cannot imagine happiness, even in Heaven, if it were to be haunted by the thought of one so true who had been cast off.

The god pleads and argues, but each word only makes the sovereign more determined. His idea of manliness is involved. "To cast off one who has loved us is infinitely sinful." But also his personal pride and honour as a king are roused. He has never yet failed the terrified or the devoted, or such as have sought sanctuary with him, nor one who has begged mercy, nor any who was too weak to protect himself. He will certainly not infringe his own honour merely out of a desire for personal happiness.

Then the most sacred considerations are brought to bear on the situation. It must be remembered that the Hindu eats on the floor, and the dread of a dog entering the room is therefore easy to understand. There is evi-

GEORGE STUBBS, *Ringwood, a Brocklesby Foxhound,* 1792. English animal painter. A foxhound and a foxglove. (Earl of Yarborough)

dently an equal dislike of the same thing in Heaven. "Thou knowest," urges Indra, "that by the presence of a dog Heaven itself would be defiled." His mere glance deprives the sacraments of their consecration. Why, then, should one who has renounced his very family so strenuously object to giving up a dog?

Yudhishthira answers bitterly that he had perforce to abandon those who did not live to accompany him further, and, admitting that his resolution has probably been growing in the course of the debate, finally declares that he cannot now conceive of a crime that would be more heinous than to leave the dog.

The test is finished. Yudhishthira has refused Heaven for the sake of a dog, and the dog stands transformed into a shining god, Dharma himself, the God of Righteousness. The mortal is acclaimed by radiant multitudes, and seated in the chariot of glory, he enters Heaven in his mortal form.

REMBRANDT VAN RIJN, *Winter Scene,* 1646. Dutch painter and etcher. (Staatliche Gemäldegalerie, Kassel)

MYSTERIOUS POWERS

Whenever hound was heard to whine,
They gave the children bread and wine.

Whenever hound was heard to bark,
They thought the dead walk'd in the dark.

Whenever hound was heard to howl,
They thought they saw a corpse's cowl.

The Danish ballad *Svend Dyring*.

lthough there is no hard evidence that dogs can perceive things outside the realm of human awareness, there are many anecdotes that say they can. Leaving the validity of these stories for others to debate, they are still fascinating as examples of people's beliefs and of the dog's possible capabilities, no matter how unlikely. The stories generally fall into several categories: dogs traveling great distances to find their owners; dogs receiving information over long distances, such as knowing about the death of their owner; dogs sensing impending dangers and attempting to avoid or prevent them or having early knowledge of their owner's future death; and dogs sensing the presence of spirits. Also related to these are stories of dog ghosts.

There are many anecdotes about dogs who have been left behind and managed to find their owners many miles away. One collie is said to have found his way 3000 miles across the United States. Another story tells how, in 1914, an Irish dog disappeared from the new home of his master's wife in London and reappeared at his master's side in the trenches at Armentières. To get there, he had to travel over about 60 miles of unfamiliar English countryside, cross the English Channel, find his way through about 60 miles of unfamiliar French terrain, and then make it through the barrage of artillery fire landing behind the trenches.

Dogs are often said to sense things the people around them are oblivious to. Mrs. T. P. O'Connor related how she believed her dog, Max, almost caught Jack the Ripper in 1888, when Jack the Ripper was terrorizing London's East End. Mrs. O'Connor visited one of the murder sites with Max, who became very disturbed. That night at about 10:00 he ran away. An hour later a strange man turned Max over to a night watchman, after having found the dog's address on his collar. He said he found the dog "going towards the East End," about five miles away. In describing the strange man, the watchman later said, "Looked like he might have been Jack the Ripper himself. His skin was green-white, just the colour of the stomach of a frog. He didn't have a drop of red blood in him, and his fingers were tough white roots. He had little awful eyes, an' he spoke so queer! He was a rum customer, he was, and yet Max wanted to follow him." Max was put in the watchman's room, from which he began howling. Less than two hours later, two more women were murdered near the site Max had visited earlier. Jack the Ripper was never caught.

The belief that a dog's howl precedes death is found all over the world. Some think dogs only make this howl at midnight. Others say it is when the dog holds his head down instead of up when he howls. Most stories just say the dog goes into mourning. In Ireland, it is said that invisible dogs tell the family's dog about an impending death and he in turn relays this to the family by mourning. While some people feel that a dog's howling can predict a death, others believe that the howling can drive the Grim Reaper away; in other words, the dog is trying to prevent the death it sees coming.

Throughout history, people have believed dogs can see spirits, gods, demons, and the Angel of Death, as well as being able to recognize vampires and wraiths (visible spirit doubles of someone about to die). It is also reported that dogs often refuse to go near places where a murder was committed or near trees on which someone has been hanged. One Scottish professor tells of a farmhouse where dogs were seen gathered around an empty chair wagging their tails and begging for attention.

A belief that extends from Europe to Africa is that only four-eyed dogs—dogs with a dark spot over each eye—can see spirits. Even today, it is reported that some people on the Aegean island of Icaria always take four-eyed dogs with them to warn them in case they come upon a Nereid—a beautiful but dangerous sea nymph who lures men off cliffs. It is interesting to note that some say people can also see spirits if they get behind their dog and look between his or her ears at the spirit the dog is looking at.

Some people believe spirits, demons, and even the Angel of Death will avoid dogs; thus dogs assist in preventing diseases caused by demons and in keeping death away. Some say dogs who bark for no apparent reason are actually driving off demons, death, or the plague. Zoroastrians believe that Ahura Mazda created dogs as an expeller of demons and that just the gaze of certain dogs is enough to drive demons away. In many European stories, dogs are presented as the best defense against werewolves.

British folklore says dogs can see and hear fairies, so that the fairies usually avoid them. Any dog who chases the fairies usually dies or, with luck, is only paralyzed for several months. One Irishman said, "I would easily believe [a story] about the dog having a fight with something his owner couldn't see. That often happens in this island, and that's why every man likes to have a black dog with him at night—a black dog is the best for fighting such things." This belief is echoed on the Isle of Man.

Tales of dog ghosts are found all over the world. Most dog apparitions are nonmenacing, and many are friendly. It has been said they will come when called or whistled to by former human companions if they did this during their lifetime. But if they did not respond while they were alive, they will not when they are dead.

In Wissembourg, France, a black dog with a key in its mouth is said to stand guard over hidden treasure. In

Emmettsburg, Maryland, people tell of a three-foot-tall black dog wearing a clanking chain who walked beside them for a few yards before suddenly vanishing. A headless dog has been reported along a road in Buncombe County, North Carolina. Several people said they struck at it with a stick, but the stick just passed through its body. They say this dog ghost is actually the spirit of a drunken man who died along that road.

Sticks and weapons are also said to pass through a spirit dog that appears in the county of Lancashire in England. This dog will run away when chased, but the dog's eyes always remain facing a pursuer. Eventually the dog either vanishes or sinks into the ground with a terrible shriek.

A headless dog with a bloody neck who casts no shadow in the moonlight is reported near an old house in Brushing Fork, North Carolina. It is said that the dog and his human companion were murdered by robbers and buried nearby. Although he is a terrifying sight, there are no accounts of him ever harming anyone. He just likes to follow people along a stretch of road, as if he misses human company.

WINSLOW HOMER, *The Flock of Sheep,* 1878. American landscape, marine, and genre painter. (Private collection)

ESP in Dogs

DR. J. B. RHINE (1895–1980). American psychologist and founder of modern parapsychology.

A number of astonishing cases have been reported of dogs seeming to see danger ahead, and especially danger for themselves. The following example will illustrate this foreknowledge. It is about a dog who had always leaped up eagerly to go hunting with his master whenever he saw him pick up the shotgun. But the sad day came when the dog, old and ailing, was to be "put out of his misery." This time when the gun was picked up as usual the animal had disappeared; it was found under the farthest corner of the house, trembling with fear, and unresponsive to calls.

The best and most impressive kind of case for ESP in dogs is called "psi-trailing." This occurs sometimes when a dog has been left behind when the family moves away but later finds its way to the new location, sometimes over very long distances and grueling terrain.

In one of these cases, a mongrel dog was left with a former owner in Aurora, Illinois, when the family that owned it moved to Lansing, Michigan. The dog disappeared within a matter of hours and six weeks later showed up, still wearing the same collar, and excitedly claimed the owner's attention on a street corner. Was it really the same dog? That is usually the first question which comes to mind. The collar was identified, the family recognized the dog, and even the former owners drove all the way to Lansing and satisfied their own doubts. I myself flew all the way to Michigan to see if this dog was really as easily identified as had been claimed, and I too was satisfied. One could hardly mistake a dog with such a combination of features as this one had!

But the best way to make sure about ESP in dogs or in any other species is by experiment. About 20 years ago I had an opportunity, in working with a government agency, to test the ability of dogs to locate objects (small boxes) buried four to eight inches deep in the ground. As the dog was led by his trainer over the well-raked soil it soon showed that it could successfully find the hidden objects, even when all surface traces had been removed. The next step was to bury the boxes in the sand washed by waves on a beach. Again the dog succeeded. We next buried the boxes in sand under six to eight inches of water. The dog had to walk through the water with a strong side wind blowing that would remove any possible traces of odor that might come up through the water. Again success in locating the boxes was high enough to leave no question. Strong precautions had been taken to see that there was no visible or other trace for the senses. Therefore, little doubt remained but that ESP was being demonstrated by the dog and his trainer together. But they were, of course, a team, and perhaps one may still question whether it was the dog alone that had the ESP.

The next step in this kind of research is to have animals tested so that the man is not necessary. The animal needs to be tested alone. This of course means automatic testing and we have had to wait for further developments. At present an automatic setup is being tried with mice, and there are some claims of success, still unconfirmed. If mice can be shown to have ESP the plan will be to go on to see if dogs can prove their ESP ability under similar conditions. From all we now know this should be expected to happen, but it is best to leave the final conclusion about ESP in animals until further research is completed.

MARTIN THEODORE WARD, *Portrait of a Dog,* ca. 1825.

Ancient Egyptian mural showing a slave drawing water. (Metropolitan Museum of Art, New York)

A Dog Looks for His Master by Train

ALBERT H. TRAPMAN, from *Man's Best Friend*, 1928.

In the year 1901 there was a bull terrier (Peter by name) in Egypt belonging to Mr. Jobson, an English official. Mr. Jobson was at one time stationed in upper Egypt and was accustomed from time to time to run up to Cairo by train (a fifteen-hour trip), taking Peter with him. Later Mr. Jobson was temporarily transferred to Demanhour near Alexandria in Lower Egypt, some three hours by express on the Northern (opposite) side of Cairo; soon after his transfer thither he paid a one-day visit to the Egyptian capital, leaving Peter behind. No sooner did Peter discover his master's ab-

sence than he made up his mind to seek him. He boarded
an express and duly reached Cairo where he changed platforms and also trains (including a three-hour wait) cor-
rectly and caught the train to upper Egypt, visited his
master's old quarters there, but, finding nobody whom he
recognized (except native servants), took the next train
back to Cairo. Here he had another three hours to wait. Apparently aware of this fact he spent the time visiting several
of his master's friends in the capital, one of whom detained
him and wired to his owner down-country for instructions
as to what to do with Peter. Peter, however, had his own
ideas and plans; he managed to make good his escape in
time to catch his train back to Demanhour and was delighted after his 42 hours' complicated tour to discover his
master had returned. It may here be interpolated that Peter

Roman statue of two
greyhounds carved
from marble, first or
second century A.D.

was a forbidding-looking dog to strangers and that Egyptian railway ticket collectors are not reputed for their courage in evicting ownerless dogs from first-class compartments, in which alone Peter condescended to travel. It should also be added that Peter was accustomed to travel by rail, although the change of trains and platforms was a thing he could have only experienced once before. The curious fact to notice here is that the dog did not apparently work by scent or any sense of compass direction but by sheer force of memory. When the train arrived at Demanhour station he insisted on the door being opened for him by a fellow-passenger. The recollection of the time factor in the change of trains at Cairo is illuminating, unless it is a mere coincidence, as indicating that Peter possessed some knowledge of estimating the passage of time. Bull terriers and fox terriers however are noteworthy for their roaming and homing instincts and, not being highly nervous dogs, are quite at home when traveling by train or other public conveyance. One is inclined to think that a collie or Alsatian confronted with Peter's problem would have endeavored to make the journey afoot rather than face the turmoil and noise of railway travel.

SIR EDWIN LANDSEER, *Eos, a Favorite Greyhound, the Property of H.R.H. Prince Albert,* 1841. On Eos's death, Queen Victoria wrote in her journal, "She had been his constant and faithful companion for 10 & 1/2 years and she was only six months old, when he first had her. She was connected with the happiest years of his [Prince Albert's] life, & I cannot somehow imagine him without her. She was such a beautiful & sweet creature & used to play so much with the Children, & be so full of tricks." (Her Majesty the Queen)

An Actor's Dog Senses His Assassination

An account of British actor William Terriss's (1852–1897) assassination from *Light.*

The evening of the assassination Mrs. Terriss was sitting in the drawing-room of her house at Bedford Park; she had on her knees a small fox terrier called Davie who was sleeping. Her children, William and Tom, were with her. The clock marked 7.20 p.m., when suddenly, without any reason, the dog jumped to the ground and commenced to hurl himself about all over the place growling, barking, and grinding his teeth and biting in an attitude of extraordinary rage and terror. These happenings had a tremendous effect on Mrs. Terriss who was knocked out for the rest of the evening. Strangely enough it was at 7.20 p.m. that William Terriss fell assassinated at the theatre.

His son, Tom Terriss, said:

"I was playing draughts with my brother William, the dog was asleep on my mother's knees, when all of a sudden he jumped to the ground, grinding his teeth, biting in the air. My mother was terrified and asked what was happening, what did he see. She was convinced that the rage of the dog was conducted against something invisible to us. My brother and I tried to calm him although we were completely surprised and perplexed at the extraordinary behaviour of the dog who was generally meek and mild."

ROBERT VONNOH, *Fais le Beau!,* 1890. American portrait painter who studied in France. (Berry Hill Galleries, New York)

WILLIAM HOGARTH,
The Painter and His Pug,
1745. English painter,
satirist, and engraver.
(Tate Gallery, London)

The Apparition

SAKI (H. H. MUNRO), from *The Unbearable Bassington,* 1912. Scottish
author and journalist. The apparition of a little black dog was said to
follow members of the Munro family just before they died. Saki's father died shortly after the dog's appearance, and Saki used that in the
novel from which this excerpt was taken.

"I did not know you kept a dog," said Lady Veula.

"We don't," said Comus, "there isn't one in the
house."

"I could have sworn I saw one follow you across the
hall this evening," she said.

"A small black dog, something like a schipperke?"
asked Comus in a low voice.

"Yes, that was it."

"I saw it myself tonight; it ran from behind my chair just as I was sitting down. Don't say anything to the others about it; it would frighten my mother."

"Have you ever seen it before?" Lady Veula asked quickly.

"Once, when I was six years old. It followed my father downstairs."

Lady Veula said nothing. She knew that Comus had lost his father at the age of six.

[Saki became a machine gunner in World War I. It was said a little black dog suddenly appeared and followed him just before he was killed.]

CARL GUSTAV PILO,
The Ramels Family Pug,
1749. (National Museum, Stockholm)

The Wolves of Cernogratz

SAKI (H. H. MUNRO), from *The Toys of Peace,* 1923. Scottish author.

"Are there any old legends attached to the castle?" asked Conrad of his sister. Conrad was a prosperous Hamburg merchant, but he was the one poetically-dispositioned member of an eminently practical family.

The Baroness Gruebel shrugged her plump shoulders.

"There are always legends hanging about these old places. They are not difficult to invent and they cost nothing. In this case there is a story that when any one dies in the castle all the dogs in the village and the wild beasts in the forest howl the night long. It would not be pleasant to listen to, would it?"

"It would be weird and romantic," said the Hamburg merchant.

"Anyhow, it isn't true," said the Baroness complacently; "since we bought the place we have had proof that nothing of the sort happens. When the old mother-in-law died last springtime we all listened, but there was no howling. It is just a story that lends dignity to the place without costing anything."

"The story is not as you have told it," said Amalie, the grey old governess. Every one turned and looked at her in astonishment. She was wont to sit silent and prim and faded in her place at table, never speaking unless some one spoke to her, and there were few who troubled themselves to make conversation with her. To-day a sudden volubility had descended on her; she continued to talk, rapidly and nervously, looking straight in front of her and seeming to address no one in particular.

"It is not when *any one* dies in the castle that the howling is heard. It was when one of the Cernogratz family died here that the wolves came from far and near and howled at the edge of the forest just before the death hour. There were only a few couple of wolves that had their lairs in this part of the forest, but at such a time, the keepers say, there would be scores of them, gliding about in the shadows and howling in chorus, and the dogs of the castle and the village and all the farms round would bay and howl in fear and anger at the wolf chorus, and as the soul of the dying one left its body a tree would crash down in the park. That is what happened when a Cernogratz died in his family castle. But for a stranger dying here, of course no wolf would howl and no tree would fall. Oh, no."

There was a note of defiance, almost of contempt, in her voice as she said the last words. The well-fed, much-too-well dressed Baroness stared angrily at the dowdy old woman who had come forth from her usual and seemly position of effacement to speak so disrespectfully.

"You seem to know quite a lot about the von Cernogratz legends, Fräulein Schmidt," she said sharply; "I did not know that family histories were among the subjects you are supposed to be proficient in."

The answer to her taunt was even more unexpected and astonishing than the conversational outbreak which had provoked it.

"I am a von Cernogratz myself," said the old woman, "that is why I know the family history."

"You a von Cernogratz? You!" came in an incredulous chorus.

"When we became very poor," she explained, "and I had to go out and give teaching lessons, I took another name; I thought it would be more in keeping. But my grandfather spent much of his time as a boy in this castle, and my father used to tell me many stories about it, and, of course, I knew all the family legends and stories. When one

A Chinese terra-cotta dog, 202 B.C.–A.D. 220.

ANDO HIROSHIGE, *Oji Oji Shozoku enoki Omisoka no kitsunebi (New Year's Eve Foxfires at the Changing Tree)*, from *100 Views of Edo (Tokyo)*, 1857. Japanese landscape painter and color print artist. It was said that on New Year's Eve, foxes would gather at the Changing Tree before entering the nearby shrine to receive their orders for the coming year.

has nothing left to one but memories, one guards and dusts them with especial care. I little thought when I took service with you that I should one day come with you to the old home of my family. I could wish it had been anywhere else."

There was a silence when she finished speaking, and then the Baroness turned the conversation to a less embarrassing topic than family histories. But afterwards, when the old governess had slipped away quietly to her duties, there arose a clamour of derision and disbelief.

"It was impertinence," snapped out the Baron, his protruding eyes taking on a scandalised expression; "fancy the woman talking like that at our table. She almost told us we were nobodies, and I don't believe a word of it. She is just Schmidt and nothing more. She has been talking to some of the peasants about the old Cernogratz family, and raked up their history and their stories."

"She wants to make herself out of some consequence," said the Baroness; "she knows she will soon be past work and she wants to appeal to our sympathies. Her grandfather, indeed!"

The Baroness had the usual number of grandfathers, but she never, never boasted about them.

"I dare say her grandfather was a pantry boy or something of the sort in the castle," sniggered the Baron; "that part of the story may be true."

The merchant from Hamburg said nothing; he had seen tears in the old woman's eyes when she spoke of guarding her memories—or, being of an imaginative disposition, he thought he had.

"I shall give her notice to go as soon as the New Year festivities are over," said the Baroness; "till then I shall be too busy to manage without her."

But she had to manage without her all the same, for in the cold biting weather after Christmas, the old governess fell ill and kept to her room.

"It is most provoking," said the Baroness, as her guests sat round the fire on one of the last evenings of the dying year; "all the time that she has been with us I cannot remember that she was ever seriously ill, too ill to go about and do her work, I mean. And now, when I have the house full, and she could be useful in so many ways, she goes and breaks down. One is sorry for her, of course, she looks so withered and shrunken, but it is intensely annoying all the same."

"Most annoying," agreed the banker's wife, sympathetically; "it is the intense cold, I expect, it breaks the old people up. It has been unusually cold this year."

"The frost is the sharpest that has been known in December for many years," said the Baron.

"And, of course, she is quite old," said the Baroness; "I wish I had given her notice some weeks ago, then she would have left before this happened to her. Why, Wappi, what is the matter with you?"

The small, woolly lapdog had leapt suddenly down from its cushion and crept shivering under the sofa. At the same moment an outburst of angry barking came from the dogs in the castle-yard, and other dogs could be heard yapping and barking in the distance.

"What is disturbing the animals?" asked the Baron.

And then the humans, listening intently, heard the sound that had roused the dogs to their demonstrations of fear and rage; heard a long-drawn whining howl, rising and falling, seeming at one moment leagues away, at others sweeping across the snow until it appeared to come from the foot of the castle walls. All the starved, cold misery of a frozen world, all the relentless hunger-fury of the wild, blended with other forlorn and haunting melodies to

FRANCISCO JOSÉ DE GOYA Y LUCIENTES, *A Dog,* 1820–1823. Spanish painter and etcher. Goya was a court painter for numerous Spanish rulers. (Prado, Madrid)

which one could give no name, seemed concentrated in that wailing cry.

"Wolves!" cried the Baron.

Their music broke forth in one raging burst, seeming to come from everywhere.

"Hundreds of wolves," said the Hamburg merchant, who was a man of strong imagination.

Moved by some impulse which she could not have explained, the Baroness left her guests and made her way to the narrow cheerless room where the old governess lay watching the hours of the dying year slip by. In spite of the biting cold of the winter night, the window stood open. With a scandalised exclamation on her lips, the Baroness rushed forward to close it.

"Leave it open," said the old woman in a voice that for all its weakness carried an air of command such as the Baroness had never heard before from her lips.

"But you will die of cold!" she expostulated.

"I am dying in any case," said the voice, "and I want to hear their music. They have come from far and wide to sing the death-music of my family. It is beautiful that they have come; I am the last von Cernogratz that will die in our old castle, and they have come to sing to me. Hark, how loud they are calling!"

The cry of the wolves rose on the still winter air and floated round the castle walls in long-drawn piercing wails; the old woman lay back on her couch with a look of long-delayed happiness on her face.

"Go away," she said to the Baroness; "I am not lonely any more. I am one of a great old family. . . ."

"I think she is dying," said the Baroness when she had rejoined her guests; "I suppose we must send for a doctor. And that terrible howling! Not for much money would I have such death-music."

"That music is not to be bought for any amount of money," said Conrad.

"Hark! What is that other sound?" asked the Baron, as a noise of splitting and crashing was heard.

It was a tree falling in the park.

There was a moment of constrained silence, and then the banker's wife spoke.

"It is the intense cold that is splitting the trees. It is also the cold that brought the wolves out in such numbers. It is many years since we have had such a cold winter."

The Baroness eagerly agreed that the cold was responsible for these things. It was the cold of the open window, too, which caused the heart failure that made the doctor's ministrations unnecessary for the old Fräulein. But the notice in the newspapers looked very well—

"On December 29th, at Schloss Cernogratz, Amalie von Cernogratz, for many years the valued friend of Baron and Baroness Gruebel."

Untitled Poem

CHARLOTTE BRONTË, ca. 1844. English novelist and poet. Brontë was the author of *Jane Eyre*. Her sister Emily was the author of *Wuthering Heights* and her sister Anne was the author of *Agnes Grey*.

Like wolf—and black bull or goblin hound,
 Or come in guise of spirit
With wings and long wet waving hair
And at the fire its locks will dry,
 Which will be certain sign
That one beneath the roof must die
 Before the year's decline.

Forget not now what I have said,
 Sit there till we return.
The hearth is hot—watch well the bread
 Lest haply it may burn.

SALVADOR DALI, *Apparition of Face and Fruit Dish on a Beach,* 1938. Spanish surrealist painter. (Wadsworth Atheneum, Hartford)

DONALD ROLLER WILSON, *Came From Wishing on the Front Porch Rolled Roast Tid-Bit on My Mind; Not a Green One: Red-Stuffed Green One, Want a T-Bone—Want That Kind!*, 1977. American painter. (Private collection)

Strange Noises at the Vicarage

REV. JOHN WESLEY (1703–1791), from *The Journal of Rev. John Wesley*. English evangelical preacher and founder of the Methodist Church. While living at the Vicarage at Epworth, he often heard sounds like iron or glass being hurled at the floor.

A short time afterwards our mastiff, which ordinarily was a magnificent watch, took refuge behind Mrs. Wesley. As long as the noise continued he yelped and snapped the air on both sides and often did that before anybody heard anything in the room. After a few days he shook all over and went off growling with his tail between his legs, although on any ordinary occasion he would have torn anybody to pieces. When he did this our family knew what was about to take place and this always occurred.

240

Dogs and Vampires

BRAM STOKER (ABRAHAM STOKER), from *Dracula*, 1897. Irish author. *Dracula* is considered his masterpiece.

One of the men who came up here often to look for the boats was followed by his dog. The dog is always with him. They are both quiet persons, and I never saw the man angry, nor heard the dog bark. During the [funeral] service the dog would not come to its master, who was on the seat with us, but kept a few yards off, barking and howling. Its master spoke to it gently, and then harshly, and then angrily; but it would neither come nor cease to make a noise. It was in a sort of fury, with its eyes savage, and all its hairs bristling out like a cat's tail when puss is on the war-path. Finally the man, too, got angry, and jumped down and kicked the dog, and then took it by the scruff of the neck and half dragged and half threw it on the tombstone on which the seat is fixed. The moment it touched the stone the poor thing became quiet and fell all into a tremble. It did not try to get away, but crouched down, quivering and cowering, and was in such a pitiable state of terror that I tried, though without effect, to comfort it.

HOKUSAI, from *Daily Exorcism*, 1842–1843. Japanese painter, draftsman, and wood engraver.

A Mexican Indian vessel in the form of a dog wearing a mask, ca. A.D. 300–1000. (Museo National de Anthropologia, Mexico D.F.)

Apparitions in Ireland

Two accounts as told to Lady Gregory, from *Visions and Beliefs in the West of Ireland*, 1920. Irish author and playwright.

AN OLD WOMAN:

That dog I met in the boreen at Ballinamantane, he was the size of a calf, and black, and his paws the size of I don't know what. I was sitting in the house one day, and he came in and sat down by the dresser and looked at me. And I didn't like the look of him when I saw the big eyes of him, and the size of his legs. And just then a man came in that used to make his living by making mats, and he used to lodge with me for a night now and again. And he went out to bring his cart away where he was afraid it'd be knocked about by the people going to

HANS HOLBEIN, THE YOUNGER (ca. 1497–1543), from *The Dance of Death*. German portrait and religious painter. He became a painter for England's King Henry VIII and died of the plague in London at age 46.

the big bonfire at Kiltartan cross-roads. And when he went out I looked out the door, and there was the dog sitting under the cart. So he made a hit at it with a stick, and it was in the stones the stick stuck, and there was the dog sitting at the other side of him. So he came in and gave me abuse and said I must be a strange woman to have such things about me. And he never would come to lodge with me again. But didn't the dog behave well not to do him an injury after he hitting it? It was surely some man that was in that dog, some soul in trouble.

A CHAUFFEUR:

I went to serve one Patterson at a place called Grace Dieu between Waterford and Tramore, and there were queer things in it. There was a woman lived at the lodge the other side from the gate, and one day she was looking out and she saw a wool-pack coming riding down the road of itself.

There was a room over the stable I was put to sleep in, and no one near me. One night I felt a great weight on my feet, and there was something very weighty coming up upon my body and I heard heavy breathing. Every night after that I used to light the fire and bring up coal and make up the fire with it that it would be near as good in the morning as it was at night. And I brought a good terrier up every night to sleep with me on the bed. Well, one night the fire was lighting and the moon was shining in at the window, and the terrier leaped off the bed and he was barking and rushing and fighting and leaping, near to the ceiling and in under the bed. And I could see the shadow of him on the walls and on the ceiling, and I could see the shadow of another thing that was about two foot long and that had a head like a pike, and that was fighting and leaping. They stopped after a while and all was quiet. But from that night the terrier never would come to sleep in the room again.

The Ghost Dog
of Peel Castle

SIR WALTER SCOTT, from a footnote to *Lay of the Last Minstrel*, 1805.
Scottish novelist and poet.

The ancient castle of Peel-town in the Isle of Man is surrounded by four churches, now ruinous. They say that an
apparition, called, in the Mankish language, the *Mauthe
Doog,* in the shape of a large black spaniel, with curled
shaggy hair, was used to haunt Peel-castle; and has been
frequently seen in every room, but particularly in the
guard-chamber, where, as soon as candles were lighted, it
came and lay down before the fire, in presence of all the
soldiers, who, at length, by being so much accustomed to
the sight of it, lost great part of the terror they were seized
with at its first appearance. But though they endured the
shock of such a guest when all together in a body, none

JOAN MIRÓ, *Dog Bark-
ing at the Moon,* 1926.
Spanish surrealist
painter. (Philadelphia
Museum of Art,
Philadelphia)

Roman floor mosaic at the House of the Tragic Poet, Pompeii, ca.
A.D. 79. *Cave canem* ("Beware of Dog") signs were common at entrances to Roman homes. Some say these were meant to scare away
burglars. Others say they were warnings to be aware not to step on the
family pet. A third explanation is that the Romans believed the mosaic
dogs could be as effective as real dogs in keeping demons or spirits
from entering the house. (Museo Nazionale, Naples)

cared to be left alone with it. It being the custom, therefore, for one of the soldiers to lock the gates of the castle
at a certain hour, and carry the keys to the captain, to
whose apartment . . . the way led through the church, they
agreed among themselves, that whoever was to succeed the
ensuing night his fellow in this errand, should accompany
him that went first, and by this means no man would be
exposed singly to the danger. One night a fellow, being
drunk, laughed at the simplicity of his companions; and
though it was not his turn to go with the keys, would
needs take that office upon him, to testify his courage. All
the soldiers endeavored to dissuade him; but the more they
said, the more resolute he seemed, and swore that he desired nothing more than that the *Mauthe Doog* would follow him as it had done the others; for he would try if it
were dog or devil. After having talked in a very reprobate
manner for some time, he snatched up the keys, and went
out of the guard-room. In some time after his departure, a
great noise was heard, but nobody had the boldness to see
what occasioned it, till, the adventurer returning, they demanded the knowledge of him; but as loud and noisy as he
had been at leaving them, he was now become sober and
silent enough; for he was never heard to speak more; and
though all the time he lived, which was three days, he was
entreated by all who came near him, either to speak, or, if
he could not do that, to make some signs, by which they
might understand what had happened to him, yet nothing
intelligible could be got from him, only that, by the dis-
tortion of his limbs and features, it might be guessed that
he died in agonies more than is common in a natural
death.

[Concerning this story, George Waldron says in his *History of the Isle of
Man* (1744), "I heard this attested by several, but especially by an old soldier, who assured me he had seen it oftener than he had then hairs on
his head."]

Dog Phantoms

ROBERT CHAMBERS, from *Book of Days,* 1862–1864. Scottish author and publisher.

A similar story is related of a man who lived at a village near Aylesbury, in Buckinghamshire. This man was accustomed to go every morning and night to milk his cows in a field, which was some distance from the village. To shorten his walk, he often crossed over a neighbour's field, and passed through a gap in the hedge; but one night, on approaching the gap, he found it occupied by a large, black, fierce-looking dog. He paused to examine the animal, and as he looked at him his fiery eyes grew larger and fiercer, and he had altogether such a fiend-like and "unkid" appearance, that he doubted whether he were "a dog or the bad spirit." Whichever he was, he thought he would be no pleasant antagonist to encounter. So he turned aside, and passed through a gate at the end of the field. Night after night he found the same dog in the gap, and turned aside in the same manner. One night, having fallen in with a companion, he returned homeward with him across his neighbour's field, being determined, if he found the dog in the gap, to make an attack upon him, and drive him away. On reaching the gap there stood the dog looking even fiercer and bigger than ever. But the milkman, wishing to appear valiant before his companion, put down his milk-pails, which were suspended from a yoke across his shoulders, and attempting to speak very bravely, though trembling all over, he exclaimed: "Now, you black fiend, I'll try what ye're made of!" He raised his yoke in both his hands, and struck at the dog with all his might. The dog vanished, and the milkman fell senseless to the ground. He was carried home alive, but remained speechless and paralytic to the end of his days. . . .

DONALD ROLLER WILSON

The Second Visit of the Queen
The Queen Had Landed in the Night
She Flew Behind a Witch;
(The Witch Went Back—She Flew Up to the Moon)

The Drink Was One a Cow Once Sipped
When Tricked Inside a Room;
(A Texas Shack All Silver—Lined with Tombs),

1979. American painter. (Private collection)

In the adjoining county of Hertford the same superstition prevails, and the black dog apparition is still a dreaded bogie. Within the parish of Tring, but about three miles from the town, a poor old woman was, in 1751, drowned for suspected witchcraft. A chimney-sweep, who was the principal perpetrator of this atrocious deed, was hanged and gibbeted near the place where the murder was effected. While the gibbet stood, and long after it had disappeared, the spot was haunted by a black dog. The writer was told by the village schoolmaster, who had been "abroad," that he himself had seen this diabolical dog. "I was returning home," he said, "late at night in a gig with the person who was driving. When he came near the spot where a portion of the gibbet had lately stood, we saw on the bank of the roadside, along which a ditch or narrow brook runs, a flame of fire as large as a man's hat. 'What's that?' I exclaimed. 'Hush!' said my companion, all in a tremble; and, suddenly pulling in his horse, made a dead stop. I then saw an immense black dog lying on the road just in front of our horse, which also appeared trembling with fright. The dog was the strangest looking creature I ever beheld. He was as big as a Newfoundland, but very gaunt, shaggy, with long ears and tail, eyes like balls of fire, and large, long teeth, for he opened his mouth and seemed to grin at us. He looked more like a fiend than a dog, and I trembled as much as my companion. In a few minutes the dog disappeared, seeming to vanish like a shadow, or to sink into the earth, and we drove on over the spot where he had lain."

HOUNDS OF HELL

"What three things are these, Sweet William,"
    she says.
    "That stands here at your feet?"
"It is three hell-hounds, Marjorie," he says.
    "That's waiting my soul to keep."

William Motherwell (1797–1835),
"Sweet William's Ghost."

Hellhounds can be distinguished from dog ghosts in that they were never really dogs, at least not in our world. Many were thought to be demons or spirit creatures who had taken on a doglike form. Many gods and goddesses of the dead, or of the underworld, are associated with dogs; these include the Greek goddess Hectate, who was usually accompanied by her hellhounds.

The most famous hellhound is Cerberus, the three-headed dog of Greek mythology who guards the entrance to Hades, keeping the living out and the dead in. Another example is Garm of the blood-splattered chest, the dog of Hel. Hel is the Norse goddess of the dead. Garm is chained in a cave beside the entrance to her realm, which is also called Hel, and allows good souls to enter unharmed. Mohorangi, who the Maoris of New Zealand say guards the island of the sacred reptiles, turns trespassers to stone. The people of North Borneo tell of a fiery dog guarding the land of the dead. This dog allows everyone to pass safely except for virgins, who he grabs. The Mordvins of Russia used to put clubs in their coffins so that the dead could protect themselves against the guardian dogs of underworld and pass through the gate unharmed.

Although not technically hellhounds, many other related magical or spirit creatures are said to appear as dogs. For example, in Guatemala the *cadejo* is a spirit that appears as a huge, terrifying black or white dog with flaming eyes that sometimes even knocks the observer down. In China, tree spirits were said to appear as dogs or as dogs with human faces. Elsewhere, sorcerers, witches (both good and evil), vampires, and gods are all said to have appeared in the form of dogs. One dog in New England was actually tried and executed for witchcraft in the late 17th century. The belief that vampires turn into bats probably did not exist until the late 19th century. Before that, vampires almost always transformed themselves into dogs or wolves. Also related to these beliefs is that of werewolves.

Sometimes the fairies of British folklore appeared in dog form, and they also kept dogs. Originally, fairies were nothing like the way we picture them today. They were as large as a human, and sometimes even larger; they had no wings; and they could be more frightening than any ghost and a lot more dangerous. Their dogs came in all sizes and colors. The most easily recognizable were those that gave off an eerie, greenish glow. A Welsh legend of a fairy dog was the model for Sir Arthur Conan Doyle's *Hound of the Baskervilles.*

Fairy dogs were also associated with the Fairy Ride, in which the fairies—on their horses and with their dogs—noisily stormed across the countryside in the middle of the night. This was also similar to the Wild Hunt, where human captives of fairyland would be seen—also on horses and with dogs—charging through the night in pursuit of something unknown. Similarly, the wisht hounds of Ireland and Cornwall and the yeth hounds of Devon are spectral packs of headless hounds that roam the countryside. In northern England, the Gabriel Hounds—a corruption of *Gabble Retchets,* meaning "Corpse Hounds"—are evil spirits who fly through the night hunting the souls of the dead. In Welsh mythology, Gwynn ab Nudd, the king of the afterworld, hunts the spirits of the dying with his terrible hounds. Sometimes these hounds, known as *Cwn Annwn* or "dogs of hell", are said to be seen pursuing spirits through the air. Some people have blended these beliefs with Christianity, saying the Wild Hunt involves the devil and his hounds pursuing souls. In Ireland, they tell of how the devil's dogs lie near the dying, waiting to chase the souls of sinners to hell.

It is recorded that one Sunday in 1577, thunder shook the church of Bongay in England, and suddenly a huge black dog ran among the congregation. It was said the dog "passed between two persons, as they were kneeling uppon their knees, and . . . wrung the necks of them bothe at one instant clene backward". To another man, it "gave him such a gripe on the back, that therewith all he was presently drawn togither and shrunk up, as it were a peece of lether scorched in a hot fire; or as the mouth of a purse or bag, drawen togither with a string", though it left him still alive. That same day, the Black Dog also visited the Blythburgh church in Suffolk; and what are said to be its claw marks can still be seen on one of the church's doors.

Not all hellhounds are frightening. The idea of dogs guarding the entrance to the afterworld is a common one and can be found in many cultures—including those of the Native Americans and Eskimos—but often this afterworld is heaven or paradise, which the dogs prevent evil people from entering. Yima, the Zoroastrian god of the dead, has two four-eyed dogs who guard Chinvat Bridge—the Bridge of Decision between this world and the next. It is said that these dogs will not help anyone or let anyone pass who has harmed a dog in this world.

Another common belief, which appears all over the world, is that dogs escort the dead to the next world, both protecting them and showing the way. An early example of this is Anubis, the Egyptian jackal-headed god of the dead, who guided the deceased into the afterworld to the seat (or throne) of Osiris.

In the Hebrides—the islands along the western coast of Scotland—the White Hound runs silently through the night. It is only seen by someone at the moment of death, though others can sometimes feel its presence. When the White Hound appears to them, the dying describe it as being absolutely beautiful.

Cry of the Hounds

JOHN AUBREY (1626–1697), from *Naturall History of Wiltshire.* English antiquary.

It is credibly told of many honest men, that fiue miles from *Blonsdon* in *Wiltshire,* a crie of houndes was heard in the ayre, the self same day that the first Earthquake was, and the noyse was so great that was made, that they seemed three or four score couple, whereat diuerse toke their Greyhoundes, thinking some gentlemen had bin hunting in the chase, and thoughte to course: yet some of those that went out of their houses, seeing nothing below abrode, loked vpwards to the skyes, and there espyed in the ayre fiue or sixe houndes perfectlye to be diserned.

PAUL KLEE, *Zwei Langhalshunde (Two Long-Necked Dogs),* 1907. Swiss painter. The Nazi regime officially expressed its dislike of Klee's work. He is now considered "a giant of modern art". (Klee Foundation, Bern)

SIR EDWIN LANDSEER, *A Highland Breakfast,* by 1814. English animal painter. (Victoria and Albert Museum, London)

Herald of the Fairies

MR. T. LEECE of the Isle of Man as told to Dr. W. Y. Evans-Wentz, from *The Fairy-Faith in Celtic Countries,* 1911.

This used to happen about one hundred years ago, as my mother has told me:—Where my grandfather John Watterson was reared, just over near Kerroo Kiel (Narrow Quarter), all the family were sometimes sitting in the house of a cold winter night, and my great grandmother and her daughters at their wheels spinning, when a little white dog would suddenly appear in the room. Then every one there would have to drop their work and prepare for *the company* to come in: they would put down a fire and leave fresh water for *them,* and hurry off upstairs to bed. They could hear *them* come, but could never see them, only the dog. The dog was a fairy dog, and a sure sign of their coming.

The Fairy Dogs

REV. JOHN GREGORSON CAMPBELL, from *Superstitions of the High-lands and Islands of Scotland,* 1900. Rev. Campbell was the minister of Tiree in Scotland.

The Fairy dog (*cu sìth*) is as large as a two-year-old stirk, a dark green colour, with ears of deep green. It is of a lighter colour towards the feet. In some cases it has a long tail rolled up in a coil on its back, but others have the tail flat and plaited like the straw rug of a pack-saddle. . . .

The Fairy hound was kept tied as a watch dog in the brugh, but at times accompanied the women on their expeditions or roamed about alone, making its lairs in clefts of the rocks. Its motion was silent and gliding, and its bark a rude clamour. . . . Its immense footmarks, as large as the spread of the human hand, have been found next day traced in the mud, in the snow, or on the sands. Others say it makes a noise like a horse galloping, and its bay is like that of another dog, only louder. There is a considerable interval between each bark, and at the third (it only barks thrice) the terror-struck hearer is overtaken and destroyed, unless he has by that time reached a place of safety.

Ordinary dogs have a mortal aversion to the Fairies, and give chase whenever the elves are sighted. On coming back, the hair is found to be scraped off their bodies, all except the ears, and they die soon after.

GORDON BROWNE, from *The Tale of the Cauldron,* 1927. The fairy
dogs are unleashed.

The Hound of the Baskervilles

SIR ARTHUR CONAN DOYLE, from *The Hound of the Baskervilles,* originally published in *Strand,* 1901–1902. Scottish author famous for his Sherlock Holmes stories.

Holmes stretched out his hand for the manuscript and flattened it upon his knee. . . .

I looked over his shoulder at the yellow paper and the faded script. At the head was written: "Baskerville Hall," and below, in large, scrawling figures: "1742."

"It appears to be a statement of some sort."

"Yes, it is a statement of a certain legend which runs in the Baskerville family. . . ."

Holmes leaned back in his chair, placed his finger-tips together, and closed his eyes, with an air of resignation. Dr. Mortimer turned the manuscript to the light and read in a high, cracking voice the following curious, old-world narrative:

"Of the origin of the Hound of the Baskervilles there have been many statements, yet as I come in a direct line from Hugo Baskerville, and as I had the story from my father, who also had it from his, I have set it down with all belief that it occurred even as is here set forth. And I would have you believe, my sons, that the same Justice which punishes sin may also most graciously forgive it, and that no ban is so heavy but that by prayer and repentance it may be removed. Learn then from this story not to fear the fruits of the past, but rather to be circumspect in the future, that those foul passions whereby our family has suffered so grievously may not again be loosed to our undoing.

"Know then that in the time of the Great Rebellion (the history of which by the learned Lord Clarendon I most

HENRI DE TOULOUSE-LAUTREC, *Bouboule: Mme. Palmyre's Bulldog,* 1897. French painter and lithographer. Toulouse-Lautrec broke both his legs as a child and was permanently deformed. He was highly productive but lived a life of debauchery and ended up being committed to an asylum as mentally deranged. He was released shortly before his death at age 37. He is best known for his studies of circuses, music halls, and Paris low-life. His works are now highly prized. Mme. Palmyre ran a well-known lesbian restaurant called "La Souris". (Musée Toulouse-Lautrec, Albi, France)

earnestly commend to your attention), this Manor of Baskerville was held by Hugo of that name, nor can it be gainsaid that he was a most wild, profane, and godless man. This, in truth, his neighbours might have pardoned, seeing that saints have never flourished in those parts, but there was in him a certain wanton and cruel humour which made his name a byword through the West. It chanced that this Hugo came to love (if, indeed, so dark a passion may be known under so bright a name) the daughter of a yeoman who held lands near the Baskerville estate. But the young maiden, being discreet and of good repute, would ever avoid him, for she feared his evil name. So it came to pass that one Michaelmas this Hugo, with five or six of his idle and wicked companions, stole down upon the farm and carried off the maiden, her father and brothers being from home, as he well knew. When they had brought her to the Hall the maiden was placed in an upper chamber, while Hugo and his friends sat down to a long carouse, as was their nightly custom. Now, the poor lass upstairs was like to have her wits turned at the singing and shouting and terrible oaths which came up to her from below, for they say that the words used by Hugo Baskerville, when he was in wine, were such as might blast the man who said them. At last in the stress of her fear she did that which might have daunted the bravest or most active man, for by the aid of the growth of ivy which covered (and still covers) the south wall she came down from under the eaves, and so homeward across the moor, there being three leagues betwixt the Hall and her father's farm.

"It chanced that some little time later Hugo left his guests to carry food and drink—with other worse things, perchance—to his captive, and so found the cage empty and the bird escaped. Then, as it would seem, he became as one that hath a devil, for, rushing down the stairs into the

261

dining-hall, he sprang upon the great table, flagons and trenchers flying before him, and he cried aloud before all the company that he would that very night render his body and soul to the Powers of Evil if he might but overtake the wench. And while the revellers stood aghast at the fury of the man, one more wicked or, it may be, more drunken than the rest, cried out that they should put the hounds upon her. Whereat Hugo ran from the house, crying to his grooms that they should saddle his mare and unkennel the pack, and giving the hounds a kerchief of the maid's, he swung them to the line, and so off full cry in the moonlight over the moor.

"Now, for some space the revellers stood agape, unable to understand all that had been done in such haste. But anon their bemused wits awoke to the nature of the deed which was like to be done upon the moorlands. Everything was now in an uproar, some calling for their pistols, some for their horses, and some for another flask of wine. But at length some sense came back to their crazed minds, and the whole of them, thirteen in number, took horse and started in pursuit. The moon shone clear above them, and they rode swiftly abreast, taking that course which the maid must needs have taken if she were to reach her own home.

"They had gone a mile or two when they passed one of the night shepherds upon the moorlands, and they cried to him to know if he had seen the hunt. And the man, as the story goes, was so crazed with fear that he could scarce speak, but at last he said that he had indeed seen the unhappy maiden, with the hounds upon her track. 'But I have seen more than that,' said he, 'for Hugo Baskerville passed me upon his black mare, and there ran mute behind him such a hound of hell as God forbid should ever be at my heels.' So the drunken squires cursed the shepherd and

A greyhound carved
from marble, 200 B.C.
(Louvre, Paris)

rode onward. But soon their skins turned cold, for there
came a galloping across the moor, and the black mare, dab-
bled with white froth, went past with trailing bridle and
empty saddle. Then the revellers rode close together, for a
great fear was on them, but they still followed over the
moor, though each, had he been alone, would have been
right glad to have turned his horse's head. Riding slowly
in this fashion they came at last upon the hounds. These,
though known for their valour and their breed, were
whimpering in a cluster at the head of a deep dip or goyal,
as we call it, upon the moor, some slinking away and some,
with starting hackles and staring eyes, gazing down the
narrow valley before them.

"The company had come to a halt, more sober men, as
you may guess, than when they started. The most of them
would by no means advance, but three of them, the bold-

est, or it may be the most drunken, rode forward down the goyal. Now, it opened into a broad space in which stood two of those great stones, still to be seen there, which were set by certain forgotten peoples in the days of old. The moon was shining bright upon the clearing, and there in the centre lay the unhappy maid where she had fallen, dead of fear and of fatigue. But it was not the sight of her body, nor yet was it that of the body of Hugo Baskerville lying near her, which raised the hair upon the heads of these three dare-devil roysterers, but it was that, standing over Hugo, and plucking at his throat, there stood a foul thing, a great, black beast, shaped like a hound, yet larger than any hound that ever mortal eye has rested upon. And even as they looked the thing tore the throat out of Hugo Baskerville, on which, as it turned its blazing eyes and dripping jaws upon them, the three shrieked with fear and rode for dear life, still screaming, across the moor. One, it is said, died that very night of what he had seen, and the other twain were but broken men for the rest of their days.

"Such is the tale, my sons, of the coming of the hound which is said to have plagued the family so sorely ever since. If I have set it down it is because that which is clearly known hath less terror than that which is but hinted at and guessed. Nor can it be denied that many of the family have been unhappy in their deaths, which have been sudden, bloody, and mysterious. Yet may we shelter ourselves in the infinite goodness of Providence, which would not forever punish the innocent beyond that third or fourth generation which is threatened in Holy Writ. To that Providence, my sons, I hereby commend you, and I counsel you by way of caution to forbear from crossing the moor in those dark hours when the powers of evil are exalted."

RUFINO TAMAYO, *Dos Perros (Two Dogs)*, 1941. Mexican painter. (Museum of Modern Art, Houston)

The Cardinal and the Dog

ROBERT BROWNING, from *Asolando: Fancies and Facts*, 1889. English poet and dramatist. Though he is best known for his poetry, he is also known for his romantic courtship and marriage to English poet Elizabeth Barrett Browning. This poem was written in 1842.

Crescenzio, the Pope's Legate at the High Council, Trent,
—Year Fifteen hundred twenty-two, March Twenty-five—
     intent
On writing letters to the Pope till late into the night,

Rose, weary, to refresh himself, and saw a monstrous
  sight:
(I give mine Author's very words: he penned, I re-indite.)

A black Dog of vast bigness, eyes flaming, ears that hung
Down to the very ground almost, into the chamber
  sprung
And made directly for him, and laid himself right under
The table where Crescenzio wrote—who called in fear and
  wonder
His servants in the ante-room, commanded everyone
To look for and find out the beast: but, looking, they
  found none.

The Cardinal fell melancholy, then sick, soon after died:
And at Verona, as he lay on his death-bed, he cried
Aloud to drive away the Dog that leapt on his bed-side.
Heaven keep us Protestants from harm: the rest . . . no ill
  betide!

266

The Devil in Disguise

JOHANN WOLFGANG VON GOETHE, from *Faust*, 1808. German poet, dramatist, novelist, and scientist. His scientific discoveries contributed to the theory of evolution. Goethe's interpretation of the Faust legend, which he worked on for over 30 years, has been described as "one of the greatest poetic and philosophic creations the world possesses." The following is Faust's first encounter with Mephistopheles (the Devil), who is disguised as a poodle.

FAUST:

Do you see that black dog that through the stubble
    strays?

WAGNER:

He looks quite unremarkable to me.

FAUST:

Look close! What do you take the beast to be?

WAGNER:

A poodle, searching with his natural bent
And snuffing for his master's scent.

FAUST:

Do you see how he spirals round us, snail-
shell-wise, and ever closer on our trail?
And if I'm not mistaken, he lays welts
Of fire behind him in his wake.

WAGNER:

I see a plain black poodle, nothing else;
Your eyes must be the cause of some mistake.

FAUST:

I seem to see deft snares of magic laid
For future bondage round our feet somehow.

WAGNER:

I see him run about uncertain and afraid
Because he sees two strangers, not his master now.

FAUST:

The circle narrows, he is near!

WAGNER:

You see! It's just a dog, no phantom here.
He growls, he doubts, lies belly-flat and all,
And wags his tail. All doggish protocol.

FAUST:

Come here! Come join our company!

WAGNER:

He's just a foolish pup. You see?
You stop, and he will wait for you,
You speak to him, and he'll jump up on you,
Lose something, and he'll fetch it quick,
Or go in water for a stick.

FAUST:

You must be right, I see there's not a trace
Of spirits. It's his training he displays.

WAGNER:

A sage himself will often find
He likes a dog that's trained to mind.
Yes, he deserves your favor totally,
A model scholar of the students, he.

(They go in through the city gate.)

•   •   •

JAMES WARD, *"Buff", a Black Poodle*, 1812. British romantic painter.
Buff was owned by Lt. Col. Chestmaster and went with him to Spain
during the Napoleonic Wars. (Private collection)

(Faust in his study with the poodle.)

FAUST:

> If I'm to share this room with you,
> Poodle, that howling must be curbed.
> And stop that barking too!
> I cannot be disturbed
> By one who raises such a din.
> One of us must give in
> And leave this cell we're in.
> I hate to drive you out of here,
> But the door is open, the way is clear.

But what is this I see?
Can such things happen naturally?
Is this reality or fraud?
My poodle grows both long and broad!
He rises up with might;
No dog's shape this! This can't be right!
What phantom have I harbored thus?
He's like a hippopotamus
With fiery eyes and ghastly teeth.
O, I see what's beneath!
For such a mongrel of hell
The Key of Solomon works well.[1]

---

[1]The *Key of Solomon* was a book of instructions for controlling spirits. This quasireligious work was originally written in Hebrew, and its translations were very popular from the 16th through the 18th centuries.

Cerberus and Orthus

HESIOD, from *Theogony,* ca. 700 B.C. Greek poet. In completing his 10th task, Hercules killed Geryones and drove away his cattle. He also choked Orthus, Cerberus's brother, who was Geryones' herd dog. The Greeks also told of Argus Panoptes (Argus All-Eyes), a 100-eyed monster sometimes represented as a white dog, who was sent by Hera to watch Io but was instead killed by Hermes.

Greek amphora with a painting of Hercules and Cerberus, ca. 510 B.C. (Louvre, Paris)

Men say that Typhaon [the god of disaster] the terrible, outrageous and lawless, was joined in love to her, the maid with glancing eyes [the fierce goddess Echidra, who was half nymph and half snake]. So she conceived and brought forth fierce offspring; first she bare Orthus the hound of Geryones, and then again she bare a second, a monster not to be overcome and that may not be described, Cerberus who eats raw flesh, the brazen-voiced hound of Hades, fifty-headed, relentless and strong.

● ● ●

There, in front, stand the echoing halls of the god of the lower-world, strong Hades, and of awful Persephone. A fearful hound guards the house in front, pitiless, and he has a cruel trick. On those who go in he fawns with his tail and both his ears, but suffers them not to go out back again, but keeps watch and devours whomsoever he catches going out of the gates of strong Hades and awful Persephone.

The Guardian of the Gate to Hell

VIRGIL (PUBLIUS VERGILIUS MARO), from *The Aeneid,* 30–19 B.C.
Roman poet. The *Aeneid* has been called "unquestionably one of the
greatest masterpieces of world literature." The reduction of Cerberus's
50 heads to three heads may be because of his later association with
Hectate (goddess of death), who is also portrayed as a three-headed
monster. In this excerpt, the Trojan hero Aeneas and the Amphrysian
sybil approach the gate to Hell.

[Charon, the ferryman of the River Styx] toward them
    turns around his barge
Of dusky hue, and brings it to the shore.
The ghosts that all along its benches sat,
He hurries out, and clears the boat; then place
To great Æneas gives. Beneath his weight
The hide-patched vessel groans; its leaky sides
Drink in the marshy water; till at length
The priestess and the hero, safe across
The river, land upon the slimy mud
And weeds of dingy green. Here Cerberus,
Whose triple-throated barking echoes through
These realms, lies stretched immense across his den,
Confronting their approach. The prophetess,
Seeing his neck now bristling thick with snakes,
Throws him a cake of medicated seeds
With soporiferous honey moistened. He
With rabid hunger, opening his three throats,
Snaps up the offered sop; and on the ground
His hideous limbs relaxing, sprawls, and lies
Huge, and extended all along the cave.
The sentinel thus sunk in lethargy,
Æneas gains the entrance, hastening on
Beyond the stream whence there is no return.

Greek hydria with a painting of Hercules presenting Cerberus to
King Eurystheus, ca. 530–525 B.C. (Louvre, Paris)

Cerberus Pacified and Captured

H. A. GUERBER, from *Myths of Greece and Rome,* 1893.

Orpheus hastened to the entrance of Hades, and there saw the fierce three-headed dog, named Cerberus, who guarded the gate, and would allow no living being to enter, nor any spirit to pass out of Hades. As soon as this monster saw Orpheus, he began to growl and bark savagely, to frighten him away; but Orpheus merely paused, and began to play such melting chords, that Cerberus' rage was appeased, and he finally allowed him to pass into Pluto's dark kingdom.

WILLIAM BLAKE, *Cerberus,* 1824–1827, from Dante's *Divine Comedy.*
English artist and poet. (Tate Gallery, London)

·   ·   ·

The twelfth and last task appointed by Eurystheus was the most difficult of all to perform. Hercules was commanded to descend into Hades and bring up the dog Cerberus, securely bound.

> "But for the last, to Pluto's drear abode
> Through the dark jaws of Tænarus he went,
> To drag the triple-headed dog to light."
>
> Euripides (Potter's tr.).

This command, like all the others, was speedily obeyed; but Eurystheus was so terrified at the aspect of the triple-headed dog, from the foam of whose dripping jaws the nightshade sprang, that he took refuge in a huge jar, and refused to come out until Hercules had carried the monster back to his cave.

Dante Meets the Hound of Hell

DANTE ALIGHIERI, from the *Divine Comedy*, 1302–1321. Italian poet. Dante has been called "one of the great figures of world literature." The *Divine Comedy* is his masterpiece. In it, Dante is conducted on a tour of Hell, Purgatory, and Heaven. One of his guides is the Roman poet Virgil.

. . . Upon the putrid earth. A monster fierce,
The direful Cerberus with triple throat,
Barks doglike o'er the people here submerged.
Red are his eyes; his beard befouled and dark,
His belly large, his paws with talons armed;
He claws the spirits, flays and quarters them.
The endless downpour makes them howl like dogs;
Trying with one side to protect the other,
The abject wretches often writhe and turn
In vain attempt to find relief from pain.
　　When Cerberus took heed of our approach,
He opened wide his jaws with horrid fangs,
And quivering with rage in every limb
Stood thwart our path; and then my noble leader
Stretched forth his hands, and picking up some earth,
He hurled it full within the rabid jaws.
Just as a hungry dog that barks for food
Is quieted when first he gnaws his meat,
Thinking and striving but to devour it:
Just so were stilled the jaws of Cerberus,
That demon whose loud, raucous bark so stuns
The spirits, that they wish that they were deaf.

Early Christianity and Cerberus

From a 12th-century Latin bestiary, which was copied from a variety of older sources.

Before we were redeemed, we were under the power of the Enemy and we had lost the shouting voice. We, though our sins needed it, were inaudible and did not cry out to the saints to help us. But after the all-merciful God had qualified us in the person of his Son, we threw off the old man

Ancient Egyptian statue.

in baptism, i.e. the clothes, and with his acts we put on the new man, who is created according to God. At this point we picked up stones in our hands, which we strike against each other. This is how we reverberate the saints of God, who are already reigning in heaven with Jesus Christ our Lord, with the exhortation of our mouths. We do this in order to strike the ears of the Judge and to obtain pardon for our sins—lest Cerberus, whom we cannot outspeak, rejoicing at our demise, should swallow us up.

The Hellhounds of God

JOHN MILTON, from *Paradise Lost,* 1667. English poet. Milton was a Puritan who wrote *Paradise Lost* through secretaries after he became blind. He followed it with another epic poem, *Paradise Regained.* Milton is considered one of England's greatest poets.

Almightie seeing,
From his transcendent Seat the Saints among,
To those bright Orders utterd thus his voice.

ARTHUR RACKHAM, *They stood outside, filled with savagery and terror,* from James Stephens's *Irish Fairy Tales,* 1920. English illustrator and water colorist.

See with what heat these Dogs of Hell advance
To waste and havoc yonder World, which I
So fair and good created, and had still
Kept in that State, had not the folly of Man
Let in these wastful Furies, who impute
Folly to mee, so doth the Prince of Hell
And his Adherents, that with so much ease
I suffer them to enter and possess
A place so heav'nly, and conniving seem
To gratifie my scornful Enemies,
That laugh, as if transported with some fit
Of Passion, I to them had quitted all,
At random yielded up to their misrule;
And know not that I call'd and drew them thither
My Hell-hounds, to lick up the draff and filth
Which mans polluting Sin with taint hath shed
On what was pure, still cramm'd and gorg'd, nigh burst
With suckt and glutted offal, at one sling
Of thy victorious Arm, well-pleasing Son,
Both *Sin,* and *Death,* and yawning *Grave* at last
Through *Chaos* hurld, obstruct the mouth of Hell
For ever, and seal up his ravenous Jawes.
Then Heav'n and Earth renewd shall be made pure
To sanctitie that shall receive no staine:
Till then the Curse pronounc't on both precedes.

THE NATURE
OF DOGS

"Hot dog," whispered Hydrangea.

Elliot Paul, *Mayhem in B-Flat,* 1940.

M any people think dogs are much smarter than they let on. One belief that appears among peoples all over the world—from Africans to Haitians and from Australian aborigines to Native Americans—is that dogs understand everything we say and can talk whenever they want to. In 1941, a study of the Yurok and Hupa Indians of California found they rarely talked to their dogs for fear the dogs might answer—which would be an omen of death or disaster. Thus they limited themselves to giving commands and directions. The Hupa relate the story of one woman who told her dog to let her husband know dinner was ready. The dog did, in easily understandable words, and the family died soon afterward. Other people run away when a dog talks, for fear they will turn to stone if they listen. The Irish did not have this fear, though. They thought you could understand dogs when they spoke if you were wearing a four-leaf clover, but that dogs only talked just prior to a disaster. Most of these beliefs have disappeared in the modern world, but many people still think dogs understand more than they let on. And everyone will admit they clearly understand some words, but is it possible they have their own language?

Our words are based on different vocal sounds because we are able to produce a much wider variety of sounds than we can of other forms of communication (hand signals, facial expressions, and so on). The variety of tones we can produce is much more limited, and so we use these to indicate our general state of mind. For example, we use high tones when talking to babies or when excited and low tones when we are serious or concerned.

The situation is somewhat reversed for dogs. Physically, they are only able to make a few types of sounds; they are essentially limited to barks, howls, whines, whimpers, and so forth. They can make these few sounds in a wide variety of tones, and their sensitive hearing can distinguish the subtleties of these tones much better than we can. The sounds they use seem to indicate their general state; they growl when mad, whine when upset, and whimper when hurt. Could they be using combinations of tones to form their "words"?

It has been pointed out that dogs actually respond more to the tone of our voice than to our words. Vance Packard suggested this experiment in his book *Animal IQ:* "Select some command which he [your dog] normally obeys and which he seems to understand, such as 'Rover, roll over!' But change your tone. For example, say it softly and casually. If the psychologists are right, Rover will just stare at you. Or, better still, stick to your usual tone and gestures but use nonsense words such as 'Blowbar, mole lobber!' Then, presumably, Rover will roll over, unless he happens to be an extraordinarily alert dog".

Some hunters who spend a lot of time with their dogs have noticed that dogs alter their tones depending on the type of prey they have spotted and that further modulations indicate where the prey fled—down a hole, up a tree, or under bushes. In his book *Man's Best Friend,* A. H. Trapman points out, "In a given district the same dog-words—or should we say rather dialect?—are used by all dogs of the vicinity and, apparently, perfectly understood by each other, but certainly readily recognized by their human auditors".

In *Never Cry Wolf*—which is the most fascinating of all the books I have come across on either dogs or wolves—Farley Mowat presents some very convincing anecdotes that demonstrate the Eskimos' ability to understand the wolves' communication network. Mowat's interpreter explained that "the wolves not only possessed the ability to communicate over great distances but, so he insisted, could 'talk' almost as well as he could. He admitted that he himself could neither hear all the sounds they made, nor understand most of them, but he said some Eskimos, and Ootek in particular, could hear and understand so well that they could quite literally converse with wolves."

Mowat tells how Ootek heard the wolves passing information that the caribou were at a specific spot 40 miles away and that this was later confirmed. In another instance, his interpreter said, "Ootek says that wolf you call George, he send a message to his wife. Ootek hear it good. He tell his wife the hunting is pretty bad and he going to stay out longer. Maybe not get home until the middle of the day". The wolf did stay out longer than usual, returning at 12:17 P.M. In a third example, one of the wolves he was watching heard a message from a northwesterly direction. Although the wolf seemed uninterested, Ootek became very excited, saying, "Eskimos come!" and headed off to the northwest. That evening the wolves headed east to hunt instead of heading north or northwest as they normally would. Sometime later, Ootek showed up with the three Eskimos the wolves said were coming and who he had gone to meet.

Although this evidence is circumstantial, it is compelling and definitely worth further investigation. While many of their good qualities are obvious, it is possible there is much more to both wolves and dogs than we are normally aware of.

Socrates on Dogs

PLATO (ca. 427–347 B.C.), from the *Republic*. Greek philosopher. Plato was a student and friend of Socrates. Here Plato records a debate between Socrates and Glaucon. Plato and Socrates are considered two of the world's greatest philosophers.

You surely have observed in well-bred hounds that their natural disposition is to be most gentle to their familiars and those whom they recognize, but the contrary to those whom they do not know.

I am aware of that.

The thing is possible, then, said I, and it is not an unnatural requirement that we are looking for in our guardian.

It seems not.

WILHELM TRÜBNER,
At the Swimming Hole,
ca. 1900.

285

And does it seem to you that our guardian-to-be will also need, in addition to the being high-spirited, the further quality of having the love of wisdom in his nature?

How so? he said. I don't apprehend your meaning.

This too, said I, is something that you will discover in dogs and which is worth our wonder in the creature.

What?

That the sight of an unknown person angers him before he has suffered any injury, but an acquaintance he will fawn upon though he has never received any kindness from him. Have you never marveled at that?

I never paid any attention to the matter before now, but that he acts in some such way is obvious.

But surely that is an exquisite trait of his nature and one that shows a true love of wisdom.

In what respect, pray?

In respect, said I, that he distinguishes a friendly from a hostile aspect by nothing save his apprehension of the one and his failure to recognize the other. How, I ask you, can the love of learning be denied to a creature whose criterion of the friendly and the alien is intelligence and ignorance?

SIR EDWIN LANDSEER, *A Scene at Abbotsford,* by 1827. English animal painter. Abbotsford was Sir Walter Scott's mansion. Scott's dog, Maida, is lying with his head on the armor breastplate. Behind sits Landseer's deerhound. (Tate Gallery, London)

Attributes of a Dog

SIR WALTER SCOTT, from *The Talisman,* 1832. Scottish novelist and poet.

Recollect that the Almighty, who gave the dog to be companion of our pleasures and our toils, hath invested him with a nature noble and incapable of deceit. He forgets neither friend nor foe—remembers, and with accuracy, both benefit and injury. He hath a share of man's intelligence, but no share of man's falsehood. You may bribe a soldier to slay a man with his sword, or a witness to take life by false accusation; but you cannot make a hound tear his benefactor—he is the friend of man, save when man justly incurs his enmity.

Canine Intelligence

PLUTARCH, from *Moralia,* ca. A.D. 70. Greek essayist and biographer.

A certain fellow slipped into the temple of Asclepius, took such gold and silver offerings as were not bulky, and made his escape, thinking that he had not been detected. But the watchdog, whose name was Capparus, when none of the sacristans responded to its barking, pursued the escaping temple-thief. First the man threw stones at it, but could not drive it away. When day dawned, the dog did not approach close, but followed the man, always keeping him in sight, and refused the food he offered. When he stopped to rest, the dog passed the night on guard; when he struck out again, the dog got up and kept following, fawning on the other people it met on the road and barking at the man and sticking to his heels. When those who were investigating the robbery learned this from men who had encountered the pair and were told the colour and size of the dog, they pursued all the more vigorously and overtook the man and brought him back from Crommyon. On the return the dog led the procession, capering and exultant, as though it claimed for itself the credit for pursuing and capturing the temple-thief. The people actually voted it a public ration of food and entrusted the charge of this to the priests in perpetuity.

•　•　•

I am not unaware that you will think that my examples are rather a hodge-podge; but it is not easy to find naturally clever animals doing anything which illustrates merely one of their virtues. Their probity, rather, is revealed in their love of offspring and their cleverness in their nobility; then, too, their craftiness and intelligence is inseparable from their ardour and courage. Those, nevertheless,

PIERRE-AUGUSTE RENOIR, *Bather with a Griffon*, 1870. French Impressionist painter. (Museu de Arte, São Paulo, Brazil)

who are intent on classifying and defining each separate occasion will find that dogs give the impression of a mind that is at once civil and superior when they turn away from those who sit on the ground—which is presumably referred to in the lines

> The dogs barked and rushed up, but wise Odysseus
> Cunningly crouched; the staff slipped from his hand;[1]

for dogs cease attacking those who have thrown themselves down and taken on an attitude that resembles humility. . . .

Still, I believe that I should not pass over one example at least of a dog's learning, of which I myself was a spectator at Rome. The dog appeared in a pantomime with a dramatic plot and many characters and conformed in its acting at all points with the acts and reactions required by the text. In particular, they experimented on it with a drug that was really soporific, but supposed in the story to be deadly. The dog took the bread that was supposedly drugged, swallowed it, and a little later appeared to shiver and stagger and nod until it finally sprawled out and lay there like a corpse, letting itself be dragged and hauled about, as the plot of the play prescribed. But when it recognized from the words and action that the time had come, at first it began to stir slightly, as though recovering from a profound sleep, and lifted its head and looked about. Then to the amazement of the spectators it got up and proceeded to the right person and fawned on him with joy and pleasure so that everyone, and even Caesar himself (for the aged Vespasian[2] was present in the Theatre of Marcellus), was much moved.

---

[1]Homer (8th century B.C.), from the *Odyssey*.

[2]Vespasian was emperor of Rome, A.D. 69–79.

In Cineam (excerpt)

SIR JOHN DAVIES (1569–1626), from *Epigrammes and Elegies.* English poet and solicitor (lawyer). Davies was appointed solicitor general for Ireland and was knighted by King James I.

Thou dogg'd Cineas, hated like a dog,
For still thou grumblest like a masty[3] dog,
Compar'st thyself to nothing but a dog;
Thou say'st thou art as weary as a dog,
As angry, sick and hungry as a dog,
As dull and melancholy as a dog,
As lazy, sleepy, idle as a dog.
And why dost thou compare thee to a dog
In that for which all men despise a dog?
I will compare thee better to a dog;
Thou art as fair and comely as a dog,
Thou art as true and honest as a dog,
Thou art as kind and liberal as a dog,
Thou art as wise and valiant as a dog.

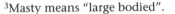

[3]Masty means "large bodied".

CHARLES TREVOR GARLAND, *Bosom Friends,* 1881. English painter. (Private collection)

SIR EDWIN LANDSEER, *Windsor Castle in Modern Times,* 1841–1845. English animal painter. Queen Victoria and Prince Albert are shown here with their first child, Princess Victoria, when she was just over a year old. The princess later became Empress Frederick of Germany. The dogs (left to right) are Cairnach, Islay, Dandie, and Eos. It is said that Queen Victoria was so fond of her dogs that after her coronation—as soon as she changed out of her ceremonial robes—her first act as the new queen was to give one of her dogs a bath. (Her Majesty the Queen)

On a Dog of Lord Eglinton's

ROBERT BURNS (1759–1796). Scottish poet. Burns came from a poor farming family and is best known for his poetry in the rural Scottish dialect. He is the author of "Tam o'Shanter", "Comin' thro' the Rye", and "Auld Lang Syne". He died at age 37.

I never barked when out of season,
  I never bit without a reason;
I ne'er insulted weaker brother,
  Nor wronged by force or fraud another.
We brutes are placed a rank below;
  Happy for man could he say so.

292

SIR EDWIN LANDSEER, *Her Majesty at Osborne,* 1867. English animal painter. Queen Victoria is shown dressed in black after the death of Prince Albert in 1861. John Brown is holding her horse, and Prince is the dog who is sitting up. On the bench are two of her daughters, Princess Helena (later Princess Christian of Schleswig-Holstein) and Princess Alice (later Duchess of Argyll). Osborne was the queen's favorite residence, but her son, King Edward VII, hated it and gave it to the nation. (Her Majesty the Queen)

Bishop Doane on His Dog "Cluny"

GEORGE WASHINGTON DOANE (1799–1859). American poet and Episcopal bishop of New Jersey.

I am quite sure he thinks that I am God—
Since he is God on whom each one depends
For life, and all things that His bounty sends—
My dear old dog, most constant of all friends;
Not quick to mind, but quicker far than I
To Him whom God I know and own; his eye,
Deep brown and liquid, watches for my nod;
He is more patient underneath the rod
Than I, when God His wise corrections sends.

He looks love at me, deep as words e'er spake;
And from me never crumb nor sup will take
But he wags thanks with his most vocal tail;
And when some crashing noise wakes all his fear,
He is content and quiet, if I am near,
Secure that my protection will prevail.
So, faithful, mindful, thankful, trustful, he
Tells me what I unto my God should be.

Inseeing

RAINER MARIA RILKE, from *Neue Gedichte (New Poems)*, 1907–1908.
German lyric poet. He died from blood poisoning after being pricked
by the thorn of a rose.

I love inseeing. Can you imagine with me how glorious it
is to insee, for example, a dog as one passes by. *Insee* (I
don't mean in-spect, which is only a kind of human gym-
nastic, by means of which one immediately comes out
again on the other side of the dog, regarding it merely, so
to speak, as a window upon the humanity lying behind it,
not that,)—but to let one's self precisely into the dog's very
center, the point from which it becomes a dog, the place in
it where God, as it were, would have sat down for a moment when the dog was finished, in order to watch it
under the influence of its first embarrassments and inspi-
rations and to know that it was good, that nothing was
lacking, that it could not have been better made.

FRANK WESTON BEN-
SON, *Summer Afternoon,*
1906. American etcher
and painter. (Private
collection)

A Lame Dog

JAMES HERRIOT (JAMES ALFRED WIGHT), from "Rip", *James Herriot's Dog Stories*, 1986. English author and veterinarian. Author of *All Creatures Great and Small.*

It was in October, when the trees around the Scott farm were bursting into a blaze of warm colour, that he hailed me as I drove past his gate.

"Will ye stop for a minute and see Rip?" His face was anxious.

"Why, is he ill?"

"Naw, naw, just lame, but I can't mek it out."

I didn't have to go far to find Rip—he was never far from his master—and I experienced a shock of surprise when I saw him because his right foreleg was trailing uselessly.

"What's happened to him?" I asked.

"He was roundin' up t'cows when one of 'em lashed out and got him on the chest. He's been gettin' lamer ever since. The funny thing is, ah can't find a thing wrong with his leg. It's a mystery."

Rip wagged vigorously as I felt my way up his leg from foot to shoulder. There was no pain in the limb, no wound or injury, but he winced as I passed my hand over his first rib. Diagnosis was not difficult.

"It's radial paralysis," I said.

"Radial . . . what's that?"

"The radial nerve passes over the first rib and the kick must have damaged rib and nerve. This has put the extensor muscles out of action so that he can't bring his leg forward."

"Well, that's a rum 'un." The farmer passed a hand over the shaggy head and down the fine white markings of the cheeks. "Will he get better?"

THEODORE ROBINSON, *Miss Motes and Her Dog Shep,* 1893. American landscape painter. (Private collection)

"It's usually a long job," I replied. "Nervous tissue is slow to regenerate and it could take weeks or months. Treatment doesn't seem to make much difference."

The farmer nodded. "Awright, we'll just have to wait. There's one thing," and again the bright smile flooded his face, "he can still get round them cows, lame or not. It 'ud break 'is heart if he couldn't work. Loves 'is job, does Rip."

On the way back to the car he nudged me and opened the door of a shed. In the corner, in a nest of straw, a cat was sitting with her family of tiny kittens. He lifted two out, holding one in each of his roughened hands. "Look at them little fellers, aren't they lovely!" He held them against his cheeks and laughed.

As I started the engine I felt I ought to say something encouraging. "Don't worry too much about Rip, Jack. These cases usually recover in time."

But Rip did not recover. After several months his leg was as useless as ever and the muscles had wasted greatly. The nerve must have been irreparably damaged and it was an unhappy thought that this attractive little animal was going to be three-legged for the rest of his life.

Jack was undismayed and maintained stoutly that Rip was still a good working dog.

The real blow fell one Sunday morning as Siegfried and I were arranging the rounds in the office. I answered the door bell and found Jack on the step with his dog in his arms.

PIERRE-AUGUSTE RENOIR, *Tama, the Japanese Dog,* ca. 1876. French Impressionist painter. (Sterling and Francine Clark Art Institute, Williamstown, Massachusetts)

QUEEN VICTORIA, from the queen's sketchbook, 1850. Queen of England (1837–1901) and empress of India (1876–1901). In 1840 she married her cousin, Prince Albert of Saxe-Coburg. Shown are Archie and Annie MacDonald, the daughters of Prince Albert's personal servant, in the kennels at Balmoral, Scotland.

"What's wrong?" I asked. "Is he worse?"

"No, Mr Herriot." The farmer's voice was husky. "It's summat different. He's been knocked down."

We examined the dog on the surgery table. "Fracture of the tibia," Siegfried said. "But there's no sign of internal damage. Do you know exactly what happened?"

Jack shook his head. "Nay, Mr Farnon. He ran on to the village street and a car caught 'im. He dragged 'imself back into t'yard."

"Dragged?" Siegfried was puzzled.

"Aye, the broken leg's on the same side as t'other thing."

My partner blew out his cheeks. "Ah yes, the radial paralysis. I remember you told me about it, James." He looked at me across the table and I knew he was thinking the same thing as I was. A fracture and a paralysis on the same side was a forbidding combination.

"Right, let's get on," Siegfried murmured.

We set the leg in plaster and I held open the door of Jack's old car as he laid Rip on the back seat.

The farmer smiled out at me through the window. "I'm takin' the family to church this mornin' and I'll say a little prayer for Rip while I'm there."

I watched until he drove round the corner of the street and when I turned I found Siegfried at my elbow.

"I just hope that job goes right," he said thoughtfully. "Jack would take it hard if it didn't." He turned and carelessly dusted his old brass plate on its new place on the wall. "He's a truly remarkable chap. He says he's going to say a prayer for his dog and there's nobody better qualified. Remember what Coleridge said? 'He prayeth best who loveth best all things both great and small.' "

"Yes," I said. "That's Jack, all right."

The farmer brought his dog into the surgery six weeks later for the removal of the plaster.

"Taking a cast off is a much longer job than putting it on," I said as I worked away with my little saw.

Jack laughed. "Aye, ah can see that. It's hard stuff to get through."

I have never liked this job and it seemed a long time before I splayed open the white roll with my fingers and eased it away from the hair of the leg.

I felt at the site of the fracture and my spirits plummeted. Hardly any healing had taken place. There should have been a healthy callus by now but I could feel the loose ends of the broken bones moving against each other, like a hinge. We were no further forward.

I could hear Siegfried pottering among the bottles in the dispensary and I called to him.

He palpated the limb. "Damn! One of those! And just when we didn't want it." He looked at the farmer. "We'll have to try again, Jack, but I don't like it."

We applied a fresh plaster and the farmer grinned confidently. "Just wanted a bit more time, I reckon. He'll be right next time."

But it was not to be. Siegfried and I worked together to strip off the second cast but the situation was practically unchanged. There was little or no healing tissue around the fracture.

We didn't know what to say. Even at the present time, after the most sophisticated bone-pinning procedures, we still find these cases where the bones just will not unite. They are as frustrating now as they were that afternoon when Rip lay on the surgery table.

I broke the silence. "It's just the same, I'm afraid, Jack."

"You mean it 'asn't joined up?"

"That's right."

The farmer rubbed a finger along his upper lip. "Then 'e won't be able to take any weight on that leg?"

"I don't see how he possibly can."

"Aye . . . aye . . . well, we'll just have to see how he goes on, then."

"But Jack," Siegfried said gently, "he can't go on. There's no way a dog can get around with two useless legs on the same side."

The silence set in again and I could see the familiar curtain coming down over the farmer's face. He knew what was in our minds and he wasn't going to have it. In fact I knew what he was going to say next.

"Is he sufferin'?"

"No, he isn't," Siegfried replied. "There's no pain in the fracture now and the paralysis is painless anyway, but he won't be able to walk, don't you see?"

But Jack was already gathering his dog into his arms. "Well, we'll give him a chance, any road," he said, and walked from the room.

Siegfried leaned against the table and looked at me, wide-eyed. "Well, what do you make of that, James?"

"Same as you," I replied gloomily. "Poor old Jack. He

ÉDOUARD MANET, *Follette*, 1882–1883. French Impressionist painter. Manet's work was received with hostility throughout his life. He is now considered one of the masters. He was friends with the painter Claude Monet. (Private collection)

THOMAS LANDSEER after Sir Edwin Landseer, with extensive retouching by Sir Edwin, *A Distinguished Member of the Humane Society,* by 1838. Thomas Landseer was Sir Edwin's eldest brother and the engraver of many of his works. (British Museum, London)

always gives everything a chance, but he's got no hope this time."

But I was wrong. Several weeks later I was called to the Scott farm to see a sick calf and the first thing I saw was Rip bringing the cows in for milking. He was darting to and fro around the rear of the herd, guiding them through the gate from the field, and I watched him in amazement.

He still could not bear any appreciable weight on either of his right limbs, yet he was running happily. Don't ask me how he was doing it because I'll never know, but somehow he was supporting his body with his two strong left legs and the paws of the stricken limbs merely brushing the turf. Maybe he had perfected some balancing feat like a one-wheel bicycle rider but, as I say, I just don't know. The great thing was that he was still the old friendly Rip, his tail swishing when he saw me, his mouth panting with pleasure.

Jack didn't say anything about "I told you so", and I wouldn't have cared, because it thrilled me to see the little animal doing the job he loved.

• • •

I suppose the things I pick out to write about are the unusual ones. Jack Scott is the only farmer I have known who resolutely refused to have any animal put down, and Rip was the only dog in my experience who could run about despite two useless legs on one side. I always think of Jack as the man who had faith, and it was good to see that faith rewarded in the case of Rip.

Byrd's Dogs

REAR ADMIRAL RICHARD BYRD, from *Little America,* 1930. American aviator and polar explorer. Byrd was the first person to fly over the North and South Poles. He led five expeditions to Antarctica, where he established his base, "Little America".

Digging these tunnels was a back-breaking order. For the housing of 80 primitive dogs involves its own problems. Unlike brow-beaten humans, who can be herded into groups without grievous friction, Eskimo dogs remain individualists to the last. They may dwell in the peaceful affinity of brothers for days on end; but for the favor of a lady or a hunk of frozen seal meat they will enthusiastically rend one another limb from limb. We had had half a dozen bloody brawls, due to the fact that some dogs were allowed to roam loose, partly because of carelessness or inexperience on the part of the drivers; and during this period two splendid dogs, Shackleton and Muskeg, were killed in a pitched battle over a female.

The crates, then, had to be sufficiently spaced apart to allow the dogs to move freely on a chain, and not near enough to permit them to come within fighting distance. We therefore staggered them on opposite sides of the tunnels.

It would be well to tell here the story of Spy. Spy was one of Vaughan's dogs. Toward the end of March I found him in his crate, in a pitiful condition. He had pulled his heart out during the unloading, and now was so lame he could hardly walk. For some strange reason his coat failed to grow in thick, as with the other dogs, so his resistance to cold was low. Vaughan, who loved him as a brother, was of the opinion he should be shot: it would put him out of his misery. But it was decided to bring him into the house, where it was warm, and put him on a special diet.

Aztec statue found in the Valley of Mexico, ca. 1325–1521.

We gave him canvas to sleep on. The only available space in the camp at the time was in my room, and old Spy lay there for two days very much to the disgust of Igloo who attacked him whenever my back was turned. His joints were so crippled by cold that he could not stir, but he was on the mend. Saturday, March 30th, we took him out for a bit of exercise. It happened that his old team went by, with black Dinty in the lead, and his boon companions, Watch and Moody, in the traces. Spy watched them go rollicking past, and a spirit like that of the Old Guard must have taken possession of his pain-stiffened limbs, for he went out in a gallant spurt, overtook the team and with a final summoning up of strength forced his way to his place in the team.

It was one of the most beautiful things I have ever seen: and for a penny I would pluck a moral from it. The whole camp stopped working at the sight, and watched with wonder how Moody and Watch muzzled the veteran, and laid their paws on him in a most extraordinary gesture. That these wild and untrammeled animals should be capable of harboring so deep and lasting a sentiment was beyond understanding.

Spy gradually grew better and soon was sufficiently recovered to return to his crate.

SIR EDWIN LANDSEER, *Her Majesty's Favorite Dogs and Parrot* (also called *Dash, Hector, Nero, and Lory*), 1837–1838. English animal painter. Shown are some of Queen Victoria's pets. (Her Majesty the Queen)

An Obituary for a Dog

WARREN G. HARDING, from the Marion *Star,* ca. 1895. The 28th president of the United States. The *Star* was a small Ohio daily newspaper where Harding was the editor for 17 years. He wrote this after Hub, his Boston terrier, was poisoned.

It isn't orthodox to ascribe a soul to a dog. But Hub was loving and loyal, with a jealousy that tests its quality. He was reverent, patient, faithful. He was sympathetic, more than humanly so sometimes, for no lure could be devised to call him from the sick bed of mistress or master. He minded his own affairs—especially worthy of human emulation. He was modest and submissive where these were becoming, yet he assumed a guardianship of the home he sentineled until entry was properly vouched. He couldn't speak our language, though he somehow understood. But he could be and was eloquent with uttering eye and wagging tail and the other expressions of knowing dogs. No, perhaps he had no soul, but in these things are the essence of soul and the spirit of lovable life.

Whether the Creator planned it so or environment and human companionship made it so, men may learn richly through the love and fidelity of a brave and devoted dog. Such loyalty might easily add luster to a crown of immortality.

A QUESTION OF QUALITY

The more I see of men, the more I admire dogs.

Madame Roland (?), 1792. This has also
been attributed to Madame de Sévigné,
Ouida, and Frederick the Great.

To be, as it were, a dog at all times.

William Shakespeare, *The Two Gentlemen
of Verona*, 1591.

ogs are often called "man's best friend". This is an appellation they generally live up to and occasionally surpass. Unfortunately, the reverse is often not the case. Few people are as devoted to their dogs as their dogs are to them. For many people, the saying "familiarity breeds contempt" more accurately describes their relationship to their dog.

It is not uncommon for a person to call someone a "dog" as a demonstration of their disrespect. The term *bitch* has taken on a whole new meaning and is considered even more offensive. Few people rarely even associate this word with dogs anymore. With all of the dog's many wonderful characteristics, you would think it would be considered a compliment to be called a "dog". This discourtesy toward "man's best friend" says a lot more about people than it does about dogs.

Usually someone is considered to be a good person if he or she assists others who need help. Some people, like Mother Teresa, are noted throughout the world for this because it is unusual for people to be more concerned for the welfare of others than for themselves. It is our nature to devote our energies to getting ahead and to improving our lives. In fact, it is so much a part of our nature that we do not know when to stop. People who have made it to the top rarely devote their lives to those who never had a chance. More often they are extremely selfish and conceited.

It is not surprising that people who devote their lives to others are considered special. But Henry David Thoreau was not impressed. He wrote in *Walden* that "a man is not a good man to me because he will feed me if I should be starving, or warm me if I should be freezing, or pull me out of a ditch if I should ever fall into one. I can find you a Newfoundland dog that will do as much".

Devoting their lives to others is not unusual for dogs; in fact, it is the selfish, inconsiderate dog who is unusual.

Once a dog near Brisbane, Australia, took a break from nursing her pups and went out hunting. After chasing a rabbit to her hole, she started digging. Eventually the rabbit fled from another hole and the dog caught and killed her. Returning to the hole, she continued to dig. Soon she discovered 10 newborn bunnies. Realizing they would die without their mother and that she was responsible, she carried them home and nursed them herself. From that day on, she was never seen chasing another rabbit.

People have a hard time achieving happiness in their lives. They tend to get wrapped up in their own little world. People get confused because they do not know what they need or want, and then depression sets in. Dogs do not have this problem. They know exactly what makes them happy—doing something for someone. They will do everything they can think of to please their human companion, and any signs that they have been successful make them very happy.

Timon, in Shakespeare's *Timon of Athens,* is someone who feels that the qualities of dogs far outshine those of people. At one point in the play, Alcibiades meets Timon and asks, "What is thy name? Is man so hateful to thee, thou art thyself a man?" To which Timon replies, "I am *Misanthropos,* and hate mankind. For thy part, I do wish thou wert a dog, that I might love thee something".

Perhaps all the glories of our knowledge and technology are just a smokescreen for problems that lie hidden beneath—problems such as unfaithfulness, deceit, vanity, and even the innocent little games we play that often end in harm. Sure, we have the power to completely alter the entire planet—we have proven over and over again that we can destroy entire species—but even with all this power and knowledge at our fingertips, something vital seems to be missing. Maybe there are some areas where, when we are compared to dogs, we come up short. Being called a "dog" might not be such a bad thing after all.

The Image of Dogs and Wolves

EDMUND BURKE, from *Philosophical Enquiry into the Origin of Our Ideas of the Sublime and Beautiful,* 1756. Irish statesman and political writer. As a member of British parliament, he spoke out against taxation in America (1774) and revealed the injustices going on in India.

The race of dogs, in many of their kinds, have generally a competent degree of strength and swiftness; and they exert these and other valuable qualities which they possess, greatly to our convenience and pleasure. Dogs are indeed the most social, affectionate, and amiable animals of the whole brute creation; but love approaches much nearer to contempt than is commonly imagined; and accordingly, though we caress dogs, we borrow from them an appellation of the most despicable kind, when we employ terms of reproach; and this appellation is the common mark of the last vileness and contempt in every language. Wolves have not more strength than several species of dogs; but, on account of their unmanageable fierceness, the idea of a wolf is not despicable; it is not excluded from grand descriptions and similitudes. Thus we are affected by strength, which is *natural* power.

Robert Louis Stevenson on Dogs

ROBERT LOUIS STEVENSON, from "The Character of Dogs", *Memories and Portraits,* 1887. Scottish novelist, poet, and essayist. Stevenson was the author of *Treasure Island, Kidnapped,* and *The Strange Case of Dr. Jekyll and Mr. Hyde.*

The civilisation, the manners, and the morals of dog-kind are to a great extent subordinated to those of his ancestral master, man. This animal, in many ways so superior, has accepted a position of inferiority, shares the domestic life, and humors the caprices of the tyrant. But the potentate, like the British in India, pays small regard to the character of his willing client, judges him with listless glances, and condemns him in a byword. Listless have been the looks of his admirers, who have exhausted idle terms of praise, and buried the poor soul below exaggerations. And yet more idle and, if possible, more unintelligent has been the attitude of his express detractors; those who are very fond of dogs "but in their proper place"; who say "poo' fellow, poo' fellow," and are themselves far poorer; who whet the knife of the vivisectionist or heat his oven; who are not ashamed to admire "the creature's instinct"; and flying far beyond folly, have dared to resuscitate the theory of animal machines. The "dog's instinct" and the "automaton-dog," in this age of psychology and science, sound like strange anachronisms. An automaton he certainly is; a machine working independently of his control, the heart like the mill-wheel, keeping all in motion, and the consciousness, like a person shut in the mill garret, enjoying the view out of the window and shaken by the thunder of the stones; an automaton in one corner of which a living spirit is confined: an automaton like man. Instinct again he certainly possesses. Inherited aptitudes are his, inherited frailties. Some things he at once views and understands, as though he were awakened from a sleep, as though he came "trailing clouds of glory." But with him, as with man, the field of instinct is limited; its utterances are obscure and occasional; and about the far larger part of life both the dog and his master must conduct their steps by deduction and observation.

The leading distinction between dog and man, after and perhaps before the different duration of their lives, is that the one can speak and that the other cannot. The absence of the power of speech confines the dog in the development of his intellect. It hinders him from many speculations, for words are the beginning of metaphysic. At the same blow it saves him from many superstitions.

GUSTAVE DORÉ, detail of an illustration for *Fables,* 1867. French illustrator, engraver, painter, and sculptor. He is one of the world's best-known illustrators.

Elegy on the Death of a Mad Dog

OLIVER GOLDSMITH, from his only novel, *The Vicar of Wakefield,* 1766. Irish poet, dramatist, and novelist. This novel is considered his masterpiece.

Good people all, of every sort,
   Give ear unto my song;
And if you find it wondrous short
   It cannot hold you long.

In Islington there was a man,
  Of whom the world might say,
That still a godly race he ran,
  Whene'er he went to pray.

A kind and gentle heart he had,
  To comfort friends and foes;
The naked every day he clad,
  When he put on his clothes.

And in that town a dog was found,
  As many dogs there be,
Both mongrel, puppy, whelp, and hound,
  And curs of low degree.

This dog and man at first were friends;
  But when a pique began,
The dog, to gain some private ends,
  Went mad and bit the man.

Around from all the neighboring streets
  The wond'ring neighbors ran,
And swore the dog had lost his wits,
  To bite so good a man.

The wound it seem'd both sore and sad
  To every Christian eye;
And while they swore the dog was mad,
  They swore the man would die.

But soon a wonder came to light,
  That show'd the rogues they lied:
The man recover'd of the bite,
  The dog it was that died.

WINSLOW HOMER, *High Tide: The Bathers,* 1870. American landscape, marine, and genre painter. (Metropolitan Museum of Art, New York)

A Village Tale

MAY SARTON, from *A Private Mythology,* 1961–1966. American poet and author.

Why did the woman want to kill one dog?
Perhaps he was too lively, made her nervous,
A vivid terrier, restless, always barking,
And so unlike the gentle German shepherd.
She did not know herself what demon seized her,
How in the livid afternoon she was possessed,
What strength she found to tie a heavy stone
Around his neck and drown him in the horse-trough,
Murder her dog. God knows what drove her to it,
What strength she found to dig a shallow grave
And bury him—her own dog!—in the garden.

And all this while the gentle shepherd watched,
Said nothing, anxious nose laid on his paws,
Tail wagging dismal questions, watched her go
Into the livid afternoon outside to tire
The demon in her blood with wine and gossip.
The gate clanged shut, and the good shepherd ran,
Ran like a hunter to the quarry, hackles raised,
Sniffed the loose earth on the haphazard grave,
Pressing his eager nose into the dust,
Sensed tremor there and (frantic now) dug fast,
Dug in, dug in, all shivering and whining,
Unearthed his buried friend, licked the dry nose
Until a saving sneeze raised up the dead.
Well, she had to come back sometime to face
Whatever lay there waiting, worse than horror:
Two wagging tails, four bright eyes shifting—
Moment of truth, and there was no escape.
She could face murder. Could she face redeeming?
Was she relieved? Could she perhaps pretend
It had not really happened after all?
All that the village sees is that the dog
Sits apart now, untouchable and sacred,
Lazarus among dogs, whose loving eyes
Follow her back and forth until she dies.
She gives him tidbits. She can always try
To make them both forget the murderous truth.

But he knows and she knows that they are bound
Together in guilt and mercy, world without end.

THOMAS EAKINS, *A Lady with a Setter Dog (Mrs. Eakins),* 1885. American painter and sculptor. (Metropolitan Museum of Art, New York)

Lord Byron's Dog

LORD BYRON (GEORGE GORDON NOEL BYRON), from a monument in the garden of his ancestral home, Newstead Abbey. English poet and sixth Baron of Byron. Byron was lame from birth and spent years in poverty before he succeeded to the title and moved into Newstead Abbey. He is best known for *Don Juan,* which is considered his masterpiece. He had his dog buried in a tomb he had intended for himself. Two of his wills stated that he was to be interred beside Boatswain (pronounced "BO-sun"), but he deleted this clause after deciding to sell Newstead Abbey.

Near this spot
Are deposited the Remains
of one
Who possessed Beauty
Without Vanity,
Strength without Insolence,
Courage without Ferocity,
And all the Virtues of Man
Without his Vices.

This Praise, which would be unmeaning flattery
If inscribed over Human Ashes,
Is but a just tribute to the Memory of
"Boatswain," a Dog
Who was born at Newfoundland,
May, 1803,
And died at Newstead Abbey
Nov. 18, 1808.

ANTOINE LE MOITURIER, *Tomb of Philippe Pot,* ca. 1475–1500.
(Louvre, Paris)

When some proud son of man returns to earth,
Unknown to glory, but upheld by birth,
The sculptor's art exhausts the pomp of woe,
And storied urns record who rests below.
When all is done, upon the tomb is seen,
Not what he was, but what he should have been.
But the poor dog, in life the firmest friend,
The first to welcome, foremost to defend,

GIACOMO BALLA,
Leash in Motion, 1912.
Italian futurist painter.
Balla was primarily self-taught. (Albright-Knox
Art Gallery, Buffalo)

Whose honest heart is still his master's own,
Who labors, fights, lives, breathes for him alone,
Unhonored falls, unnoticed all his worth,
Denied in heaven the soul he held on earth—
While man, vain insect! hopes to be forgiven,
And claims himself a sole exclusive heaven.

Oh man! thou feeble tenant of an hour,
Debased by slavery, or corrupt by power—
Who knows thee well must quit thee with disgust,
Degraded mass of animated dust!
Thy love is lust, thy friendship all a cheat,
Thy smiles hypocrisy, thy words deceit!
By nature vile, ennobled but by name,
Each kindred brute might bid thee blush for shame.

Ye, who perchance behold this simple urn,
Pass on—it honors none you wish to mourn.
To mark a friend's remains these stones arise;
I never knew but one—and here he lies.

The Dog

Author unknown, written prior to 1946.

I've never known a dog to wag
   His tail in glee he didn't feel,
Nor quit his old-time friend to tag
   At some more influential heel.
The yellowest cur I ever knew
Was, to the boy who loved him, true.

I've never known a dog to show
   Halfway devotion to a friend;
To seek a kinder man to know,
   Or richer; but unto the end
The humblest dog I ever knew,
Was, to the man that loved him, true.

I've never known a dog to fake
   Affection for a present gain,
A false display of love to make,
   Some little favor to attain.
I've never known a Prince or Spot
That seemed to be what he is not.

But I have known a dog to fight
   With all his strength to shield a friend,
And whether wrong or whether right
   To stick with him until the end.
And I have known a dog to lick
The hand of him that men would kick.

And I have known a dog to bear
    Starvation pangs from day to day
With him who had been glad to share
    His bread and meat along the way.
No dog, however mean or rude
Is guilty of ingratitude.

The dog is listed with the dumb,
    No voice has he to speak his creed.
His messages to humans come
    By faithful conduct and by deed.
He shows, as seldom mortals do,
A high ideal of being true.

WILLIAM MERRITT CHASE, *Good Friends,* ca. 1891. American painter. (Private collection)

The Twa Dogs: A Tale

ROBERT BURNS, 1784–1785. On the night before his father died, Burns's dog, Luath, was cruelly killed for no reason. He wrote this as a tribute to his dog, creating the fictional Caesar. I have provided his original along with a version I have modernized. The original—in the Scottish dialect—is given for beauty of its rhythm and rhyme. The modernized version is given so its meaning may be more easily understood.

'Twas in that place o
   Scotland's Isle,
That bears the name of
   auld King Coil,
Upon a bonie day in June,
When wearin thro the
   afternoon,
Twa dogs, that were na
   thrang at hame,
Forgathered ance upon a
   time.

The first I'll name, they
   ca'd him Caesar,
Was keepit for 'his
   Honor's' pleasure:
His hair, his size, his
   mouth, his lugs,
Shew'd he was nane o
   Scotland's dogs;
But whalpit some place
   far abroad,
Whare sailors gang to fish
   for cod.

'Twas in that place of
   Scotland's Isle,
That bears the name of
   old King Kyle,
Upon a pretty day in June,
When passing through
   the afternoon,
Two dogs, that were not
   busy at home,
Encountered once upon
   a time.

The first one—they called
   him Caesar—
Was kept for "his
   Honor's" pleasure:
His hair, his size, his
   mouth, his ears,
Showed he was not of
   Scotland's dogs;
But born some place far
   abroad,
Where sailors go to fish
   for cod.

SIR EDWIN LANDSEER (1802–1873), *The Connoisseurs*. English animal painter. This is a self-portrait with two of his dogs. (Her Majesty the Queen)

His lockèd, letter'd, braw
   brass collar
Shew'd him the
   gentleman an scholar;
But tho he was o high
   degree,
The fient a pride, nae
   pride had he;
But wad hae spent an
   hour caressin,

His snug, lettered,
   splendid brass collar
Showed him the
   gentleman and scholar,
But though he was of
   high degree,
To the devil with pride,
   no pride had he;
But would have spent an
   hour caressing,

SIR EDWIN LANDSEER (1802–1873), *The Twa Dogs*. English animal painter. This painting was inspired by Burns's poem. Caesar is on the left and Luath on the right. (South Kensington Museum, London)

Ev'n wi a tinkler-gipsy's
    messin:
At kirk or market, mill or
    smiddie,
Nae tawted tyke, tho e'er
    sae duddie,
But he wad stan't, as glad
    to see him,
An stroan't on stanes an
    hillocks wi him.

The tither was a
    ploughman's collie,
A rhyming, ranting,
    raving billie,
Wha for his friend an
    comrade had him,
And in his freaks had
    Luath ca'd him,
After some dog in
    Highland sang,
Was made lang syne—
    Lord knows how lang.

Even with a gipsy
    repairman's cur:
At church or market, mill
    or smithy,
No matted mongrel,
    though ever so ragged,
But he would stand, as
    glad to see him,
And pissed on stones and
    mounds with him.

The other was a farmer's
    collie,
A rhyming, ranting,
    raving fellow,
Who for his friend and
    comrade had him,
And with caprice had
    called him Luath,
After some dog in
    Highland song,
Was made long ago—
    Lord knows how long.[1]

[1]Burns is making fun of James MacPherson's alleged translations of the ancient works of Ossian.

He was a gash an faithfu
   tyke,
As ever lap a sheugh or
   dyke.
His honest, sonsie,
   baws'nt face
Ay gat him friends in
   ilka place;
His breast was white, his
   tousie back
Weel clad wi coat o
   glossy black;
His gawsie tail, wi upward
   curl,
Hung owre his hurdies
   wi a swirl.

Nae doubt but they were
   fain o ither,
And unco pack an thick
   thegither;
Wi social nose whyles
   snuff'd an snowkit;
Whyles mice an moudie-
   worts they howkit;
Whyles scour'd awa in
   lang excursion,
An worry'd ither in
   diversion;
Till tir'd at last wi monie
   a farce,
They set them down
   upon their arse,
An there began a lang
   digression
About the 'lords o the
   creation.'

He was a wise and faithful
   dog,
As ever leaped over a
   ditch or wall.
His honest, sweet, white-
   streaked face
Always got him friends in
   every place;
His breast was white, his
   rumpled back
Well clad with coat of
   glossy black;
His handsome tail, with
   upward curl,
Hung over his hips with
   a swirl.

No doubt they were
   happy with each other,
And very familiar and
   friendly together,
With social nose some-
   times sniffed and poked;
Sometimes mice and
   moles they dug up;
Sometimes ran away in
   long excursion,
And reveled further in
   diversion;
Till tired at last with many
   a farce,
They sat right down upon
   their asses,
And there began a long
   digression
About the "lords of the
   creation."

THOMAS GAINSBOR-OUGH, *The Woodsman*, ca. 1787–1788. English portrait and landscape painter. This was Gainsborough's last great "fancy picture". The woodsman watching the approaching storm had a personal meaning for Gainsborough, since after completing it, he was bedridden and soon died of cancer. This is his small version of the painting, the much larger original having been destroyed by fire in 1810. (Private collection)

•   •   •

By this, the sun was out
  o sight,
An darker gloamin
  brought the night;
The bum-clock humm'd
  wi lazy drone;
The kye stood rowtin
  i' the loan;
When up they gat an
  shook their lugs,
Rejoic'd they were na
  men but *dogs;*
An each took aff his
  several way,
Resolv'd to meet some
  ither day.

By this, the sun was out
  of sight,
And darker twilight
  brought the night;
The beetle hummed
  with lazy drone;
The cattle stood lowing
  in the pasture;
When up they got and
  shook their ears,
Rejoiced they were not
  men but dogs;
And each took off his
  separate way,
Resolved to meet some
  other day.

I'm the Dog

GRENVILLE KLEISER, from *The Christian Science Monitor,* 1940.

I'm only a dog,—
Not much, you say?
But I have great sport,
I play all day.

I'm only a dog,—
You're sorry for me?
I sleep well at night,
From worry I'm free.

I'm only a dog,—
Sad lot, do you think?
I've good things to eat,
And plenty to drink.

I'm only a dog,—
When I see men at strife,
I'm thankful to God
I lead a dog's life!

GEORGE STUBBS, *King Charles Spaniel,* 1776. English animal painter.
(Private collection)

Sonnet for My Dog

THOMAS CURTIS CLARK (1877–1953), from *The Linebook.*

In distant lands the statesmen scheme and plot.
A war is in the making. Terror grips
The people and their masters. But you, Spot,
Are undisturbed by guns and battleships.
For you the thrills of life, without a care!
Long months of play in lush green grass await.
The world is good, for you; all days are fair—
You are no citizen of any state!
Rejoice, in your dog-kingdom happy, blest,
And woo us from the bitterness of life.
We, lordly men, with terrors are oppressed;
Our greed for gold and power brings hate and strife.
Wise little dog, be happy while you can;
Ignore the brutal idiot called man!

Artist unknown, ca. 1861. This is a painting of Lootie, one of five Pekinese that were captured by the British when the Summer Palace in Beijing was taken in 1860. Lootie was given to Queen Victoria by Capt. Dunne, who was later promoted to general.

Conversation with a Dog

STING (GORDON SUMNER), 1987. English singer, musician, and song-
writer.

I asked my dog what he thought the best in man
He said, "The love you dispense to me twice daily from
    a can."
I said, "Why do you think my question funny?
And where would you be without my money?"
I said, "There may be some quality in us you must
    treasure."
"It's despair," he said, "of which your money is the
    measure."

Walk like a dog   Like anybody can

I said, "What about our politics, philosophy, our
    history?"
He said, "If there is something admirable in these it is
    a mystery."
"But there must be something in our system tell me at
    your leisure."
"It's despair," he said, "of which your borders are the
    measure."

Walk like a dog   Talk like a man
Walk like a dog   Like anybody can

I said, "What about technology, computers, nuclear
    fission?"
"I'm terrified of radiation, hate the television."
I said, "There must be something in our scientific
    treasure."
"It's despair," he said, "of which your weapons are the
    measure."

FRANZ MARC, *Hund Vor der Welt (Dog before the World)* (originally titled *This Is How My Dog Sees the World*), 1912. German Postimpressionist landscape and animal painter. Marc was killed in World War I. (Private collection)

"Feed me, you can beat me. I will love you till I die.
But don't ask for admiration and don't ever ask me why."
I said, "Why wait till now to demonstrate displeasure?"
"It's despair," he said, "of which my silence was the
    measure."

Walk like a dog   Talk like a man
Walk like a dog   Like anybody can

To a Dog Dreaming

LORD DUNSANY (EDWARD JOHN MORETON DRAX PLUNKET), from
Mirage Water, 1938. Irish fantasy author, soldier, and 18th Baron of
Dunsany.

What golden rabbits do you chase
   In emerald fields of far away,
Or through what forests do you race
   With unicorns, as swift as they,

All shimmering through the silent gloom,
   Where unimagined flowers grow
And glitter downward, bloom on bloom,
   From grand trees that no men know?

No answer comes from lands of dream—
   Only the twitching of your limbs
And hunting cries, that fainter seem,
   As though, so soon, your dreamland dims,

As though the strange horizons melt
   And all the dreamy valleys fade,
And there comes back your bit of felt,
   Before the fire that men have made,

We shall not see your unicorns
   Where, like a multitude of towers,
Lifts up the splendor of their horns;
   We shall not even paint the flowers;

We shall not know the beasts you hunt,
   Only this knowledge shall we find:
The dream, the dream is far in front,
   And you, and we, pant on behind.

A DOG'S LIFE

The country is going to the dogs.

Bernard Shaw, *Augustus Does His Bit,* 1917.

The world is going to the dogs.

Theodora Dubois, *Death Comes to Tea,*
1940.

Don't let's go to the dogs tonight,
For mother will be there.

A. P. Herbert, *Don't Let's Go to the Dogs.*

I n 1986, U.S. Representative Gerald Solomon wrote, "[My dog] can bark like a congressman, fetch like an aide, beg like a press secretary, and play dead like a receptionist when the phone rings." With such versatility, maybe dogs should be running the world. It would not take much to surpass our track record. For the present, though, dogs seem content to leave it all up to us.

Dogs do not seem to mind doing what we tell them to do. They seem content to have complete trust in us . . . but there are times when this can be a problem. The Germans trained their military dogs to respond to four hand signals, one of which was the traditional palm forward signal for "halt". It is reported that after Hitler came to power, the dogs were part of a parade that passed Hitler in review. When they saw the Führer's salute, they immediately responded by sitting down and the troops marching up from behind promptly stumbled over them. All the dogs had to be retrained. Although it is possible this story was a bit of wartime propaganda, it is a humorous note on the obedience of dogs.

Obedience does have its limits, even for dogs. During World War II, the Nazis constantly used messenger dogs along the Maginot Line. The French tried to shoot these dogs, but it was "like trying to hit a white jackrabbit zigzagging over the snow". One French dog handler decided to release a small liaison dog, who had just gone into heat, to see what would happen. That evening she returned, followed by a dozen normally obedient German dogs who had discovered something more important than war.

Sometimes a well-intentioned dog can misunderstand a situation, with dire consequences. It is said that the Earl of Wiltshire decided to take his toy spaniel along with him in about 1530, when King Henry VIII sent him to the pope with a petition. The king wanted to annul his marriage to Catherine of Aragon, the daughter of Ferdinand and Isabella of Spain, so that he could marry Anne Boleyn. At the beginning of his audience, Lord Wiltshire knelt to kiss the pope's foot, as custom required. To assist in this process, the pope shifted his food forward so that it would be more accessible. The lord's spaniel spotted this and concluded the pontiff was going to kick her master in the face. Responding to the threat, she immediately launched an attack on the offending holy digits. The pope was not pleased. In fact, one historian of the time described the subsequent scene as "riotous".

It is not known what effect the spaniel had on the pope's decision, but Lord Wiltshire returned home without the divorce. King Henry VIII decided the Catholic Church was not for him and organized the Church of England, which was glad to grant his divorce. One of the results of all this is the continuing conflict in Northern Ireland.

No doubt dogs find much of what we do baffling and incomprehensible, to say the least. Still, they put up with us no matter how out of touch with reality we seem to be. Perhaps they are impressed by our gadgets and the way we can manipulate our environment. Maybe they just hope we know what we are doing, no matter how strange our behavior seems.

At any rate, their lives and ours are inextricably tied together. For good or ill, dogs are stuck with us.

ELLIOT ERWITT.

Going to the Dogs

Unknown author,[1] ca. 1905.

My grandad, viewing earth's worn cogs,
Said, "Things are going to the dogs";
His grandad in his house of logs
Swore things were going to the dogs;
His grandad in the Flemish bogs
Swore things were going to the dogs;
His grandad in his old skin togs
Said, "Things are going to the dogs."
Well, there's one thing I have to state:
Those dogs have had a good long wait.

---

[1]This is sometimes wrongly attributed to George B. Cutten.

A Business Partner

EDGAR ALLAN POE (1809–1849), from "The Business Man". This is probably based on an actual bootblack and his poodle who lived in Pont Neuf, France, during the 19th century.

I was making money at this business when, in an evil moment, I was induced to merge in the Cur-Spattering—a somewhat analogous, but, by no means, so respectable a profession. My location, to be sure, was an excellent one, being central, and I had capital blacking and brushes. My little dog, too, was quite fat and up to all varieties of snuff. He had been in the trade a long time, and, I may say, understood it. Our general routine was this:—Pompey, having

ÉDOUARD MANET, *Tama, the Japanese Dog,* ca. 1875. French Impressionist painter. (Private collection)

rolled himself well in the mud, sat upon end at the shop door, until he observed a dandy approaching in bright boots. He then proceeded to meet him, and gave the Wellingtons a rub or two with his wool. Then the dandy swore very much, and looked about for a bootblack. There I was, full in his view, with blacking and brushes. It was only a minute's work, and then came a sixpence. This did moderately well for a time;—in fact, I was not avaricious, but my dog was. I allowed him a third of the profit, but he was advised to insist upon half. This I couldn't stand— so we quarrelled and parted.

THOMAS EAKINS, *Arcadia* (detail), 1883. American painter and sculptor. (Private collection)

An Independent Dog

WILL ROGERS, from *The Autobiography of Will Rogers*, 1921–1935. American humorist known as the "cowboy philosopher". Rogers died in a plane crash in 1935.

When I finally got into Amarillo the whole country around was covered with trail herds waiting for cars to ship them away. There was plenty of grass and water everywhere.

I hit up every trail boss I could find for a job, but they didn't want me. At night I'd go out a piece from town, stake out my horse, and sleep, then the next morning go back.

While I dident have anything else to do, I got to watching an old spotted dog. He was just an ordinary dog, but when I looked at him close, he was alert and friendly with everyone. Got to inquiring around and found out he'd been bumped off a freight train and seemed to have no owner. He made himself at home and started right in business. When a crowd of cowboys would go into a saloon, he would follow em in and begin entertaining. He could do all kinds of tricks—turn somersaults, lay down and roll over, sit up on his hind feet, and such like.

He would always rush to the door and shake hands with all the newcomers. The boys would lay a coin on his nose, and he'd toss it high in the air and catch it in his mouth and pretend to swallow it. But you could bet your life he dident swallow it—he stuck it in one side of his lip and when he got a lip full of money, he'd dash out the back door and disappear for a few minutes. What he really done was hide his money. As soon as he worked one saloon, he would pull out and go to another place.

I got to thinking while watching this old dog, how much smarter he is than me. Here I am out of a job five hundred miles from home, and setting around and cant find a thing to do, and this old dog hops off a train and starts right in making money, hand over fist.

Me and some boys around town tried to locate his hidden treasure, but this old dog was too slick for us. He never fooled away no time on three or four of us boys that was looking for work. He seemed to know we was broke, but he was very friendly. As he was passing along by me, he'd wag his tail and kinda wink. I must a looked hungry and forlorn. I think he wanted to buy me a meal.

When times was dull and he got hungry, he would mysteriously disappear. Pretty soon he'd show up at a butcher shop with a dime in his mouth and lay it on the counter and the butcher would give him a piece of steak or a bone. He always paid for what he got in the line of grub. Pretty soon he seemed to get tired of the town, and one morning he was gone. A railroad man told us later that he seen this same dog in Trinidad, Colorado.

THOMAS GAINSBOROUGH, *Lady Hamilton as "Nature"*, 1782. English portrait and landscape painter. Emma married the much older and somewhat senile Lord Hamilton and then became the mistress of Admiral Lord Nelson.

ALPHONSE MUCHA,
for Anatole France's
Cleo, 1900. Czech Art
Nouveau painter.

From Pillar to Post

or

How to Raise a Dog

(edited)

JACK ALAN (JACK GOODMAN AND ALAN GREEN), from *How to Do Practically Anything,* 1942.

Dog owners, arise! Too long has the actual head of your family not even paid an income tax. Too long have you tried to conceal from your dog the fact that he really owns you. Too long have you searched in vain for the counsel you so sorely need when, panting and tongue hanging out, you fall back into the nearest chair and finally admit to yourself that the lively little fellow isn't going to sit up

341

and beg, hasn't the slightest intention of leaving that frayed end of the tapestry alone, and is unshakeably convinced that the mathematical center of the living-room rug is the Comfort Station Supreme.

You can expect no help from dog books or dog doctors. In this all-important emergency, all they do is back away, muttering incoherent statements about Training and Psychology. And you are left holding the bag, one end of which has already been chewed away, like everything else you own.

I am no expert. I might as well tell you right now that I generally go to sleep with a large, greasy bone under my pillow because I have failed to sway my dog in his opinion that there isn't a better spot in town for bone hiding. My house is thoroughly dog-broken. But I do not intend to leave my fellow man with his dog having the upper paw in the household.

I believe my predicament to be an average one, a valuable case history. I will show you how I deal with my dog. Maybe you will be able to discover where along the line something went terribly, terribly wrong.

Things started badly when I bought him. I didn't select him, he selected me. When I went to the kennel, I had decided definitely against buying four or five puppies, as I wanted to do. Phyllis claims that this is too many for a small apartment. Cunningly, however, I planned to get around this by getting as much dog as possible for my money—a great Dane.

I looked critically at the batch of puppies, which, while only three months old, were the size of Airedales. Then one detached himself from the mob. He had a lot of filling out to do. He took, I noticed, several steps before his skin started moving along with him. He galloped over, sat down heavily on my feet, and looked me over carefully. I couldn't move, so I had to look at him, too. He was obvi-

SIR EDWIN LANDSEER, *Pincher, the Property of Montague Gore, Esq.,* by 1848. English animal painter. (Private collection)

ously admiring me. His next step was to take my trouser leg in his mouth and shake it, possibly to test the quality of the material. Then he gave several pleased body wiggles, attempted to climb up on me, and washed my hand thoroughly with a salmon-pink tongue. Then he sat down again on my feet and admired me some more.

I had been chosen.

Several months have passed, and we have learned much about each other. Neither of us regrets his choice, although my training methods seem to lack something.

I have found that the very first step must be to Gain His Confidence. To accomplish this, I sit on the floor next to him and say, "*Good* little dog!" This is a flat lie and he knows it, being well aware that he is neither little nor good. He backs away several feet, presses himself close to the floor, and turns up his eyes at me with a wary "You-are-up-to-something-tricky-and-I'm-not-going-to-like-it" expression.

I reach out reassuringly and pat his nearest paw. He withdraws the paw and licks it off fastidiously.

I attempt now to get his attention by cupping both hands and saying coyly: "Guess what I've got here?"

Showing signs of interest, he nuzzles into my hands. I am caught flat-footed with nothing in them. I run to get a dog biscuit to absolve myself. Meanwhile he stalks off bitterly to a corner of the room, tenses his forelegs, digs a hole in the carpet, and lies down in it.

I now change my approach, deciding to try the Great Big Playmate tactic. Crouching on all fours, I advance on him, barking several times with mock ferocity. He decides to humor me by pretending he thinks I'm a huge, dangerous dog. With a happy yelp, he flashes around a chair and dashes upon me from behind. Since he weighs roughly eighty-two pounds at the moment, I am now flat on the floor with him on top of me. He wants to pretend he is

343

PABLO PICASSO, *The Painter and His Model,* 1963. Spanish Cubist
painter. (Private collection)

shaking me by the neck. This is too difficult unless he actually does shake me by the back of the neck. So he does.

I get up and brush myself off. I brush him off me, too,
several times. I have now succeeded in gaining his confidence and showing him that I am a regular fellow who
doesn't mind a good, clean romp, so I am through. But he
isn't. He likes it too well to quit. He gets my tie in his teeth
and hangs from it. It is some time before I get my breath.

He still refuses to stop. It is therefore time for me to
Punish Him. I decide to lock him in the bathroom. This
consists of the following steps:

1. He instantly senses my purpose and scrambles into the bedroom and under the bed.
2. I rush after him and say, "Come out from under there this minute!"
3. He doesn't.
4. I get down on the floor and look under the bed. We face each other silently for a moment, each trying to outstare the other. I blink, which gives him the round.
5. I mutter several dire threats. So does he.
6. I hold out my handkerchief, hoping he will grab it and pull, thereby enabling me to drag him out.
7. He grabs it and pulls.
8. We are now both under the bed.
9. I seize him firmly and wriggle out.
10. A head bumps severely against the box spring. It is not his.
11. I shove and pull him into the bathroom and back out, closing the door.
12. I stop closing the door to avoid catching his nose in it.
13. I shove him back and close the door, catching my hand in it.
14. We both howl simultaneously.

Returning to the living room, tired but victorious (look up Pyrrhic in any good encyclopedia), I now proceed to describe my dog to you. He is still a puppy, seven months old. He is a good dog to have for a case history because, although a thoroughbred, he has a character which is practically a cross section of that of America's dogs.

Although large and getting larger, it is his opinion that he is a lap dog and as such entitled to climb on my chair whether I am in it or not. When I can catch him to give him a bath, he emerges as a dull gold in color with a

DANIELE RANZONI (1843–1889), *The Trubetskoy Children*. Italian painter. Ranzoni suffered from physical and mental problems and so produced few pictures. (Galleria Nazionale d'Arte Moderna, Rome)

mouth fringed with black. This mouth is already large enough to contain my arm and, when I am giving him a bath, does. Like all his breed, he has a short coat, but he sheds it with the success of the collie. He has a way of searching out tidbits in his food which probably reveals that in spite of his pedigree he contains a trace of ant-eater. He has a beery sort of baritone. And he is very democratic in his ideas about love.

When I first got him I called him Gilbert, the name I still introduce him by. The only word he will always answer to, however, is Food, so I generally call him that.

Food, or Gilbert, is still in the bathroom, you will recall. This is my golden opportunity to get something to eat unbeknownst to him. Let me explain.

Since I have known Gilbert, I have had few square meals at home. This is because Gilbert is an adept at a quiet, effective sort of bullying. When I am eating, he is too wily to use strong-arm tactics, realizing that force will be answered with force. He therefore just looks at me tragically. He keeps looking at me. He meditates on man's inhumanity to dog. He sighs. Beginning to feel like a heartless gourmand, I transfer my little morsel of food to my mouth. His glance never wavers. He drools slowly.

As a result, I spend a large part of my time at my dinner table chewing things up a little for Gilbert. Then I give them to him, cursing.

But now that Gilbert is in the bathroom, I turn on the radio full blast and enter the kitchen singing loudly, hoping that both noises will distract him.

It is a losing game. Gilbert, who would sleep soundly through a collision with another planet, easily detects the noiseless opening of the electric icebox. No sooner do I reach a guilty hand to a roast-beef bone than Gilbert utters a series of agonized cries, giving the entire neighborhood the impression that I am murdering him by inches. In self-defense I rush to the bathroom to make him stop.

He is very happy as I open the door, particularly since a well-timed move enables him to snatch the beef bone from my hand and rush back to the bathroom.

I am about to follow him to get back my bone when the doorbell rings.

It is Mrs. Garble, a middle-aged woman I do not like. She is the president of Phyllis' club. She is also a cat lover. She expresses relief at being able to come in for once and not have that great brute of a dog jumping all over her.

GEORGE STUBBS, *Portrait of a Spanish Dog Belonging to Mr. Cosway*, 1775. English animal painter. A papillon and a butterfly. Papillon, which means "butterfly", are so named because their head markings often resemble a butterfly. (Private collection)

Looking around nervously, she asks where he is. I tell her.

"What in the world is he doing in the bathroom?" she says.

"Well, really, Mrs. Garble," I reply primly, "he *said* he wanted to wash his hands."

This keeps her quiet for a moment. It then develops that she wants to see Phyllis, who isn't home. She looks at the carpet, which has no more than a normal amount of Gilbert's hair on it.

"Goodness gracious!" she says, clucking, "I don't see *how* you can keep a great Dane in a city apartment! Why, I'd just as soon keep a horse in one!"

I bristle and stifle a desire to say, "Oh, so you don't think I ought to keep my horse, either?"

Gilbert chooses this moment to enter. And not, to my surprise, with his usual attitude, which practically says, "Oh my chin and whiskers! What wonderful things have I been missing!" Instead, he comes in with measured dignity. He casts a sedate glance at Mrs. Garble.

"He seems to be getting much better manners," she says grudgingly. "You certainly are training him to behave like a gentleman!"

I decide that Mrs. Garble, too, seems to be getting better manners. I warm toward her, as I do to all types of characters who have a kind word to say for Gilbert. I even toy with the idea of giving her a drink.

I watch with paternal pride as Gilbert walks slowly over to her. He sniffs at her leg in a genteel way. I beam reassuringly. Mrs. Garble smiles back uncertainly. Gilbert seems about to walk past her. He doesn't. He stops. Trained to observe such matters, I suddenly notice an uncertain attitude, a slight quivering of the muscles of Gilbert's left hind leg.

"GILBERT!" I cry, in the nick of time.

GEORGES SEURAT, *Study for La Grande-Jatte: Landscape with Dog,*
ca. 1884–1885. French Postimpressionist painter. Seurat developed the
technique called *pointillism,* where a painting is constructed of tiny
dots of pure colors. (British Museum, London)

There is no need to go into the next five minutes. It will serve no purpose for me to repeat my weak explanation to the outraged Mrs. Garble that Gilbert, being still in the experimental stage, was merely about to test out a comparatively new idea. And that there was no personal malice or intended criticism involved. . . .

All right. Now that I have revealed my relationship to my dog in all its squalor, the curious may inquire why I have a dog at all. The curious may, but not the wise.

The answer, of course, is simple. In Gilbert I have found a being to whom I am superior in many ways, in spite of the fact that Phyllis insists that a lot more people stop to admire him than me on the street. Gilbert cannot drive a car. I can. Gilbert cannot wash dishes, pour drinks for people, run errands, or do dozens of other things around the house Phyllis considers necessary. Above all, Gilbert is a living, breathing answer to her contention that I am the most inefficient form of life yet devised.

He is also the finest dog in town, even if he did tear up the very best parts of this piece.

DIEGO RODRÍGUEZ DE SILVA Y VELÁZQUEZ, *Las Meninas (The Maids of Honor)*, 1656. Spanish court painter. (Museo del Prado, Madrid)

The Dreaded Bath

FARLEY MOWAT, from *The Dog Who Wouldn't Be*, 1957. Canadian writer and biologist.

Summer drew on and the sloughs again grew dry and white; the young grain wizened and burned, and another season of drought was upon us. A film of dust hung continuously in the scorching air and we were never free of the gritty touch of it, except when we stripped off our clothing and went to soak in the bathtub. For Mutt there was no such relief. His long coat caught and trapped the dust until the hair became matted and discolored, assuming a jaundiced saffron hue, but he would not, in those early days, voluntarily turn to water to escape his misery.

He was a true son of the drought. I suppose that he had seen so little water in his first months of life that he had a right to be suspicious of it. At any rate he shied away from water in any quantity, as a cayoose shies from a rattlesnake. When we decided to force a bath upon him, he not only became argumentative and deaf, but if he could escape us, he would crawl under the garage floor, where he would remain without food or drink until we gave in and solemnly assured him that the bath was off.

Not the least difficult part of the bath was the devising of a plan whereby Mutt might be lured, all unsuspecting, into the basement where the laundry tubs stood waiting. This problem required a different solution each time, for Mutt had a long memory, and his bath suspicions were easily aroused. On one occasion we released a live gopher in the cellar and then, encountering it "unexpectedly," called upon Mutt to slay it. This worked once.

The bath itself was a severe ordeal to all who were involved. During the earlier attempts we wore raincoats, sou'westers, and rubber boots, but we found these inadequate. Later we wore only simple breechclouts. Mutt never gave up, and he would sometimes go to incredible lengths to cheat the tub. Once he snatched a piece of naphtha soap out of my hand and swallowed it, whether accidentally or not I do not know. He began frothing almost immediately, and we curtailed the bath and called the veterinary.

The veterinary was a middle-aged and unimaginative man whose practice was largely limited to healing boils on horses and hard udders on cows. He refused to believe that Mutt had voluntarily swallowed soap, and he left in something of a huff. Mutt took advantage of the hullabaloo to vanish. He returned twenty-four hours later looking pale and emaciated—having proved the emetic efficacy of naphtha soap beyond all question.

FRANCISCO JOSÉ DE GOYA Y LUCIENTES, *Las Meninas after Velázquez*, 1778. Spanish court painter and etcher. (Museo del Prado, Madrid)

The decision to bathe Mutt was never lightly made, and we tended to postpone it as long as possible. He was long overdue for a cleansing when, in late July, I went away to spend a few days at a friend's cottage on Lake Manitou.

I enjoyed myself at Manitou, which is one of the saltiest of the west's salt sloughs. My friend and I spent most of our days trying to swim, despite the fact that the saline content of the water was so high that it was impossible to sink deep enough to reach a point of balance. We slithered about on the surface, acquiring painful sunburns and bad cases of salt-water itch.

I was in a carefree and happy mood when, on Monday morning, I arrived back in Saskatoon. I came up the front walk of our house whistling for Mutt and bearing a present for him—a dead gopher that we had picked up on the road home. He did not respond to my whistle. A little uneasily I pushed through the front door and found Mother sitting on the chesterfield, looking deeply distressed. She stood up when she saw me and clutched me to her bosom.

"Oh, darling," she cried, "your poor, *poor* dog! Oh, your *poor*, poor dog!"

A lethal apprehension overwhelmed me. I stiffened in her arms. "What's the matter with him?" I demanded.

Mother released me and looked into my eyes. "Be brave, darling," she said. "You'd better see him for yourself. He's under the garage."

I was already on my way.

Mutt's grotto under the garage was his private sanctuary, and it could be reached only through a narrow burrow. I got down on my hands and knees and peered into the gloom. As my eyes became accustomed to the darkness, I could discern a vague but Muttlike shape. He was curled up in the farthest recess, his head half hidden by his tail, but with one eye exposed and glaring balefully out of the murk. He did not seem to be seriously damaged and I ordered him to emerge.

He did not move.

In the end I had to crawl into the burrow, grasp him firmly by the tail, and drag him out by brute force. And then I was so startled by his appearance that I released my grip and he scuttled back to cover.

Mutt was no longer a black and white dog, or even a black and yellow one. He was a vivid black and blue. Those sections of his coat that had once been white were now of an unearthly ultramarine shade. The effect was ghastly, particularly about the head, for even his nose and muzzle were bright blue.

PABLO PICASSO, *Las Meninas after Velázquez* (first version), 1957. Spanish Cubist painter. (Picasso Museum, Barcelona)

Mutt's transformation had taken place the day I left for Manitou. He was indignant and annoyed that he had been left behind, and for the rest of that day he sulked. When no one gave him the sympathy he felt was due him, he left the house, and he did not return home until evening. His return was notable.

Somewhere out on the broad prairie to the east of town he found the means with which to revenge himself upon humanity. He found a dead horse in that most satisfactory state of decomposition which best lends itself to being rolled upon. Mutt rolled with diligence.

He arrived home at a little after nine o'clock, and no doubt he trusted to the dusk to conceal him until he could reach his grotto. He was caught unawares when Father leaped upon him from ambush. He made a frantic effort to escape and succeeded briefly, only to be trapped in the back yard. Squalling bitterly, he was at last dragged into the basement. The doors were closed and locked and the laundry tubs were filled.

Father has never been willing to describe in any detail the events that followed, but Mother—although she did not actually descend into the basement herself—was able to give me a reasonably circumstantial account. It must have been an epic struggle. It lasted almost three hours and the sounds and smells of battle reached Mother, via the hot-air registers, without appreciable diminution. She told me that both my father and Mutt had become hoarse and silent by the end of the second hour, but that the sounds of water sluicing violently back and forth over the basement floor testified clearly that the struggle was not yet at an end.

It was nearly midnight before Father appeared alone at the head of the cellar stairs. He was stripped to the buff, and close to exhaustion. After a stiff drink and a bath of his own, he went to bed without so much as hinting to Mother of the dreadful things that had happened on the dank battleground downstairs.

Mutt spent the balance of the night outside, under the front porch. He was evidently too fatigued even to give vent to his vexation by an immediate return to the dead horse—although he probably had this in mind for the morrow.

But when dawn came, not even the lure of the horse was sufficient to make him forgo his usual morning routine.

It had long been his unvarying habit to spend the hours between dawn and breakfast time going his rounds through the back alleys in the neighborhood. He had a regular route, and he seldom deviated from it. There were certain garbage cans that he never missed, and there were, of course, a number of important telephone poles that had to be attended to. His path used to take him down the alleyway between Ninth and Tenth Avenues, thence to the head of the New Bridge, and finally to the rear premises of the restaurants and grocery stores in the neighborhood of the Five Corners. Returning home, he would proceed along the main thoroughfare, inspecting fireplugs en route. By the time he started home, there would usually be a good number of people on the streets, bound across the river to their places of work. Mutt had no intimation of disaster on this particular morning until he joined the throng of south-bound workers.

Mother had no warning either until, at a quarter to eight, the telephone rang. Mother answered it and an irate female voice shouted in her ear, "You people should be put in jail! You'll see if it's so funny when I put the law onto you!" The receiver at the other end went down with a crash, and Mother went back to making breakfast. She was always phlegmatic in the early hours, and she assumed that this threatening tirade was simply the result of a wrong number. She actually smiled as she told Father about it over the breakfast table. She was still smiling when the police arrived.

There were two constables, and they were pleasant and polite when Mother answered the door. One of them explained that some "crank" had telephoned the station to report that the Mowats had painted their dog. The policemen were embarrassed, and they hastened to explain that it was the law that all such complaints had to be investigated, no matter how ridiculous they might seem. If

ROSA BONHEUR (1822–1899), *"Barbaro" after the Hunt.* French animal painter. Bonheur is the most famous woman painter of the 19th century. (Philadelphia Museum of Art, Philadelphia)

Mother would assure them, simply for form's sake, they said, that her dog was still his natural color, they would gladly depart. Mother at once gave them the requisite assurance, but, feeling somewhat puzzled, she hastened to the dining room to tell my father about it.

Father had vanished. He had not even finished his morning coffee. The sound of Eardlie grunting and snorting in the back alley showed that he was departing in haste.

Mother shrugged her shoulders, and began carrying the dishes out to the kitchen. At that moment Mutt scratched on the screen door. She went to let him in.

Mutt scurried into the house, with his head held low and a look of abject misery about him. He must have had a singularly bad time of it on the crowded street. He fled directly to my room, and vanished under the bed.

Father was not yet at his office when Mother phoned the library. She left an agitated message that he was to return home at once, and then she called the veterinary.

Unfortunately it was the same one who had been called in when Mutt ate the naphtha soap. He came again—but with a hard glint of suspicion in his eye.

Mother met him at the door and rushed him into the bedroom. Then the two of them tried to persuade Mutt to come out from under the bed. Mutt refused. Eventually the veterinary had to crawl under the bed after him—but he did this with a very poor grace.

When he emerged he was momentarily beyond speech. Mother misinterpreted his silence as a measure of the gravity of Mutt's condition. She pressed the doctor for his diagnosis. She was not prepared for the tirade he loosed upon her. He forgot all professional standards. When he left the house he was bitterly vowing that he would give up medicine and return to the wheat farm that had spawned him. He was so angry that he quite forgot the bill.

Mother had by now put up with quite enough for one morning, and she was in no condition to be further trifled with when, a few minutes later, Father came cautiously through the back door. He was almost as abject as Mutt had been. He saw the look in my mother's eye and tried to forestall her.

"I swear I didn't even guess it would do that," he explained hastily. "Surely it will wash out?" There was a pleading note in his voice.

The light of a belated understanding began to dawn on Mother. She fixed her husband with her most baleful glare.

"Will *what* wash out?" she demanded, leaving Father with no room for further evasion.

"The bluing,"[2] said my father humbly.

It was little wonder that Mother was distressed by the time I returned from my holiday. The telephone had rung almost incessantly for three days. Some of the callers were

[2]Bluing is a chemical used to whiten clothes.

360

SIR EDWIN LANDSEER, *Suspense* (also called *The Friend in Suspense*), by 1834. English animal painter. (Victoria and Albert Museum, London)

jovial—and these were undoubtedly the hardest to bear. Others were vindictive. Fortunately the reporters from the *Saskatoon Star-Phoenix* were friends of my father's and, with a notable restraint, they denied themselves the opportunity for a journalistic field day. Nevertheless, there were not many people in Saskatoon who did not know of, and who did not have opinions about, the Mowats and their bright blue dog.

By the time I arrived home Father had become very touchy about the whole affair, and it was dangerous to question him too closely. Nevertheless, I finally dared to ask him how much bluing he had actually used.

"Just a smidgen," he replied shortly. "Just enough to take that damned yellow tint out of his fur!"

I do not know exactly how much a "smidgen" is, but I do know that when Mother asked me to clean the clogged basement drain a few days later, I removed from it a wad of paper wrappers from at least ten cubes of bluing. Some of them may, of course, have been there for some time.

The Bath

R. C. LEHMANN.

Hang garlands on the bathroom door;
    Let all the passages be spruce;
For, lo, the victim comes once more,
    And, ah, he struggles like the deuce!

Illumination from Count Gaston de Foix's *Le Livre de Chasse (The Book of Hunting),* ca. 1440. Count de Foix was a French general and the nephew of King Louis XII. (Bibliothèque Nationale, Paris)

362

Bring soaps of many scented sorts;
  Let girls in pinafores attend,
With John, their brother, in his shorts,
  To wash their dusky little friend.

Their little friend, the dusky dog,
  Short-legged and very obstinate,
Faced like a much-offended frog,
  And fighting hard against his fate.

Vain are his protests—in he goes.
  His young barbarians crowd around;
They soap his paws, they soap his nose;
  They soap wherever fur is found.

And soon, still laughing, they extract
  His limpness from the darkling tide;
They make the towel's roughness act
  On back and head and dripping side.

They shout and rub and rub and shout—
  He deprecates their odious glee—
Until at last they turn him out,
  A damp, gigantic bumble-bee.

Released, he barks and rolls, and speeds
  From lawn to lawn, from path to path,
And in one glorious minute needs
  More soapsuds and another bath.

A Dog's Eye View

AMELIA JOSEPHINE BURR.

The people whom I take to walk
   I love and yet deplore,
Such things of real importance
   They persistently ignore.
The sights and smells that thrill me
   They stolidly pass by,
Then stop and stare in rapture
   At nothing in the sky.

They waste such time in stopping
   To look at things like flowers.
They pick the dullest places
   To settle down for hours.
Sometimes I really wonder
   If they can hear and smell;
Such vital things escape them—
   And yet they mean so well!

ARISTIDE SARTORIO,
The Child of Pleasure,
ca. 1889.

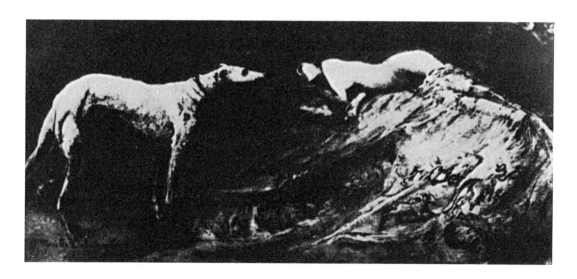

Memoirs of a Yellow Dog

O. HENRY (WILLIAM SIDNEY PORTER), from *The Four Million*, 1906. American short story writer. O. Henry was originally a banker but in 1896 he was accused of embezzling and he fled to Honduras. He returned to the United States and spent three years in prison. He then became a writer. This short story is reprinted here in its entirety.

I don't suppose it will knock any of you people off your perch to read a contribution from an animal. Mr. Kipling and a good many others have demonstrated the fact that animals can express themselves in remunerative English, and no magazine goes to press nowadays without an animal story in it, except the old-style monthlies that are still running pictures of Bryan and the Mont Pelée horror.

But you needn't look for any stuck-up literature in my piece, such as Bearoo, the bear, and Snakoo, the snake, and Tammanoo, the tiger, talk in the jungle books. A yellow dog that's spent most of his life in a cheap New York flat, sleeping in a corner on an old sateen underskirt (the one she spilled port wine on at the Lady 'Longshoremen's banquet), mustn't be expected to perform any tricks with the art of speech.

I was born a yellow pup; date, locality, pedigree, and weight unknown. The first thing I can recollect, an old woman had me in a basket at Broadway and Twenty-third trying to sell me to a fat lady. Old Mother Hubbard was boosting me to beat the band as a genuine Pomeranian-Hambletonian-Red-Irish-Cochin-China-Stoke-Pogis fox terrier. The fat lady chased a V around among the samples of grosgrain flannelette in her shopping bag till she cornered it, and gave up. From that moment I was a pet—a mamma's own wootsey squidlums. Say, gentle reader, did you ever have a 200-pound woman breathing a flavour of Camembert cheese and Peau d'Espagne pick you up and wallop her nose all over you, remarking all the time in an

PAUL GAUGUIN (1848–1903), *The Red Dog.* French Postimpressionist
painter. (Louvre, Paris)

Emma Eames tone of voice: "Oh, oo's um oodlum, dood-
lum, woodlum, toodlum, bitsy-witsy skoodlums?"

From a pedigreed yellow pup I grew up to be an
anonymous yellow cur looking like a cross between an An-
gora cat and a box of lemons. But my mistress never tumbled. She thought that the two primeval pups that Noah
chased into the ark were but a collateral branch of my ancestors. It took two policemen to keep her from entering
me at the Madison Square Garden for the Siberian bloodhound prize.

I'll tell you about that flat. The house was the ordinary thing in New York, paved with Parian marble in the entrance hall and cobblestones above the first floor. Our flat was three fl—well, not flights—climbs up. My mistress rented it unfurnished, and put in the regular things—1903 antique upholstered parlour set, oil chromo of geishas in a Harlem tea house, rubber plant and husband.

By Sirius! there was a biped I felt sorry for. He was a little man with sandy hair and whiskers a good deal like mine. Henpecked?—well, toucans and flamingoes and pelicans all had their bills in him. He wiped the dishes and listened to my mistress tell about the cheap, ragged things the lady with the squirrel-skin coat on the second floor hung out on her line to dry. And every evening while she was getting supper she made him take me out on the end of a string for a walk.

If men knew how women pass the time when they are alone they'd never marry. Laura Jean Libbey, peanut brittle, a little almond cream on the neck muscles, dishes unwashed, half an hour's talk with the iceman, reading a package of old letters, a couple of pickles and two bottles of malt extract, one hour peeking through a hole in the window shade into the flat across the air-shaft—that's about all there is to it. Twenty minutes before time for him to come home from work she straightens up the house, fixes her rat so it won't show, and gets out a lot of sewing for a ten-minute bluff.

I led a dog's life in that flat. 'Most all day I lay there in my corner watching that fat woman kill time. I slept sometimes and had pipe dreams about being out chasing cats into basements and growling at old ladies with black mittens, as a dog was intended to do. Then she would pounce upon me with a lot of that drivelling poodle palaver and kiss me on the nose—but what could I do? A dog can't chew cloves.

DONALD ROLLER WILSON, *RICHARD WAS CONCERNED ABOUT HIS BIG TRIP TO HOLLY'S*, 1984. (Private collection)
The words in the picture read:

SHIRLEY AND KATHLEEN (BUT MAINLY SHIRLEY) MADE RICHARD WEAR A DRESS DURING LUNCH AND THEY MADE HIM SIT IN HIS CHAIR FROM 12:00 to 1:00 AGAINST THE WALL IN THE HALL OPPOSITE THE DOOR LEADING TO MRS. LAMAR JENKINS' ROOM THINKING IT WOULD BE VERY SCARY AND A GOOD TRICK ON HIM BECAUSE THEY THOUGHT HIS OVERPOWERING FEAR WOULD BE THAT MRS. JENKINS WOULD CATCH HIM IN THE DRESS (MAYBE LOOKING OUT THROUGH HER KEYHOLE AND SEEING HIM) BUT WHAT SHIRLEY AND KATHLEEN (BUT MAINLY SHIRLEY) DIDN'T KNOW WAS THAT WHILE RICHARD WAS AWARE OF THE POTEN-TIAL EMBARRASSMENT IN THAT EPISODE, HIS <u>WORRY</u> WAS OF GO-ING TO HOLLY SOLOMON'S IN NEW YORK AND BEING DISCOVERED BY JOHN GLUECK, GRACE BRENSON, KIM LARSON, KATE DeAk, PETER LINKER, EDIT LEVIN, MICHAEL RUSSELL, ROBERTA SCHJELDAHL, KAY SMITH, OR MRS. HEINZ (ALPHABETI-CALLY LISTED) ALL WHOM, FOR INDIVIDUAL REASONS, MIGHT GET AFTER HIM • 5:44P.M. FRIDAY • OCTOBER 12 • DONALD ROLLER WILSON • 1984/16 ♥

I began to feel sorry for Hubby, dog my cats if I didn't. We looked so much alike that people noticed it when we went out; so we shook the streets that Morgan's cab drives down, and took to climbing the piles of last December's snow on the streets where cheap people live.

One evening when we were thus promenading, and I was trying to look like a prize St. Bernard, and the old man was trying to look like he wouldn't have murdered the first organ-grinder he heard play Mendelssohn's wedding-march, I looked up at him and said, in my way:

"What are you looking so sour about, you oakum trimmed lobster? She don't kiss you. You don't have to sit on her lap and listen to talk that would make the book of a musical comedy sound like the maxims of Epictetus. You ought to be thankful you're not a dog. Brace up, Benedick, and bid the blues begone."

EDWARD GOREY, from Jan Wahl's *The Cobweb Castle,* 1968. American illustrator. Gorey is considered one of the greatest contemporary illustrators.

The matrimonial mishap looked down at me with almost canine intelligence in his face.

"Why, doggie," says he, "good doggie. You almost look like you could speak. What is it, doggie—Cats?"

Cats! Could speak!

But, of course, he couldn't understand. Humans were denied the speech of animals. The only common ground of communication upon which dogs and men can get together is in fiction.

In the flat across the hall from us lived a lady with a black-and-tan terrier. Her husband strung it and took it out every evening, but he always came home cheerful and whistling. One day I touched noses with the black-and-tan in the hall, and I struck him for an elucidation.

"See here, Wiggle-and-Skip," I says, "you know that it ain't the nature of a real man to play dry nurse to a dog in public. I never saw one leashed to a bow-wow yet that didn't look like he'd like to lick every other man that looked at him. But your boss comes in every day as perky and set up as an amateur prestidigitator doing the egg trick. How does he do it? Don't tell me he likes it."

"Him?" says the black-and-tan. "Why, he uses Nature's Own Remedy. He gets spifflicated. At first when we go out he's as shy as the man on the steamer who would rather play pedro when they make 'em all jackpots. By the time we've been in eight saloons he don't care whether the thing on the end of this line is a dog or a catfish. I've lost two inches of my tail trying to sidestep those swinging doors."

The pointer I got from that terrier—vaudeville please copy—set me to thinking.

One evening about 6 o'clock my mistress ordered him to get busy and do the ozone act for Lovey. I have concealed it until now, but that is what she called me. The black-and-tan was called "Tweetness." I consider that I have the bulge on him as far as you could chase a rabbit. Still "Lovey" is something of a nomenclatural tin can on the tail of one's self-respect.

At a quiet place on a safe street I tightened the line of my custodian in front of an attractive, refined saloon. I made a dead-ahead scramble for the doors, whining like a dog in the press despatches that lets the family know that little Alice is bogged while gathering lilies in the brook.

"Why, darn my eyes," says the old man, with a grin; "darn my eyes if the saffron-colored son of a seltzer lemonade ain't asking me in to take a drink. Lemme see—how long's it been since I saved shoe leather by keeping one foot on the foot-rest? I believe I'll——"

I knew I had him. Hot Scotches he took, sitting at a table. For an hour he kept the Campbells coming. I sat by his side rapping for the waiter with my tail, and eating free lunch such as mamma in her flat never equalled with her homemade truck bought at a delicatessen store eight minutes before papa comes home.

When the products of Scotland were all exhausted except the rye bread the old man unwound me from the table leg and played me outside like a fisherman plays a salmon. Out there he took off my collar and threw it into the street.

"Poor doggie," says he; "good doggie. She shan't kiss you any more. 'Sa darned shame. Good doggie, go away and get run over by a street car and be happy."

I refused to leave. I leaped and frisked around the old man's legs happy as a pug on a rug.

"You old flea-headed woodchuck-chaser," I said to him—"you moon-baying, rabbit-pointing, egg-stealing old beagle, can't you see that I don't want to leave you? Can't you see that we're both Pups in the Wood and the missis is the cruel uncle after you with the dish towel and me with the flea liniment and a pink bow to tie on my tail. Why not cut that all out and be pards forever more?"

Maybe you'll say he didn't understand—maybe he didn't. But he kind of got a grip on the Hot Scotches, and stood still for a minute, thinking.

A Chinese terra-cotta effigy from a tomb, 202 B.C.–A.D. 220. (Cernuschi Museum)

GEORGE STUBBS, *A Water Spaniel,* 1769. English animal painter. The English water spaniel is now extinct. (Yale Center for British Art)

"Doggie," says he, finally, "we don't live more than a dozen lives on this earth, and very few of us live to be more than 300. If I ever see that flat any more I'm a flat, and if you do you're flatter; and that's no flattery. I'm offering 60 to 1 that Westward Ho wins out by the length of a dachshund."

There was no string, but I frolicked along with my master to the Twenty-third Street ferry. And the cats on the route saw reason to give thanks that prehensile claws had been given them.

On the Jersey side my master said to a stranger who stood eating a currant bun:

"Me and my doggie, we are bound for the Rocky Mountains."

But what pleased me most was when my old man pulled both of my ears until I howled, and said:

"You common, monkey-headed, rat-tailed, sulphur-colored son of a door mat, do you know what I'm going to call you?"

I thought of "Lovey," and I whined dolefully.

"I'm going to call you 'Pete,' says my master; and if I'd had five tails I couldn't have done enough wagging to do justice to the occasion.

A Mexican Indian terra-cotta statue, third century A.D.

A Sense of Humor

From the New York *Telegram,* ca. 1920s.

The PROPRIETOR of a Third Avenue store owns a little black kitten that has a habit of squatting on its haunches, like a bear or a kangaroo, and then sparring with its fore paws as if it had taken lessons from a pugilist.

A gentleman took into the store the other evening an enormous black dog, half Newfoundland, half collie, fat, good-natured and intelligent. The tiny black kitten, instead of bolting at once for shelter, retreated a few paces, sat erect on its hind legs, and "put its fists" in an attitude of defiance. The contrast in size between the two was intensely amusing. It reminded one of Jack the Giant Killer preparing to demolish a giant.

Slowly and without a sign of excitability the huge dog walked as far as his chain would allow him, and gazed intently at the kitten and its odd posture. Then, as the comicality of the situation struck him, he turned his head and shoulders around to the spectators, and if an animal ever laughed in the world, that dog assuredly did so, then and there. He neither barked nor growled, but indulged in a low chuckle, while his eyes and mouth beamed with merriment.

GEORGE STUBBS, *White Poodle in a Punt,* ca. 1780. British animal painter. (Private collection)

The Legend of Pan Hu

Attributed to KAN PAO, from *Sou-shen chi (In Search of the Supernatural),* 4th century A.D.

In the reign of King Hsin, one of the princes named Fang plotted to usurp the throne. The former offered a reward of a thousand catties [ounces] of gold and a number of pretty women in his harem to anyone who brought back the head of the latter. One day King Hsin's dog Pan Hu disappeared. It had gone to the headquarters of Prince Fang, who was greatly pleased with the new arrival. He told his aids, saying "I am sure King Hsin will fall. His own dog has deserted him." So he celebrated the good omen with a banquet and when he was lying drunk, the dog killed him. It bit off his head and carried it back to King Hsin, who was overjoyed and fed the dog with a great deal of meat. But the dog would not touch it and continued to abstain from eating for a day, besides refusing to respond to his master's call. At last the king said, "Are you unhappy? Do you want to be rewarded according to my offer?" Upon this the dog jumped up in jubilation. So the King gave it five women and called it the marquis of Kweilin [Kwangsi].

[Pan Hu is said to have had six children whose descendants are the aboriginal peoples of China.]

DEVELOPMENT OF DOG BREEDS

T he first members of the order *Carnivora* (which includes wolves, bears, raccoons, weasels, civets, hye-
nas, and cats) evolved about 55 million years ago.
The earliest members of the family *Canidae*
(wolves, foxes, and wild dogs) appeared 25–30 million
years ago in North America. The genus *Canis* (wolves, jackals, domestic dogs) first appeared 10 million years ago and
migrated to Eurasia about 6 million years ago. The first
wolves evolved 300,000 years ago, and current estimates
say that dogs appeared 15,000 to 25,000 years ago. Skeletons that are 14,000 years old have been found in the Middle East and some that are 10,500 years old in North
America. New discoveries continue to push back the dates
for the first dog further into the past.

In the early stages of the evolution of dogs, differences
between individual dogs were based solely on their ancestry. It was not until much later that humans began mold-
ing their characteristics through selective breeding.

It is very difficult to determine when individual breeds
first appeared; this chart is designed to give you a general
idea, but it is far from exact. For the origins of the older
breeds, the dates given by the experts often vary by a thousand years or more. I have tried to place each breed at its
earliest reasonably reliable date. These dates are based on
skeletons, art, and written descriptions, the first being the
most accurate and the last generally being the vaguest. Origins, lineage, and even what constitutes a breed are all
hotly debated, which adds to the confusion. Figures on the
number of breeds vary from about 120 to over 800, and
this does not include the many breeds that have become
extinct.

The breeds are broken down by their theoretical wolf
ancestors. Since there has been extensive cross-breeding,
these lines are very blurred, though one ancestor usually
leaves a greater imprint. I have tried to place each breed
with the majority of its ancestors or those that left the
strongest imprint. Some breeds have changed over time
and are no longer exactly like their ancestors (for example, the King Charles spaniel); others, such as the Saluki,

have remained unchanged for thousands of years. Many breeds were altered on purpose—for instance, when ear cropping was outlawed, many of these breeds were bred for erect ears at the expense of other qualities.

Normally charts of this type are placed on a logarithmic time scale, since much more space is required to list the many recent breeds than to list the fewer ancient breeds. Unfortunately, altering the time scale in this manner tends to warp one's perception by making it appear that the ancient breeds develop much more rapidly than they actually did. I have decided to overcome this problem by maintaining arithmetical time scales and by dividing the time line into three separate charts of different increments: one-thousand-year, one-hundred-year, and ten-year increment charts. I hope this presents the time scale in a more realistic manner.

Thousand-Year-Increment Chart

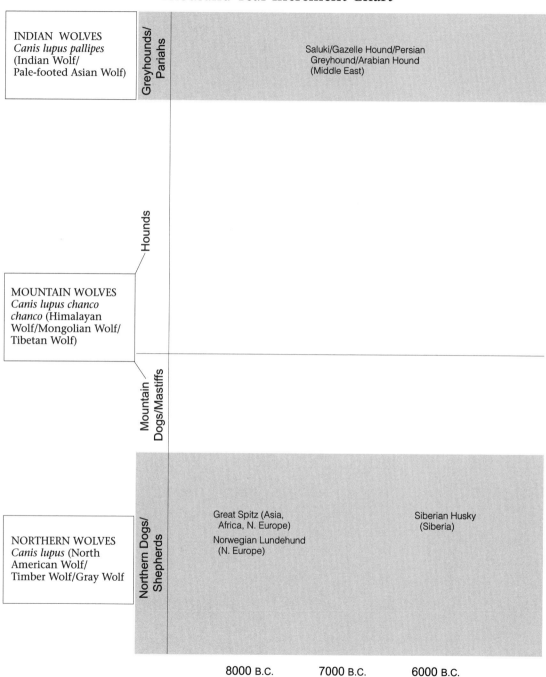

INDIAN WOLVES
Canis lupus pallipes
(Indian Wolf/
Pale-footed Asian Wolf)

Greyhounds/
Pariahs

Saluki/Gazelle Hound/Persian
Greyhound/Arabian Hound
(Middle East)

Hounds

MOUNTAIN WOLVES
*Canis lupus chanco
chanco* (Himalayan
Wolf/Mongolian Wolf/
Tibetan Wolf)

Mountain
Dogs/Mastiffs

NORTHERN WOLVES
Canis lupus (North
American Wolf/
Timber Wolf/Gray Wolf

Northern Dogs/
Shepherds

Great Spitz (Asia,
Africa, N. Europe)

Norwegian Lundehund
(N. Europe)

Siberian Husky
(Siberia)

8000 B.C.   7000 B.C.   6000 B.C.

Thousand-Year-Increment Chart

Greyhound (Mesopotamia or N. Africa)

Ibizan Hound (Egypt, then to Spain)

Dingo (Australia)[2]

Pharaoh Hound (Egypt)

Basenji (C. Africa)

Sicilian Hound/Cirneco dell'Etna (Italy)

Irish Wolfhound (Britain)[1]

Afghan Hound (Sinai Peninsula)

pointers (India)

spaniels (Babylon/Assyria)

Dachshund? (Egypt, then to Germany)

Bloodhound? (Babylon)

Basset Hound? (Egypt)

Cardigan Welsh Corgi (Wales)

Tibetan Mastiff (Tibet)

Great Dane? (Egypt, then to Greece/Italy)

Great Pyrenees/ Pyrenean Mountain Dog (C. Asia or Babylon?, then to Europe)

Mastiff/Old English Mastiff? (Asia, then to Babylon/Assyria/Italy)

Anatolian Sheepdog/ Karabash (Babylon, then Turkey)

Norwegian Elkhound (Scandinavia)

Swedish Elkhound/Jämthund (Sweden)

Small Gray Elk Dog (Scandinavia)

Pekinese (Korea/China)

Chow Chow (China)

Maltese? (Egypt, then to Europe)

5000 B.C. 4000 B.C. 3000 B.C. 2000 B.C. 1000 B.C.

381

Hundred-Year-Increment Chart

Greyhounds/Pariahs

Celtic Swifthound/Celtic War Dog (Germany)[4]

Smooth-coated Chihuahua? (arrives in Malta from N. Africa)

Italian Greyhound (arrives in Rome from Egypt)

Slough (N. Africa or Arabia)

Hounds

hounds (Scandinavia)

Bracco italiano (Italy)

Basset Hound? (Turkey)

Beagle? (Greece)

Dalmatian (Egypt/Greece)

Sabuseso Español (Phoenicia or Spain)

Italian Hound (Gaul, then to Italy)

Mountain Dogs/Mastiffs

Molossus (Greece/Italy)[5]

Northern Dogs/Shepherds

Lhasa Apso (Tibet)

Tibetan Terrier (Tibet)[3]

terriers (Britain)

Hokkaidoken (Japan)

Collie? (Britain)

Pomeranian (arrived in Greece/Italy from N. Europe)

Bergamasco (Phoenicia)

800 B.C.   600 B.C.   400 B.C.

Hundred-Year-Increment Chart

Mexican Hairless?
(in Mexico, across the
Bering Strait from
China/Xdoitzcuintle?)

English
Greyhound
(England)

Welsh Springer
Spaniel
(Wales)

Swiss Hound
(Switzerland)

retrievers (Italy)

Poodle? (Rome/Greece)

English Cocker Spaniel?
(England)

Papillon?
(Belgium)

Rottweiler (Mediterranean,
then to Germany)[7]

Bernese Mountain Dog
(Mediterranean, then
to Switzerland)

Shar-Pei/Chinese
Fighting Dog (China)

Great Dane? (Greece)

Neopolitan Mastiff (Italy)

Pug (China)

French
Mastiff/Dogue
de Bordeaux
(France)

Eskimo Dog (Siberia)[6]

Shiba Inu (arrived in
Japan from China)

Scottish Terrier/Scottie?
(Scotland)

Bearded Collie (Scotland)

Irish Terrier (Ireland)

Welsh Terrier (Britain)

Samoyed (Siberia)

Maremma Sheepdog
(Asia, then to Italy)

Finnish Spitz
(Scandinavia)

Shih Tzu (Tibet,
then to China)

| 200 B.C. | B.C./A.D. | A.D. 200 | A.D. 400 |

Hundred-Year-Increment Chart

Greyhounds/ Pariahs			

Scottish Deerhound (Scotland)[10]

Magyar Agár/Hungarian Greyhound (arrived in Hungary from Russia)

Hounds

Vizsla/Hungarian Pointer (Hungary)[11]

Pembroke Welsh Corgi (Wales or Sweden)

Otterhound (England)

Irish Water Spaniel (Ireland)

Harrier (England)

Saint Hubert Hound (France)[8]

Bloodhound (Belgium or England)

Talbot Hound (England)[13]

Schillerstövare (Norway?)

Mountain Dogs/Mastiffs

Komondor (arrived in Hungary from C. Asia)

Northern Dogs/ Shepherds

Puli (arrived in Hungary from C. Asia)

Vastgotaspets (Sweden)[12]

Japanese Chin/ Japanese Spaniel (China or Korea, then to Japan)[9]

Briard (Europe)

Swedish Shepherd/ Swedish Vallhund (Sweden)

Norwegian Buhund/ Norsk Buhund (Norway)

Picardy Sheepdog (France)

Polish Owczarck Nizinny Sheepdog/ PONS (Poland)

Bichon Frisé (Mediterranean, then to France by way of the Canary Islands)

A.D. 600	A.D. 800	A.D. 1000

Hundred-Year-Increment Chart

Black and Tan Terrier (England)[14]	Spanish Greyhound Galgo (Spain); Borzoi/Russian Wolfhound (Russia)		Mexican Hairless Dog/Xoloitzcuintle (China, then to Mexico); Hairless Chinese Crested Dog (in China, originally from Africa?); Powderpuff Chinese Crested Dog (in China, originally from Africa?)	Whippet (England)	
Small Continental Spaniel (Italy); Foxhound (England); Hovawart (Germany)[15]; Papillon (Italy)	Bleu de Gascogne (France); Griffon (France); English Cocker Spaniel (England); English Setter (England); French Spaniel (France)	English Springer Spaniel (England); Lucernese Hound (Switzerland); Beagle (England); Poodle (Germany/Russia); Toy Poodle (Germany); setters (France)	Basset Hound (France); Brittany/Brittany Spaniel (France); King Charles Spaniel/English Toy Spaniel (unknown); German Rough-haired Pointer (Germany)	Braque Français/French Pointer (France); Drachsbracke (Germany); German Short-haired Pointer (Germany); Weimaraner (Germany); Pointer/English Pointer (England or Spain); Gordon Setter (Scotland); Poitevin (France)[17]	Bengal Pointer (England)[18]; French Spaniel (France); Braque Dupuy (France); Finnish Hound (Finland); Catahoula Leopard Dog (Louisiana); King Charles Spaniel—Blenheim Spaniel variety/English Toy Spaniel (England)[19]; Smooth-coated Dachshund (Germany); Old Danish Pointer (arrived in Denmark from Spain)
English Bulldog (England); Komondor (Hungary); Kuvasz (Hungary)	Short-hair Saint Bernard (Switzerland); Great Dane (Germany/France/Italy)	Great Swiss Mountain Dog (Switzerland)	Boxer? (Holland); English Bulldog (England)	Newfoundland/Newf (Canada)	Fila Brasileiro (Brazil); Mastiff/Old English Mastiff (Britain)
Bolognese (Italy); Barbet (France)	Schnauzer (Germany)	Belgian Sheepdog? (Europe); Belgian Griffon (Belgium); Maltese (Europe); Cairn Terrier (Scotland); Schipperke (Belgium)	Spinone/Italian Griffon (France or Italy); Löwchen/Little Lion Dog (S. Europe); Skye terrier (Scotland)	Akita Inu (Japan); Dandie Dinmont Terrier (Scotland)[16]; Wolf-Spitz (Germany); Pinscher (Germany); Border Collie (Scotland); Affenpinscher? (Germany); West Highland White Terrier/Westie (Scotland); Miniature Pinscher (Germany); Shetland Sheepdog/Sheltie (Scotland); Keeshond (Holland)	Pumi (Europe); Bouvier des Ardennes (France/Belgium); Volpino Italiano (Italy); Smooth-coated Collie (England); Rough-coated Collie (England); Scottish Terrier/Scottie (Scotland); Estrela Mountain Dog (Portugal); Bouvier des Flandres (France/Belgium)[20]; Soft-coated Wheaten Terrier (England); Karelian Bear Dog (Finland, then to Russia)

1200	1400	1600	1800

Ten-Year-Increment Chart

	1740	1760	1780
Greyhounds/ Pariahs	Manchester Terrier (England)	Kerry Blue Terrier/Irish Blue Terrier (Ireland)	Toy Manchester Terrier/English Toy Terrier (England)
Hounds	Wire-haired Fox Terrier (England) / Clumber Spaniel (England) / Plott Hound (Great Smoky Mountains, United States)	Braque d'Auvergne (arrived in France)	Smooth-coated Fox Terrier (England) / Pont Audener Spaniel (France)[22] / Wire-haired Dachshund (Britain?) / Sussex Spaniel (England) / Irish Setter (Ireland) / Porcelaine (France)
Mountain Dogs/Mastiffs			
Northern Dogs/ Shepherds	Tibetan Spaniel (Tibet)[21] / Old English Sheepdog (England)		Smooth-coated Chihuahua (arrived in Mexico from Asia) / Bedlington Terrier (England)

Ten-Year-Increment Chart

Rhodesian Ridgeback (South Africa, then to Zimbabwe)

Cumberland Spaniel (France)
Flat-coated Retriever (England)
Somerset Harrier (England)
Labrador Retriever (Canada)
American Foxhound (United States)[23]
Stabyhoun (Holland)

Jack Russell Terrier (England)
Long-haired Dachshund (Germany)
Dunker/Norwegian Hound (Norway)

Redbone Coonhound (Georgia)
Gascon Saintongeois (France)

American Water Spaniel (United States)
Golden Retriever (Scotland)

Braque Saint-Germain/Saint Germain Pointer (France)
King Charles Spaniel—Prince Charles variety/English Toy Spaniel (England)
Corded Poodle (France)[25]

Walker Coonhound (Kentucky)
Curly-coated Retriever (England)
Beauceron (France)
Wire-haired Styrian Mountain Hound (Austria)

Bullmastiff (England)

Landseer (England)[24]
Staffordshire Bull Terrier (England)

Leonberger (Germany)

Boxer (Germany)
Brindle Boxer (Germany)
Tawny Boxer (Germany)
Toy Bulldog (England)

Long-haired Saint Bernard (Switzerland)
Bull Terrier (England)

Boston Terrier (Boston)

Airedale Terrier (England)
Yorkshire Terrier/Yorkie (England)
Sealyham Terrier (Wales)
Long-haired Chihuahua (Mexico)

Border Terrier (England/Scotland)

Armant/Egyptian Sheepdog (Egypt)

Australian Cattle Dog/Blue Cattle Dog (Australia)

Lakeland Terrier (England)

| 1800 | 1820 | 1840 | 1860 |

Ten-Year-Increment Chart

	1880	1900	1920
Greyhounds/Pariahs	Australian Kelpie/Australian Collie/the Barb (Australia)		
Hounds	Wetterhoun (Holland); Pont-Audemère Spaniel (France); Levesque (France); Field Spaniel (England); Trigg Hound (Kentucky); Wire-haired Pointing Griffon/Korthals Griffon (Holland/Germany/France); American Cocker Spaniel (United States); Chesapeake Bay Retriever (Chesapeake Bay, Maryland); Pudelpointer/Poodle Pointer (Germany)[26]; German Wire-haired Pointer (Germany); King Charles Spaniel—Ruby variety/English Toy Spaniel (England); Long-coated Pointing Griffon/Boulet Griffon (France); Billy (France); Styrian Mountain Hound (Austria)	Treeing Walker Coonhound (Kentucky/Virginia); Black and Tan Coonhound (United States); Picardy Spaniel (France); German Hunting Terrier/Jagdterrier (Germany); Estonian Hound (Estonia); Bosnian Hound (Yugoslavia); Kooikerhondje (Holland); German Long-haired Pointer (Germany); Hanover Hound/Hanoverian Schweisshund (Germany); Hygenhund (Norway); Drever (Sweden); Toy Fox Terrier/American Toy Fox Terrier/Amertoy (United States)	German Spaniel (Germany); Grosser Münsterländer (Germany); Kleiner Münsterländer (Germany); Ariégeois (France); Miniature Dachshund (England)
Mountain Dogs/Mastiffs	French Bulldog (France); Pit Bull Terrier/American Staffordshire Terrier (England); Tosa (Japan)		
Northern Dogs/Shepherds	Australian Terrier (Australia); Soft-coated Griffon (France); Affenpinscher (Germany); Brussels Griffon/Belgium Griffon (Belgium); Griffon Brabançon/Belgium Griffon (Belgium); Cão da Serra de Aires (Portugal); German Shepherd (Germany); Norwich Terrier (England)	Mudi (Hungary); Belgian Malinois (Belgium); Belgian Tervuren (Belgium); Groenendael/Belgian Sheepdog (Belgium); Scottish Terrier—modern version (Scotland); Australian Silky Terrier/Silky Toy Terrier (Australia); Affenpinscher (Germany); Dobermann (Germany)[27]; Miniature Schnauzer (Germany); Giant Schnauzer (Germany); Schapendoes (Holland); Australian Shepherd (United States); Grand Basset Griffon Vendéen (France); Pyrenean Sheepdog (France)	Sanshu (Japan); Briquet Griffon Vendéen (France); Kromfohrländer (Germany)

Ten-Year-Increment Chart

Cavalier King Charles
Spaniel (England)[28]

Chien Français
(France)

American Hairless Terrier
(Louisiana)[31]

Miniature Bull Terrier
(England)

Miniature Shar-Pei/
  Miniature Chinese Fighting Dog
  (United States)

Toy Shar-Pei
(United States)

Glen of Imaal Terrier
(Ireland)

Chinook (New
  Hampshire)[29]

Norfolk Terrier
(England)[30]

Eurasier (Germany)

Chesky Terrier/
  Bohemian Terrier
  (Czechoslovakia)

Kyi-Leo (California)

Havanese (Cuba)

Petit Basset Griffon
  Vendéen (France)

Silky Terrier/Sidney Silky
  (Australia)

Miniature Australian
  Shepherds (California)

1940   1960   1980

[1]The Irish wolfhound almost became extinct and was reestablished in the 1860s.

[2]Recent discoveries show that the dingo was originally a domestic dog that later became semiwild, not a wild dog who has been domesticated.

[3]The Tibetan terrier is not a true terrier.

[4]The Celtic swifthound, a relative of the wolf and deerhounds, is now extinct.

[5]The molosus, a fierce mastiff-type breed, is now extinct.

[6]Eskimo dogs are still very closely related to wolves, and the two are often still bred together.

[7]Rottweilers almost vanished by 1905, and the breed had to be reestablished.

[8]The Saint Hubert hound, a variety of bloodhound, became extinct in the 19th century.

[9]The Japanese spaniel is not a true spaniel and so is now more commonly called the Japanese chin.

[10]The Scottish deerhound almost became extinct and was reestablished in the 19th century.

[11]The vizsla almost vanished in World War II.

[12]The vastgotaspets almost became extinct around 1950.

[13]The Talbot hound, a variety of bloodhound, became extinct in the early 19th century.

[14]The Black and Tan terrier is probably extinct, though some people think it still exists as the Welsh terrier or the Manchester terrier.

[15]The hovawart had almost vanished but was reestablished around the 1920s.

[16]The Dandie Dinmont terrier is named after a character in a novel by Sir Walter Scott.

[17]The poitevin disappeared in the French Revolution and had to be rebred.

[18]The Bengal pointer, a breed similar to the Dalmatian, is now extinct.

[19]Originally the Blenheim spaniel was a separate breed from the King Charles spaniel, but they have since been bred together, so that now they can only be distinguished by their color.

[20]The Bouvier des Flandres was almost destroyed in World War I. It was reestablished in 1923.

[21]The Tibetan spaniel is not a true spaniel.

[22]The Pont Audener spaniel has almost vanished.

[23]The American foxhound may be descended from French staghounds owned by George Washington.

[24]The Landseer almost became extinct and was reestablished in Germany during the 1920s.

[25]The corded poodle is now extinct.

[26]The pudelpointer has almost vanished.

[27]The "pinscher" (which means "terrier") has been dropped from Dobermann pinscher because it is not a true terrier.

[28]By the early 20th century, King Charles spaniels no longer looked like their ancestors of the 16th century, so between 1920 and 1945, they were rebred to their former appearance. These rebred dogs are called Cavalier King Charles spaniels.

[29]The chinook almost became extinct and has since been reestablished.

[30]The Norfolk terrier almost became extinct during World War II.

[31]This unique breed is descended solely from Manchester terriers and is not related to any of the other hairless breeds. Unlike the other hairless breeds, this one does not have a lethal gene, so two American Hairless Terriers can be bred together with the entire litter surviving. The gene is recessive; only a quarter of the puppies are hairless. Actually the puppies are born with hair, but when they are about a week old, it begins to fall off at their nose and gradually works back to their tail, so that they are hairless by about their sixth week. They are normal in every other way. Toys have also been bred.

CREDITS

My thanks to the following, who have granted permission to reprint copyrighted material. Every effort has been made to reach owners of copyrighted material. I apologize for any inadvertent omissions and will be grateful if such are brought to my attention.

Page 17: "Fashions in Dogs" by E. B. White. From THE FOX OF PEAPACK AND OTHER STORIES by E. B. White. Copyright © 1932 by E. B. White. Reprinted by permission of HarperCollins Publishers.

Page 28: The New Puppy by D. H. Lawrence. Excerpted from "Rex", from PHOENIX: THE POSTHUMOUS PAPERS OF D. H. LAWRENCE by D. H. Lawrence and edited by Edward McDonald. Copyright © 1936 by Frieda Lawrence, renewed © 1964 by The Estate of the late Frieda Lawrence Ravagli. Used by permission of Viking Penguin, a division of Penguin Books USA Inc.

Page 30: Puppies Adopted by Cats by Sarah J. Eddy. Copyright © 1929 by Marshall Jones Inc. Reprinted by permission of Marshall Jones Inc.

Page 49: Hemingway's Dog by Ernest Hemingway. Reprinted by permission of Charles Scribner's Sons, an imprint of Macmillan Publishing Company, from BY-LINE: ERNEST HEMINGWAY by William White. Copyright © 1954 by Ernest Hemingway. Copyright © 1967 by Mary Hemingway.

Page 60: Puppies Adopted by Cats by Sarah J. Eddy. Copyright © 1929 by Marshall Jones Inc. Reprinted by permission of Marshall Jones Inc.

Page 115: Saint Bernards by Albert Heim. Excerpted with permission of Howell Books, an imprint of Macmillan Publishing Company, from THE NEW COMPLETE SAINT BERNARD by E. Georgean Raulston and Rex Roberts. Copyright © 1963, 1966, 1973 by Howell Book House, Inc.

Page 136: "The Turkish Trench Dog" by Geoffrey Dearmer. Copyright © 1918 by Geoffrey Dearmer. Reprinted by permission of the author.

INDEX